HOT SPOTS GUIDEBOOK

GREAT PLACES TO WATCH TRAINS

Kalmbach Books
21027 Crossroads Circle
Waukesha, Wisconsin 53186
www.Kalmbach.com/Books

Published in 2012
16 15 14 13 12   1 2 3 4 5

Manufactured in China

ISBN: 978-0-89024-805-8

Front cover photo: Belmont, Nebraska, by Tom Danneman
Back cover photo: Belen, New Mexico, by William P. Diven

Editor: Randy Rehberg
Art Director: Tom Ford
Illustrators: Bill Metzger, Rick Johnson

Publisher's Cataloging-In-Publication Data

Hot spots guidebook : great places to watch trains / [From the publisher of Trains magazine].

   p. : ill. (some col.), maps ; cm.

 "Trains books"--Cover.
 ISBN: 978-0-89024-805-8

   1. Railroads--United States--Guidebooks. I. Kalmbach Publishing Company. II. Title: Trains magazine.

HE2727 .H68 2012
385/.0973

Contributors

The following people provided editorial content and/or photos for the hot spots described in this guidebook:

Kevin Andrusia, Bruce Barrett, Marshall Beecher, Mike Blaszak, Ken Borg, Brad Buecker, Paul Burgess, Joseph Calisi, Gerry Callison, Jeff Carlson, Steve Carter, Mike Condren, Dave Crosby, Andy Cummings, Dan Cupper, Mike Danneman, Tom Danneman, Charlie Dischinger, Bill Diven, Dick Dorn, Ken Fitzgerald, Ron Flanary, Steve Forrest, Fred Frailey, Steve Freer, Steve Glischinski, Phil Gosney, Chase Gunnoe, Chris Guss, Drew Halverson, Mike Harbour, Woody Harrison, Scott Hartley, Eric Hendrickson, David Hoge, Thom Horvath, Kevin Keefe, Bruce Kelly, Tom Kline, Dave Kuntz, Elrond Lawrence, Carl Lehman, Shawn Levy, Stefan Loeb, Scott Lothes, David Lustig, Alex Mayes, Greg McDonnell, Rob McGonigal, Ron Mele, Hal Miller, Dan Munson, Michael Murray, Tom Murray, Scott Muskopf, Tom Nanos, Don Nickel, Mick Nussbaum, Dave Patch, Sam Phillips, Eric Powell, Zach Pumphery, Clint Renegar, John Roskoski, Craig Sanders, Mike Schaller, Robert Scott, Dave Stanley, Dave Syffe, Nick Tharalson, Casey Thomason, Nick Trimburger, Matt Van Hattem, Ralcon Wagner, David Warner, Steven Welch, Dale Woodland, Jim Wrinn, and Mike Yuhas

About this guide

The *Hot Spots Guidebook* is written by TRAINS staff and contributors from across the country, using their first-hand knowledge of the sites. Each listing gives an overview of the site, points out the best viewing spots, describes the types of and number of trains you can see, and shows how to get there. Also included are radio frequencies, any safety concerns, additional activities found in the area, a general reference map, and a photo. Some hot spots are described in shorter listings. These condensed listings provide the basic train-watching information without a map and photo.

We have provided the most up-to-date information available for each train-watching location. Some of the hot spots have been previously featured in TRAINS and may contain additional material. You can look for any of these articles or find corrections and additions to this book on TrainsMag.com.

Contents

Introduction. 7

Six ways to be a smarter
train watcher 8

Staying safe 11

Basics of
photographing trains. 12

ALABAMA
Decatur 17
Mobile 17
Birmingham. 18

ALASKA
Anchorage 20

ARIZONA
Williams. 22
Cienega Creek Bridge. 24
Holbrook. 24

ARKANSAS
Little Rock. 25
Mammoth Spring 26

CALIFORNIA
Beaumont. 28
Dunsmuir 28
Fullerton 29
Redding. 29
Cajon Pass. 30
Feather River Canyon 32
Pinole. 34
Roseville 36
Stockton 38
Tehachapi 40
Truckee 42

COLORADO
Denver. 44
Grand Junction. 46

CONNECTICUT
New Haven. 48
New London 50

FLORIDA
Jacksonville 52
St. Augustine. 53
Callahan 54
Tampa 56

GEORGIA
Austell 58
Cartersville 58
Cordelle. 59
Jesup 59
Atlanta. 60
Folkston. 62
Manchester 64
Marietta. 66

IDAHO
Sandpoint. 68

ILLINOIS
Elmhurst 70
Gibson City. 70
Hinsdale 70
Homewood 71
Kankakee 71
Matteson. 71
Centralia 72
Danville 74
East Dubuque 76
Galesburg. 78
Joliet. 80
La Grange 82
Rochelle. 84
Savanna. 86
West Chicago. 88

INDIANA
Lafayette. 90
Michigan City. 90
Porter 90
Princeton 91
Terre Haute. 91
Wellsboro 91
Hammond 92
Muncie 94

IOWA
Clinton 96
Ottumwa 98
Nevada 100

KANSAS
Hutchinson 101
Topeka 101
Emporia 102
Mulvane 104
Paola 106
Wichita 108

KENTUCKY
Burnside Bridge 110
La Grange 112
Bowling Green 114
Corbin 114

LOUISIANA
New Orleans 115
Blanchard 116

MAINE
Brownville Junction 118

MARYLAND
Hyattsville 119
Cumberland 120
Perryville 122
Point of Rocks 124

MASSACHUSETTS
Palmer 126
Boston, South Station 128
Springfield 128

MICHIGAN
Detroit 129
Durand 130

MINNESOTA
Iron Junction 132
St. Paul 134
Hastings 136
Winona 136

MISSISSIPPI
Jackson 137
Meridian 138

MISSOURI
Eureka 140
Kansas City, Union Station . . . 140
La Plata 140
Neosho 141
Scott City (Thebes Bridge) . . . 141
Birmingham 142
Kansas City, West Bottoms . . . 144
Springfield 146

MONTANA
Essex 148
Helena 150
Missoula 152
Billings 154
Livingston 154

NEBRASKA
Hastings 155
Belmont 156
Fremont 158
Lincoln 160
North Platte 162
Omaha 164

NEVADA
Winnemucca 166

NEW JERSEY
Bridgeport 167
Bound Brook 168
Three Bridges 170

NEW MEXICO
Abo Canyon 172
Belen 174
Vaughn 176

NEW YORK
Binghampton 177
Bear Mountain Bridge 178
New York City,
Jamaica Station 180

NORTH CAROLINA
Old Fort.....................182
Salisbury....................184
Hamlet......................186
Selma.......................186

NORTH DAKOTA
Dickinson...................187
Fargo.......................188
Minot.......................190

OHIO
Alliance.....................192
Deshler.....................192
Fostoria.....................192
Greenwich...................193
Toledo......................193
Berea.......................194
Marion......................196

OKLAHOMA
Wagoner....................198
Heavener....................200
Tulsa.......................200
Waynoka....................200

OREGON
Albany......................201
Columbia River Valley.......202

PENNSYLVANIA
Allentown...................204
Erie........................204
Holmesburg Junction........205
Reading.....................205
Scranton....................205
Harrisburg..................206
Horseshoe Curve............208
Sand Patch Grade...........210

TENNESSEE
Chattanooga................212
Cowan......................214
Frisco......................216
Harriman....................218
Memphis....................220
Nashville...................222

TEXAS
El Paso.....................224
Flatonia....................225
Sweetwater.................225
Big Sandy...................226
Dallas......................228
Jefferson...................230
Rosenberg..................232
Saginaw.....................234
San Antonio.................236
Texarkana...................238

UTAH
Echo Canyon................240

VIRGINIA
Doswell.....................242
Lynchburg..................244
Roanoke....................246
Arlington....................248
Clifton Forge................248

WASHINGTON
Tacoma.....................249
Edmonds....................250
Spokane....................252
Vancouver...................254

WEST VIRGINIA
Harpers Ferry...............256
Kenova.....................258
Shenandoah Junction.......260
Magnolia Cutoff............262
Thurmond..................262

WISCONSIN
Milwaukee..................263
La Crosse...................264
Saunders Junction..........266
Stevens Point...............268

WYOMING
Cheyenne...................270

Introduction

More than 140,000 miles of railroad tracks crisscross the United States, and they offer a great opportunity to observe America's fascinating railroads. This is a great show for so many reasons! The giant locomotives that pack more than 4,000 horsepower each are amazing machines. The trains are always different, whether they're mixed freight, intermodal shipping containers, unit coal trains, new autos, or something else. And the cargoes can be equally fascinating—from ubiquitous grain to make bread and coal to burn for making electrical power to airliner fuselages. Best of all, American railroads are busier than ever in the 21st century. They're the primary conduits for manufactured goods, raw materials, and in some corridors, people. The chance of seeing trains is good—if you know where to go to watch.

Finding a good spot to see this traveling show of commerce can be difficult.

The community depot and the knowledgeable freight or passenger agent residing within are things of the past. Railroad yards are private property, and they can be dangerous if you're not savvy to the comings and goings of freight cars. Security around railroad tracks is tighter than ever, and some states have strict no-trespassing laws when it comes to railroads.

This hot spots guidebook can point you toward the best places to watch trains: America's busy junctions, its most scenic locations, and the growing number of formalized train-watching pavilions that have been built to welcome you. Whether you are a novice train watcher or a veteran railfan, this guide gives you the most basic tool for a successful train-watching experience—good information.

Prepared by experienced railfans who know the areas and the railroads, you'll learn the best places to watch trains from one end of the country to the other. Have fun watching America's railroads, be safe, and we'll see you trackside!

Jim Wrinn

Jim Wrinn, Editor
Trains

Six ways to be a smarter train watcher *by Fred Frailey*

The book you hold in your hands is your invitation to do hands-on train watching. We tell you where to go to find the action, what to expect—sometimes even where to go to eat. But beyond all that, there are some things you can do to enhance your train-watching experience. I've boiled it down to six simple bits of advice. Well, maybe not always so simple…

1. Learn the territory

You need good reference material (yes, even more than this book can tell you). Start with good maps. On train-chasing trips, my gold standard is a DeLorme Atlas & Gazetteer, which are published for each state. They're sold at truck stops, on Amazon.com, and directly by the publisher at delorme.com (most for $19.95). Every dirt path is documented, meaning you should never wonder where the tracks are. Or maybe you want to go digital. Call up Google Maps on your iPad and let it show you where you and the railroad are as you travel.

If possible, get employee timetables for the lines you are watching. Ask fellow railfans (or fans who are railroaders) whether they have current or recently outdated copies in PDF form. Or look at listings on eBay.com. The timetable does not need to be up to date, but it helps to know siding lengths and locations, speed limits, placement of defect detectors, and signaling. Some are available from Altamont Press (altamontpress.com/store) that cover states in the West. They contain the same information as employee timetables in a convenient, spiral-bound format.

2. Make friends

I am amazed by the ease with which railfans, especially younger ones, network over the Internet. TrainsMag.com and trainorders.com both have wide-ranging forums divided into general topics. But really serious networkers also join any of probably thousands of rail-oriented Yahoo discussion groups. For instance, I subscribe to one whose several hundred members follow the Buckingham Branch Railroad in Virginia. I subscribe to several dozen in all, usually preferring to get daily digests of messages exchanged by members. But when I'm out watching trains, I might change my preference to instant delivery. I wager that Matt Rose at BNSF Railway and Jim Young at Union Pacific would be stunned by the detail of information exchanged on Yahoo boards about their railroads. (I am also thinking of another Class I CEO who would not be surprised, because he probably belongs to at least a couple.)

3. Don't fly blind

Why miss trains because you're not in the right place at the right time? Once, you could stop by the nearest yard office and ask for a train lineup. Those days are over. But something even better, in my opinion, is available. I'm talking about a Yahoo group called ATCS Monitor. ATCS is the acronym for a public protocol for sending centralized traffic control commands to distant signals and switches. An industrious army of railfans has decoded radio-based ATCS commands for thousands of miles of railroad. This means you can view a real-time dispatcher's display of a railroad subdivision showing the locations of trains. Alas, train numbers or symbols are not revealed.

To take advantage of ATCS, you must first be accepted by the ATCS Monitor group on Yahoo. Then after downloading appropriate files, you can either view on the Internet the translated code that fans broadcast from radio intercepts or equip your own vehicle with an ATCS-enabled radio and antenna and find trains yourself on your laptop computer anywhere from 5 to 50 miles away.

4. Own a good radio

Rulebooks generally require crews to broadcast their presence when they come upon restricting signals. Radios also tell you when and where an operating problem erupts. Radio Shack and Bearcat are the primary suppliers of scanners, but there are better products. A fellow fan I encountered a few years ago was pulling down conversations that my Shack scanner couldn't get a peep from. By nightfall, I had bought my first iCom IC-V82 handheld scanner (I now own two), and within a week, UPS dropped off a Larsen Kulduckie HQ antenna tuned to 160 MHz. The difference between the ordinary scanner and the iCom is night and day. Ham radio shops sell them, and they cost only a bit more than a Shack or Bearcat scanner. When we meet, you will thank me for this advice.

5. Leave your camera behind

Try mixing things up. Sometimes try engaging the trains you see with all your senses and not just with what you see through a viewfinder. It can make a huge difference. My most enjoyable moments while train watching are driving, with the window down, beside a freight train with its locomotives pegged to Run 8. The thrust and power and noise all stir my soul, and not a whiff of this can you hear in a photograph. I'm all for photography, but don't let that be the be-all and end-all of your train-watching experiences.

6. Don't become part of the action

I needn't tell you that we live in a time of heightened anxiety. So why stand out more than necessary? And why do things that endanger yourself? For example, it's not necessary to violate speed limits to enjoy watching trains. Safe driving protects you and helps not call attention to yourself by law enforcement officers, who may next ask why you have antennas sprouting from your car's roof and all that. And stay off railroad property unless you have permission, which brings me to this little gem of advice: any time you can join a railroad's community of friends, do so. I'm talking about BNSF's Citizens for Rail Security, for example, and Partners for Amtrak Safety and Security (https://pass.amtrak.com). I carry both membership cards in my wallet; who knows when it might convince a deputy sheriff I'm not out to sabotage the next train to go by.

And finally, it's wise to carry with you the phone numbers of railroad police when you're out and about. When you see an unsafe condition (for instance, a malfunctioning crossing gate or an open door on a van or container), you can call at once. Here's how to reach the larger railroads:

Amtrak: 800-331-0008
BNSF Railway: 800-832-5452
Canadian National: 800-465-9239
Canadian Pacific: 800-716-9132
CSX: 800-232-0144
Kansas City Southern: 877-527-9464
Norfolk Southern: 800-453-2530
Union Pacific: 888-877-7267

Railfanning should be an enjoyable activity. The purpose of this book is to make it more so. Get the most out of it, and have fun out there.

Fred W. Frailey is a TRAINS *columnist and author of* Twilight of the Great Trains.

Staying safe

Because of a growing number of photographers taking high school graduation or wedding photos with railroad tracks as a setting, and some placing video cameras on the tracks, the Union Pacific recently crafted a new policy on taking photos. It provides sound advice for railfans in general. Here is a summary of the policy's main points:

- When taking pictures, stay off Union Pacific Railroad property. This includes tracks, bridges, buildings, and signal towers.
- Obey all safety rules, regulations, and instructions provided by law enforcement and Union Pacific employees.
- Violators are subject to a citation for trespassing on railroad property.
- Union Pacific will seek removal from publication any photograph or video that violates this policy.

The UP also suggested that if railroad property cannot be determined, take the safe way and photograph from identifiable public property, such as the shoulder of a public road. Mark Davis, a spokesman for the UP (in an interview with TRAINS correspondent Don Phillips), said the Union Pacific welcomes fans and the thousands of photos they take. He added that even if UP police see railfans trespassing inadvertently or in some nonthreatening way, they will merely point out where the property line is and guide them to public property. No one at UP is looking to harass or be unfriendly to railfans.

Here are several other safety tips to remember when railfanning:

- Make sure all sets of tracks are clear after a train passes. There may be a second one.
- It takes at least 1 mile for a train to stop.
- Trains overhang the tracks by at least 3 feet in both directions. Don't get too close.
- It is safest to cross tracks at a designated public crossing.
- In remote areas, carry a first aid kit, bring food and water, and charge your cell phone.

Basics of photographing trains _by Jeff Wilson_

Photography has long been a popular pastime among railfans. Railroad photography is also an art form, as witnessed by the beautiful images captured by many rail photographers and showcased in various books and magazines.

Photography has evolved dramatically since the digital camera revolution of the early 2000s. There are still film shooters out there, but by and large, photography is now the realm of pixels.

There's no way that a short article like this one can summarize all you need to know about photography, but it touches on the basics, starting with the camera itself.

Cameras

Digital cameras fall into two broad categories: point-and-shoot (PAS) and single-lens-reflex (DSLR).

Point-and-shoot cameras are the most common. They're designed to be fully automatic, they have built-in zoom lenses, their price tag is generally less than DSLRs, and most are compact and easy to carry. Most PAS cameras use live view on a rear-mounted LCD video screen to allow you to see the subject being photographed.

Digital single-lens-reflex (DSLR) cameras operate like film SLRs. When looking through the viewfinder, you're looking out through the lens, so you see the exact scene that will be captured. Although more expensive, DSLRs offer many advantages, including access to many interchangeable lenses, larger image sensors, more features, and better image quality. About the only DSLR disadvantage is the size: They can be cumbersome to carry, especially if you have multiple lenses.

A DSLR is much more preferable for railfan photography. Along with the above advantages, with a DSLR, the response time when pressing the shutter button is almost instantaneous (there's often a lag with PAS cameras).

Canon, Nikon, Olympus, Pentax, and Sony all offer reasonably priced starter kits (body and small zoom lens) that will get you into the DSLR world.

This sunny-day photo was taken at 1/400th of a second at f/8, ISO 100. The medium aperture setting kept the entire scene in focus, while the shutter speed froze the train in motion as it rolled along near Schuyler, Neb. *Jeff Wilson*

Mastering exposure

Digital cameras can appear quite complex, with a myriad of settings and options. However, a huge advantage of digital is that pixels are free—there's no film wasted as you take photos while experimenting with settings and techniques. You can also see the results instantly.

DSLRs offer a full manual setting, two semiautomatic settings—aperture-priority (Av) and shutter-priority (Tv)—and a full auto setting, program (P). Many PAS cameras don't have a manual mode, instead relying on preset modes and perhaps Av and Tv.

Although designed to make cameras easy to use, the full automatic mode is rarely the best choice for getting a great image. By using automatic settings, you're letting your camera make decisions for you. You can get good photos this way, but even the best cameras sometimes guess wrong regarding the shutter speed or aperture. The result can be a perfectly exposed image that's fuzzy from motion blur or a photo with a properly exposed sky but a foreground subject that's too dark.

Getting the proper exposure requires mastering three settings: shutter speed, aperture (f-stop), and ISO. Changing any of these requires adjusting the others. Knowing what each does and how it impacts your image will help you choose the proper settings.

Shutter speed. Measured in seconds, the shutter speed needs to be fast enough to freeze action (a moving train) and any stray camera movement. I always try to shoot action at 1/500 or faster; any slower and you risk blur. Doubling the shutter speed cuts the exposure by one stop (1/250 allows twice as much light as 1/500).

Aperture. This is a measure of the amount of light allowed in by the adjustable opening in the lens. The aperture is measured by its f-stop. The larger the number (f/16, f/22), the smaller the aperture and the less light allowed into the camera.

The aperture also controls the depth of field (depth of focus). The wider the aperture, the less depth of field your photo will have. An image at f/2.8 will have the subject in sharp focus, with the background and foreground soft. This is more noticeable and accentuated with telephoto lenses.

More often than not with train photos, you want more of the image in focus. Moving the aperture to the f/11 to f/16 range brings more of the scene in focus.

ISO. The ISO setting adjusts the light sensitivity of the sensor. A lower number requires a longer exposure but results in the sharpest, cleanest image. Each doubling of the ISO number accounts for one full stop of light (ISO 400 requires half as much light as ISO 200 and so on). In general, keep your ISO at the lowest setting possible.

Camera settings

If you're not yet comfortable with manual operation, try a semiauto setting. Because freezing motion is a priority, a good place to start is shutter-priority (Tv). Start with your camera on ISO 100 and pick a shutter speed that you know will stop the motion (let's say 1/500). Aim at the scene, press the shutter partway, and see what your camera chooses for an aperture. If it's anywhere in the mid-range of f/8 to f/16, you're OK. If it's a bright day, you may have to adjust your speed to 1/1000 or faster; under clouds or dark conditions, you may have to drop the shutter speed to 1/250 or bump up the ISO.

Try this for a few exposures. Once you have the hang of it, try all manual settings. Remember to always take a sample photo or two to make sure the image looks good before the train arrives.

When calculating an exposure, make sure you point your camera at the subject to get a reading. If your camera catches a lot of bright sky, it can throw off the meter and overexpose the subject. This is the main reason experienced photographers often choose manual operation.

Focus, focus, focus

Another key is autofocus. Most DSLR lenses focus relatively quickly. The typical method is to push the shutter button halfway to lock the focus. Pressing the shutter all the way then takes the photo. However, between the time the focus locks and the picture is taken, a moving subject (such as a train) has moved, often a considerable distance. The result: lots of railfans think there's something wrong with their camera or lens because they can't seem to take sharp photos.

One solution is to use a special DSLR focusing mode. Canon calls it AI Servo, and Nikon calls it CF or continuous focusing. When in this mode, pushing the shutter button halfway causes the focus to track the moving object. The focus will keep tracking the object until the shutter is pressed all the way, keeping the moving object in sharp focus. This method works best with just one focus point selected.

Lenses

DSLR owners have dozens of lens options available to them. What you choose is a matter of the subjects you shoot and how much you want to spend. There are two basic types of lenses: prime, which have a fixed focal length, and zoom, which can be adjusted over a range of focal lengths.

All lenses tend to have "sweet spots"—aperture and focal-length settings in which they produce especially sharp images. This is usually in the f/8 to f/11 range, with higher-quality lenses performing better throughout the entire range. Do some test shots to determine how your lenses perform at different settings.

If you already have a camera with a kit lens, I'd suggest a 50mm, f/1.8 prime lens as a good first addition, followed by a good-quality medium zoom lens. If you're in the market for a DSLR, consider buying a body only and upgrading to a zoom lens that's a step above the kit lens. Check online for lens reviews and suggestions, and talk to fellow photographers to see what they use and recommend.

What to shoot

All of the locations listed in this book offer multiple angles and possibilities for photographs.

When you get to a location, start by checking out the area. Determine where you can safely (and legally) stand to take photos.

Make sure there aren't any obstructions between you and the tracks (poles, trees, signs, weeds).

Make sure backgrounds are clean. When possible, avoid things like power lines, unrelated buildings, signs, and random people and vehicles.

Check the light. Unless you're going for a special effect, get the sun behind you and see where shadows are falling—make sure a shadow won't hit the locomotive right where you intend to photograph it. Cloudy days aren't necessarily bad. Although colors appear brighter and a photo will have more "pop" with sun, clouds allow you more leeway in choosing an angle for the photo.

Get your camera set before a train arrives. Check the mode and each exposure setting to make sure it's what you need. Check the autofocus to make sure you're in the correct mode.

How do the tracks approach? Curves and angles add interest to a photo, as can other features such as signals and bridges. Make sure you know the intended focal point of your photo. For example, cutting off the wheels of a locomotive will look awkward.

Some railfans prefer using a tripod. It allows framing a scene precisely before a train arrives and helps eliminate crooked photos and blur from camera motion.

Most simply hold the camera. To do so, stand solid, and brace your left elbow against your body to keep a firm base. Be conscious of the train entering the frame. Press the shutter button gently but firmly to avoid jerking the camera.

With any type of photography, it's easy to fall into a rut. For railfans, the three-quarters-view wedge shot of an oncoming train often becomes the "go-to" preference. It's a good fallback in most situations, but I make it a point to try something different with each train at any given location. This can mean a different lens (try a wide angle for one, and a normal or telephoto for another) or different vantage point.

This brief article can only touch on the basics of railfan photography. Search the web for additional technical info, join or view photography forums, and get to know other photographers (railfans and others) in your area. Most of all, shoot lots of photos and learn what your camera can do.

Jeff Wilson is a professional photographer, freelance writer, and railfan.

Decatur

Historic Decatur is located in north Alabama on the south bank of the Tennessee River. Decatur is served by Norfolk Southern via its main line between Memphis and Chattanooga and by CSX on its S&NA line between Nashville and Birmingham. The centerpiece of railroading in Decatur is Norfolk Southern's massive lift bridge across the Tennessee River. On average, CSX runs 30 trains a day through Decatur and NS operates 20 trains. Both NS and CSX have moderately sized yards in Decatur to serve chemical, pulp and paper, and food-related industries mostly located along the river.

Mainline traffic on both roads includes intermodals and general manifest freights. Powder River coal trains destined for power plants in Georgia run through Decatur on NS via a Union Pacific connection at Memphis. A parking area on Harborview Drive NE is a safe train-watching location for traffic on the bridge. Another location a few blocks away is at Vine Street and Railroad Street NW where the joint line splits. Decatur's extant, but unused, Union Station is located at the junction and provides a good photo prop.

Mobile

Mobile, Alabama's port city on the Gulf of Mexico, hosts seven railroads. Class I lines include CSX, CN, Norfolk Southern, and Kansas City Southern. Class III short lines include Rail America's Alabama & Gulf Coast, state-owned Terminal Railway-Alabama State Docks, and CG Railway—a railcar ferry operating between Mobile and Mexico. CSX, Mobile's busiest railroad, hosts traffic running between New Orleans and Birmingham, Atlanta, and Jacksonville.

Traffic on CSX can be viewed near the Arthur R. Outlaw Convention Center on South Water Street. The former GM&O railroad station, located on Beauregard Street, has been beautifully restored and now houses Mobile's Metro Transit Authority. Norfolk Southern's terminal yard is situated behind the station. Mobile's massive port operations include rail service for container handling; coal loading and unloading operations; and transloading steel, paper products, and other commodities. The port is well guarded, so be careful to avoid trespassing.

Birmingham

Ron Mele

The focal point of railroad activity in Birmingham is at 13th Street—the crossing point of Norfolk Southern and CSX double-tracked main lines. CSX trains through Birmingham run on the north-south ex-L&N S&NA Subdivision running between Nashville and Mobile and to Waycross, Ga., via the Lineville Subdivision. Norfolk Southern's AGS main funnels traffic running between Chattanooga and Atlanta to Mobile, New Orleans, Meridian, Miss., and Memphis. BNSF's former Frisco line from Memphis terminates in Birmingham at the East Thomas Yard. Birmingham also features two hump yards: Norfolk Southern's Norris Yard in Irondale and CSX's Boyles Yard. In addition, Birmingham has three Class III short lines. They are the Alabama & Tennessee River Railway, an Omnitrax line leased from CSX, running between Birmingham and the Tennessee River port at Guntersville; Watco's Alabama Southern, which uses CSX trackage rights between Brookwood Junction and Birmingham; and U.S. Steel's Birmingham Southern Railroad.

ACTIVITY: Roughly 50 trains a day traverse the parallel NS and CSX lines through Birmingham. These include unit coal trains, double-stack and conventional intermodals, manifests, and locals. CSX and BNSF team up on a joint intermodal run-through between Memphis and Jacksonville. Amtrak's north and southbound *Crescents* arrive in Birmingham during midday.

TRAIN-WATCHING SPOTS: The 21st Street Viaduct offers a wide-open view of NS and CSX freight action and overlooks Birmingham's Amtrak station. On-bridge

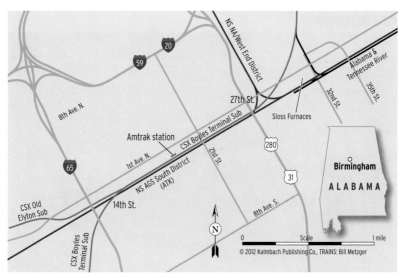

Birmingham, Alabama's largest city, is located in north-central Alabama.

parking and a sidewalk make this an ideal location. Another location nearby is a parking area at 32nd Street near Sloss Furnace where ATN and NS cross at grade. A pavilion near the southern throat of Norfolk Southern's Norris Yard in Irondale, home of the famous Irondale Café, is a popular hangout for railfans.

SAFETY: The yards, in particular, are patrolled by railroad police. While most viewing areas are relatively safe, this is an urban setting so use common sense.

RAILROAD FREQUENCIES: NS: 161.085, 161.505; CSX: 161.370, 161.220; BNSF: 160.695, 160.530; BSRR: 160.290, 160.890

TO DO: Sloss Furnace may be the only 20th century blast furnace preserved as a historic industrial site. It is open to the public for self-guided tours. Sloss is also home to a Frisco-class USRA Light 2-8-2 Mikado steam locomotive. The McWane Science Center is a hands-on museum with interactive exhibits and an IMAX Dome Theater.

NEARBY: The Heart of Dixie Museum in Calera operates excursions on former L&N track and has rolling stock displays. The Bessemer Hall of History, housed in the city's former Southern Railway station, features an operating model railroad depicting the city during the mid-20th century. Also, don't miss the annual John Henry Festival held each September at the former Southern Railway station in Leeds.

DIRECTIONS: From I-65N, take the Eighth Avenue South/University Boulevard Exit to 21st Street. Turn left onto 21st Street to the viaduct.

Anchorage

Tom Murray

Anchorage is the hub of the Alaska Railroad. Passenger trains leave from its downtown depot at Milepost 114 on the ARR main line. ARR's main freight classification yard is located a short distance north of the depot. The yard is the terminal for manifest and intermodal trains north to Fairbanks and south to Whittier.

ACTIVITY: From mid-May to mid-September, the *Coastal Classic* to Seward, *Denali Star* to Fairbanks, and *Glacier Discovery* to Whittier depart Anchorage in the morning and arrive in the evening (check alaskarailroad.com for schedules). There are also special passenger trains tied to cruise ship arrivals at Whittier and Seward, some of which pass the depot while others go to Anchorage International Airport. In each direction, 3–4 coal trains per week operate past the depot, as do 2–3 weekday gravel trains during the summer season.

TRAIN-WATCHING SPOTS: A sidewalk on C Street, immediately east of the depot, provides one vantage point. The C Street Bridge overhead also has a pedestrian sidewalk that affords views of the passenger platforms as well as yard and port tracks if you walk across its full quarter-mile length. Once you reach the north side of the bridge, continue on the public sidewalk for views of the ARR diesel shop. Elderberry Park, at Fifth Avenue and N Street near downtown Anchorage, is a good spot to see trains operating to and from Seward and Whittier. Bike rentals are available at the corner of Fifth and L, and a ride next to the ARR on the Tony Knowles Coastal Trail provides opportunities for unique photo angles. If you have a car, there are turnouts along Seward

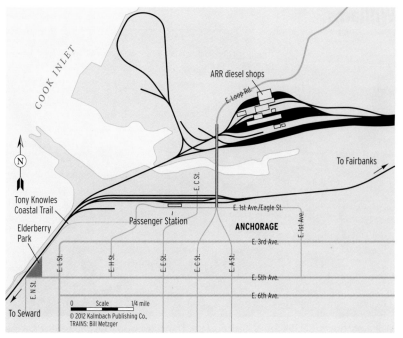

Anchorage is located in south-central Alaska on the shores of Cook Inlet and at the foot of the Chugach mountain range.

Highway south of Anchorage that provide a scenic backdrop as the railroad winds along the shore of Turnagain Arm.

SAFETY: When passenger trains are arriving and departing, pedestrian access to the station platform may be limited, and the baggage-handling area is off limits. Be observant of No Trespassing signs posted by the railroad and other property owners in the area of the depot and other railroad facilities.

RAILROAD FREQUENCIES: ARR: 164.625 (road), 165.3375 (dispatcher to train), 165.265 (yard), 161.535 (road between MP 113 & MP 91), 164.987 (yard, gravel operations), 161.415 and 161.445 (yard)

TO DO: Be sure to stop at the railroad's gift shop in the depot. The depot is a few minutes' walk from downtown Anchorage and its many restaurants, hotels and shopping opportunities.

DIRECTIONS: To reach the ARR depot from downtown Anchorage, follow E Street north to Second Avenue. The depot is down the hill from this intersection at 431 First Avenue.

Williams

Elrond Lawrence

Williams hosts BNSF's busy Chicago-LA Transcon and the railway's Peavine Line to Phoenix. It's also home to the popular Grand Canyon Railway tourist railroad. All three routes are former Santa Fe Railway trackage. The Phoenix Line and the Grand Canyon Railway both pass through Williams' charming and historic downtown. Santa Fe relocated its Chicago-Los Angeles route in 1960, and today's Transcon skirts around town on the north end.

ACTIVITY: Intermodal is king on BNSF, but manifest, unit grain, and auto trains are also a frequent sight. Between 80–100 trains roll past on the Transcon every 24 hours, while the Peavine carries 10–12 trains a day. The Grand Canyon Railway runs a daily train to its namesake attraction. Its steam power is no longer a daily sight—most trains are powered by ex-Amtrak F40PHs—but 2-8-2 No. 4960 is used on special occasions. Amtrak's daily *Southwest Chief* stops in East Williams, a few miles from town.

TRAIN-WATCHING SPOTS: Williams lies in the Kaibab National Forest and great railfanning locations abound. A popular spot is Williams Junction, a few miles east of town, where the Phoenix Line meets the Los Angeles-Chicago Transcon. To get there, drive east on old Route 66 (East Bill Williams Avenue), turn right on Mountain Man Trail (Forest Service Road 51A), and follow it to Depot Road, which heads south to the BNSF main lines. Another good spot can be found along Airport Road north of town, where Transcon freights blast by on a high fill. In downtown Williams, Grand Canyon and Peavine trains can easily be viewed at the Grand Canyon Railway's depot and Harvey House beside North Grand Canyon Boulevard.

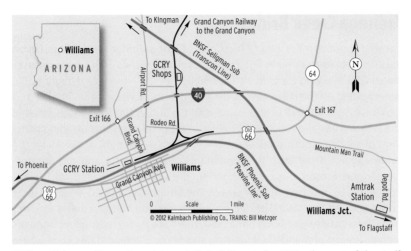

Williams is located in northern Arizona's Kaibab Forest about 30 miles west of Flagstaff.

SAFETY: Be on constant alert for high-speed BNSF trains. Several access roads have recently been gated and may not always be passable.

RAILROAD FREQUENCIES: BNSF: 160.935 (road), 160.335 and 160.260 (PBX), 161.370 (road, Phoenix); Grand Canyon: 160.350 (road)

TO DO: Williams is a Route 66 town, and its historic downtown reflects that heritage with unique shops, diners, soda fountains, and hotels both quirky and of the chain variety. Oh, and the Grand Canyon is about 60 miles away.

NEARBY: The beautiful La Posada Harvey House resort is 90 miles east in Winslow and makes for a great day-trip. Vintage FP7s and spectacular desert scenery can be found at the Verde Canyon Railroad in Clarkdale about 80 miles southeast.

DIRECTIONS: Eastbound, take Exit 161 off I-40 and drive West Bill Williams Avenue (Route 66) into downtown Williams. Westbound I-40 drivers should take Exit 165 and turn left, following Route 66 into town.

Cienega Creek Bridge

Located about 20 miles west of Tucson, the Cienega Bridge is incredible. Union Pacific's double-track main line crosses over each other. Trains have reverse-signal CTC, allowing trains in either direction to use either line. Freight traffic is everything on the railroad, including piggyback, containers, unit trains, and general freight. Amtrak uses this line with the *Sunset Limited*. Various times of the year will find the sun directly in line with the UP main line, meaning many days of shade on both sides of the trains with the sun right above. What the bridge allows is the train to momentarily change course and run approximately north-south in excellent lighting. If it's on the UP roster, you'll see it here as well as a variety of pool power. The bridge averages 40–60 trains in 24 hours. Located in a natural preserve, parking near the bridge requires a permit from Pima County (see www.pima.gov). There are three parking lots, and Lots 2 and 3 are recommended for viewing and photographing trains. Look where you're walking as snakes and other desert creatures abound.

Holbrook

Holbrook is located in northern Arizona, 90 miles east of Flagstaff along BNSF's busy LA-Chicago main line. This Route 66 town is home to a key junction between the former Santa Fe and the Apache Railway, which operates an immaculate fleet of Alco C420s. Up to 100 trains blast through every 24 hours; most are intermodal, but manifests and unit grain trains are also common. Holbrook hosts 2 daily *Southwest Chiefs*, although they no longer stop at the restored 1892 depot. The depot area at the corner of Apache Avenue and SE Central Avenue is a good place to watch the BNSF action. NW Central Avenue and SE Central Avenue also parallel the BNSF main lines. South of town, West Romero Street offers a grade crossing where you can catch Apache trains. Be sure to stay at the landmark Wigwam Motel on Route 66 and get a clear view of the line.

Little Rock

Union Station is the place in Little Rock to watch trains. At the station (1400 West Markham Street), built by Missouri Pacific in 1921, you can see 30–50 trains per day pass by on Union Pacific's busy double-track main line. Since UP operates the former Missouri Pacific line for predominately northbound traffic, the best time for photos is in the early morning. Southbound locals, manifests, and coal trains also operate through the depot headed to Pine Bluff, Texarkana, and Monroe, La. The station hosts Amtrak's *Texas Eagle* during the early morning hours, and the Little Rock & Western usually makes a daily appearance (Monday-Friday and occasionally on weekends). The LRWN makes a round trip from Perry to the UP yard in North Little Rock. Trains also stop and switch the LRWN yard at Pulaski, a short distance from Union Station.

Two bridges on either end of Union Station offer prime vantage points. Parking is either in the station parking lots or on streets nearby. The double-track Baring Cross Bridge over the Arkansas River is just north of Union Station. Union Pacific's Downing B. Jenks shop is located across the river in North Little Rock. The shops are the largest on the UP and a DDA40X Centennial is on display in front of the shops.

Mammoth Spring

Charlie Dischinger

While Thayer may be the better-known railroad name, most of the public access spots to watch trains and the best ones for photography are in Mammoth Spring. Thayer is the crew change location on the Thayer North and South Subs and usually sees more than 30 trains a day on this 300-mile-long, single-track railroad with 27 sidings. The steep Ozark Mountain grades on the Thayer North Sub require lots of power with river running along the Spring River from Mammoth Spring to Black Rock and then across the Mississippi flood plain to Memphis.

ACTIVITY: With in excess of 30 trains every day on the Thayer Subs, it is one of the busiest single-track railroads in the country. With this number of trains, a steady mixture of merchandise, intermodal, coal, and grain trains adds interest and creates an operational need to keep all trains moving at a good clip. Coal trains are usually powered with five units in a 2x3 DPU (Distributed Power Unit) configuration for 135-car trains. Grain trains and some of the 125-car coal trains run in a 2x2 DPU configuration. The rest of the trains, from Zs to merchandise, usually run with 3–5 units.

TRAIN-WATCHING SPOTS: You can generally find a place for watching trains at any of the numerous crossings along the line. While there are many good photographic locations, they can require some searching and exploring because the main roads that follow the railroad (Highways 60 and 63) do not stay in sight of it for long. You can stay at one spot or catch one train and follow it, listening to the scanner.

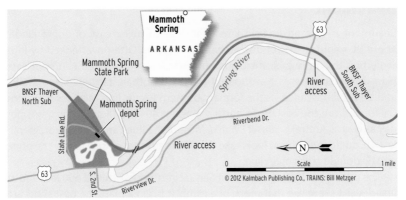

Mammoth Spring is right on the Missouri border and adjacent to Thayer, Mo., halfway between Springfield, Mo., and Memphis.

At Mammoth Spring, there are numerous Spring River access points near town that also give a nice view of the tracks. In addition, Mammoth Spring State Park has a depot with tracks running adjacent to it and the lake.

RAILROAD FREQUENCIES: BNSF: 161.100 (Springfield Yard), 160.335 (Teed to WS), 160.500 (WS to Olden), 161.415 (Olden to Madlock), 161.160 (Madlock to Tennessee Yard)

TO DO: In Mammoth Spring, you can try some homemade ice cream at the Palace Drug Soda Fountain on Main Street. Cherokee Village is nearby at Hardy, and numerous outfitters will rent you canoes and rafts for floating on the Spring River, one of the state's most popular fishing and floating rivers.

NEARBY: There are many state parks and scenic locations throughout the Ozarks. The Ozark Scenic National Waterway is close by to the north and Buffalo River National Park to the southwest.

DIRECTIONS: From Memphis, take Highway 63 north. From Springfield, take Highway 60 east to Willow Spring and then Highway 63 south. From Little Rock, take Highway 167 north to Hardy and then Highway 63 north.

Beaumont

Beaumont is located in Southern California 10 miles east of Loma Linda, about 90 minutes east of downtown Los Angeles. Often overlooked by fans preferring the more majestic Cajon and Tehachapi hot spots, Beaumont Pass (San Gorgonio Pass) is a wonderful mix of suburban, farm, low mountain, and desert landscapes, as the former Southern Pacific line accesses Southern California from the east. Here, you'll see about 40–50 Union Pacific trains per day as well as Amtrak's *Sunset Limited*. Most of the line can be seen from parallel I-10, but for a firsthand look, take the side roads that closely follow the busy, mostly double-track main line.

The peak near Beaumont, Mount San Jacinto, is just under 2,600 feet and at first doesn't seem like that much of a climb. It is. On a map, the best spots are between Indio, on the east, and San Timoteo Canyon, on the west. The area can be quite windy. Depending on the time of year, be prepared for blustery cold nights and hideously hot days. Lodging and food are everywhere, and, sadly, the open areas of the line are slowly getting choked off by urban sprawl. Chase it soon.

Dunsmuir

Located in the heart of northern California's Cascade Range, Dunsmuir is home to Union Pacific's historic Shasta route. Dunsmuir is where the Black Butte Subdivision ends from Klamath Falls, Ore., and where the Valley Division to Roseville begins. At Dunsmuir, you can see Amtrak's *Coast Starlight* daily, and on most days, 6 northbound and 6 southbound freight trains travel through. Dunsmuir Avenue is the main drag through town, and 1 block east is Sacramento Avenue, which parallels the railroad. Make sure to check out the Amtrak depot (5750 Sacramento Avenue) with its historic photos and where UP freights stop to change crews. Across from the depot is a fuel storage tank painted with Southern Pacific artwork.

You can view the horseshoe curve at Cantara Loop by going north of Dunsmuir on I-5 and exiting at Mott Road. You can also easily chase trains between Shasta Lake and Dunsmuir along I-5, taking the numerous exits almost all of which have access to the tracks. Dispatcher 66 controls all traffic through Dunsmuir. South of town use frequency 161.310 and north of town, 160.785.

Fullerton

Fullerton lies 25 rail miles southeast of Los Angeles at the junction where Metrolink's Orange Subdivision (the former Santa Fe Surf Line) joins BNSF's San Bernardino Sub, the westernmost leg of the busy Transcon. The city was named after George H. Fullerton, the Santa Fe director who was persuaded to route the railroad through the newly established town site in 1888. One of California's busiest passenger stations, Fullerton hosts up to 22 *Pacific Surfliners*, Amtrak's *Southwest Chief*, 34 Metrolink commuter trains, and 30–40 BNSF freights during a 24-hour weekday.

The primary train-watching spots along the three main tracks are the passenger platforms on the north and south sides and the pedestrian bridge that connects them. There is plenty of parking at either end of the 1930 Spanish Colonial style depot that houses a cafe with platform dining and is within easy walking distance of many downtown restaurants. Disneyland is only 4 miles south on Harbor Boulevard.

Redding

In Redding, Highway 273 lets you follow the action on Union Pacific's north-south I-5 corridor. The former Southern Pacific main line through the area is now part of UP's Valley Subdivision. Freights range from hot Z container/stack trains pulling United Parcel Service and FedEx trailers to loaded lumber trains heading south. The Redding local, based at the downtown depot, runs two shifts each day and draws a pair of GP60s. GP60s also power the Roseville to Redding turn, a Tuesday, Thursday, and Saturday departure from Redding that serves local customers along this important route. You'll also see 2 Amtrak *Coast Starlight* passenger trains.

While you're there, don't miss UP's Redding trestle. Built in 1939, this nearly three-quarter-mile-long landmark spans the Sacramento River and offers fantastic views of the river canyon, Shasta Bally Mountain, and Mount Lassen in the background. The trestle's north-south configuration makes it ideal for early morning and late day photography. Be sure to walk over the unique Sundial Bridge, a 700-foot, glass-decked pedestrian bridge that connects the Sacramento River Trail with the Turtle Bay Exploration Park and Museum.

Cajon Pass

David Lustig

Cajon Pass features heavy mountain grades for heavy mountain railroading. The conquering of Cajon Pass, which separates the San Bernardino Mountains and the San Gabriel Mountains is a 24/7 activity for the BNSF and the Union Pacific. For the BNSF, it is on the western end of its former Atchison, Topeka & Santa Fe Chicago-Los Angeles main line. For the Union Pacific, it is twofold. It is the southern end of the Utah-Los Angeles line via trackage rights over the BNSF and a separate ex-Southern Pacific route, known as the Palmdale Cutoff, between Palmdale, in the Mojave Desert, and Colton near San Bernardino.

ACTIVITY: On double- and triple-track main lines, with helpers and distributed power operations, you'll see a smorgasbord of intermodal, traditional boxcar, and unit trains. BNSF averages 70 trains per day and UP, 20. You'll also see Amtrak's *Sunset Limited* several times a day. The first few days of the week usually have lighter traffic.

TRAIN-WATCHING SPOTS: Consider Cajon Pass a hot area rather than a hot spot. Anywhere from just north of San Bernardino on the southern end to Barstow on the northern end is great train watching. If you stay at the Summit area, however, you will miss 99 percent of the adventure. Plus, Summit is not exactly fan friendly. Best bet is to watch the action from the public roads. Public side roads honeycomb the area; some are paved while others are washboard dirt. Follow the tracks and be prepared for nonstop trains. Many areas of the right-of-way are surrounded by U.S. Forest Service land. Check with the USFS before driving through their area, as sometimes a USFS day pass is required.

About an hour north of Cajon Pass is BNSF's Barstow Yard, where many side roads and overpasses allow excellent views of the railroad. Be aware that Barstow is near the U.S. Army's Fort Irwin, and you might be asked your intentions. To get to Barstow, you can hop on I-15 or follow the tracks through Oro Grande, Helendale, and Hodge to watch the action. On the

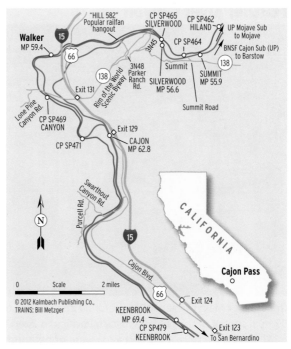

Cajon Pass is located in San Bernardino County, about an hour east of Los Angeles.

northern outskirts of Victorville is a Southwest Portland Cement facility with a private railroad and a small number of EMD road-switchers. The operation can be observed from public side roads.

SAFETY: Prepare for any kind of weather and you'll be fine. Also be careful where you step—nature has a variety of species living here, including snakes.

RAILROAD FREQUENCIES: BNSF: 161.190, 160.085; UP: 160.320, 160.740

TO DO: As well as exploring the mountains, you can explore desert areas. In San Bernardino County, you'll find Joshua Tree National Park, Mojave National Preserve, and Calico Ghost Town, a county park on I-15 northeast of Barstow.

DIRECTIONS: To get to the Summit, take I-15, exit at Highway 138, and follow the twists and turns through the mountains until you reach Summit and its overlook parking spot. For an even more scenic, and nostalgic drive, follow Route 66 (Cajon Boulevard) along the tracks.

Feather River Canyon

Dave Stanley

Once the domain of the fabled *California Zephyr* streamliner, this spectacular 89-mile stretch of the former Western Pacific has been the freight-only route for Union Pacific since 1982 and a trackage-rights corridor for BNSF since the mid-1990s. Nestled in the pines at an elevation of 4,834 feet, UP's Canyon Subdivision winds through the Sierra Nevada range on a constant 1 percent grade, perched on a ledge overlooking the north and middle forks of the Feather River. More than 30 tunnels bisect the steep terrain along with several spectacular steel and concrete bridges, allowing the railroad to traverse both the canyon and paralleling Route 70. At the hamlet of Keddie, BNSF's Gateway Subdivision branches to the north, providing an artery for traffic routed between California and the Pacific Northwest.

ACTIVITY: UP, with virtually no scheduled eastbound movements on the Canyon Sub, uses this route for westbound traffic, averaging 4 trains in a 24-hour period. Heavy lifters such as unit coal, grain, and ore, along with a manifest train, require fewer locomotives over this northern route than would be necessary on the steep grades of UP's Donner Pass crossing. At least 2 north (east) and a pair of south (west) trains comprise BNSF's daily activity through the Feather River Canyon west of Keddie. In addition, extra "bare tables" (empty intermodal wells and flats) and auto rack moves are routed via the Canyon and Gateway Subs several times a week.

TRAIN-WATCHING SPOTS: Route 70, between Oroville and Portola, follows the UP main line throughout the canyon affording numerous possibilities for train watching and photography. Pulga, Rock Creek, Tobin, Keddie wye, and Williams Loop (just east of Quincy at Spring Garden) are all visible from the

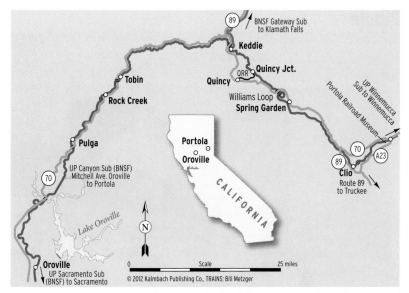

Feather River Canyon is situated between the foothill town of Oroville to the west and Portola.

highway and are popular spots with railfans. The impressive Clio trestle can be photographed from Plumas County Road A-15. At the western end of the canyon, the immense concrete arch bridge across the North Fork of the Feather River can be reached via Big Bend and Poe Powerhouse Roads off Route 70.

SAFETY: The curvature of Route 70 and truck traffic can create a treacherous environment when train chasing. Practice good driving habits. The canyon is a natural habitat for wildlife, including bears, mountain lions, and rattlesnakes.

RAILROAD FREQUENCIES: UP: 160.875 (Oroville to Keddie), 160.515 (Keddie to Portola); BNSF: 161.100 (Gateway Sub)

TO DO: Camping, fishing, and swimming are all popular pastimes along the Feather River, as is boating on Lake Oroville. For golfers, there are several courses in the Blairsden area. Activities in Reno are a 40-minute drive from Portola via Route 70 and US 395.

NEARBY: While in Portola, you can visit the Western Pacific Railroad Museum (which features a rent-a-locomotive program for those desiring throttle time).

DIRECTIONS: Oroville is between Redding and Sacramento. From Redding, take I-5 south to Highway 99 south. From Sacramento, take Highway 70 north.

Pinole

Phil Gosney

The former Southern Pacific Oakland to Sacramento main line hugs the shores of San Pablo Bay for 13 miles between San Pablo and Martinez. This is Union Pacific's main route into the Bay Area, and the line is consistently busy with Amtrak trains and various types of UP freight trains. The line is CTC controlled from Omaha with two main tracks that are signaled for movement in either direction. This is Milepost 19 on the UP Martinez Sub. Along the Bay in Pinole, you'll see majestic views of both passenger and freight trains.

ACTIVITY: On weekdays, *Capitol Corridor*, *San Joaquin*, *California Zephyr*, and *Coast Starlight* Amtrak passenger trains serving the Bay Area pass this location. Union Pacific trains consist of double-stack, automobile, manifest, and unit trains of ethanol and iron ore. While the Amtrak trains outnumber the freights in daylight hours, UP freight activity numbers 16–20 trains each day.

TRAIN-WATCHING SPOTS: Pinole Shores Park is the best location that overlooks San Pablo Bay and the UP tracks. You can walk along the paved pathway in either direction for different views and photos.

RAILROAD FREQUENCIES: UP: 160.800; BNSF: 160.560

TO DO: While in Pinole Shores Park, you can do some birdwatching (more than 100 species can be seen), hike trails through a variety of terrain, or walk along Point Pinole's 1,250-foot fishing pier. Grab a burger or soft-serve cone at Fosters Freeze, which appeared at its first location in 1946.

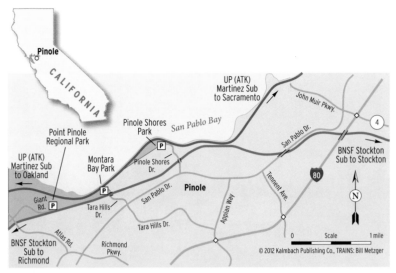

Pinole is about 17 miles north from the Oakland-Berkeley area.

NEARBY: BNSF's main line, which was the former Santa Fe line, is nearby with 16–20 trains running into the Bay Area, the majority being intermodal. This line is more inland and only skirts San Pablo Bay briefly in the town of Pinole. The tracks pass under Pinole Shore Drive, and this location is known as Gateley on the BNSF.

Martinez Station (601 Marina Vista Avenue) is located 12 miles to the east, and every Amtrak train pauses here and can be inspected closely from the station platform. There is a railroad display with a steam engine and freight cars located across from the station at Waterfront Park.

DIRECTIONS: From I-80, take Exit 21 (Appian Way). Drive west to San Pablo Avenue. Go left on San Pablo to Pinole Shores Drive. Make a right on Pinole Shores Drive and continue to end of road and park in the lot on the left.

Roseville

Dick Dorn

Roseville is home to Union Pacific's Davis Yard. UP says 98 percent of its northern California traffic moves through here. At the east end of the yard, the Roseville Subdivision begins its climb over 7,085-foot Donner Pass to Sparks, Nev. The Valley Subdivision heads north up the Sacramento Valley on the way to Oregon. To the west is the Martinez Subdivision, which runs to Oakland. Branching off the Cal P at Elvas, just east of Sacramento is the Fresno Subdivision that heads for Bakersfield toward Southern California. Amtrak's *California Zephyr* and a Auburn-Oakland *Capitol Corridor* train serve Roseville.

ACTIVITY: Davis Yard encompasses 915 acres that include 55 bowl tracks and 247 switches. The yard has 50 miles of track for manifest, unit, and intermodal trains, with a capacity for 6,500 freight cars. The yard is capable of classifying 1,800–2,300 cars per day and has eight receiving and departure tracks.

TRAIN-WATCHING SPOTS: Pacific Street has a viewing platform where you can watch trains arrive and depart both east to Donner Pass and north to Oregon. The Amtrak station (201 Pacific Street) just east of the shops has an open view into the yard. The east end of the yard is the most accessible area from which to watch and photograph trains. On the south side, you can take clear photos from Atlantic Street, across from the diesel shops. On the north side, Atkinson Street offers a view of the east end of the shops. At the west end of the yard, the only public access is along Old North Antelope Road.

RAILROAD FREQUENCIES:
Dispatcher 57 in Omaha, 160.875, controls all movements in and out of the yard. The yard and switching radios are on 161.400.

TO DO: At the Maidu Interpretive Center and Historic Site, you can walk a trail past ancient petroglyphs. Nearby in Sacramento, be sure to see the State Capitol Building, the California State Railroad Museum, Old Town Sacramento, Sutter's Fort, and the State Indian Museum. The American River Parkway offers beaches and a 15-mile biking and hiking path.

NEARBY: You can drive east on I-80 and follow the original transcontinental railroad for the Central Pacific, today UP, over Donner Pass to the town of Truckee and Donner Lake about 85 miles away.

DIRECTIONS: Roseville is a short drive along I-80 from Sacramento. Exit at Riverside Avenue, take a right on Douglas Boulevard, then a left on Oak Street, and another left on Washington Boulevard across the tracks to Pacific Street.

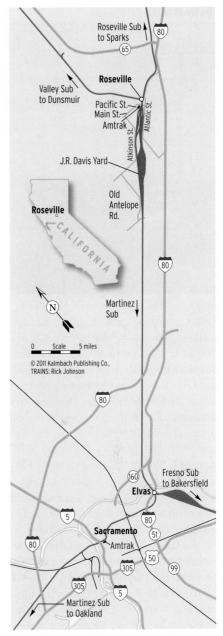

Roseville is located 16 miles east of Sacramento on I-80.

Stockton

Dave Stanley

Stockton's rail activity finds Union Pacific's Fresno Subdivision, the main north-south artery for traffic destined between Roseville and Southern California, intersecting Burlington Northern-Santa Fe's gateway from San Francisco. Stockton is home to Altamont Commuter Express (ACE) and is located on Amtrak's busy San Joaquin corridor. Central California Traction Company (CCT) operates a daily train between Stockton and Lodi and performs all the switching at the Port of Stockton. Stockton Terminal & Eastern serves the warehouse and industrial districts located in the central and eastern parts of town with an attractive MP15DC.

ACTIVITY: UP uses the former WP yard, originating 4 locals, 3 yard engines, and 3 ACE trains. BNSF's Mormon Yard dispatches a daily local running north and receives a daily turn from Riverbank. Yard engines work around Mormon including interchange moves to UP as well as deliveries to the CCT and ST&E. Roughly 35 movements a day bang across the diamonds including intermodal trains, numerous grain trains, and manifests carrying autos, plastics, steel, chemicals, lumber, perishables, and canned goods. Amtrak operates 12 *San Joaquins* through town. CCT's Lodi Turn goes on duty at noon at the old carbarn located at Cherokee and Sanguinetti. Port traffic includes unit coal, ore, and corn (for ethanol) trains. ST&E's yard engine works at the engine house on Shaw Road, just east of Highway 99.

TRAIN-WATCHING SPOTS: The interlocking plant, located southwest of Union and Scott Streets, is a popular spot to view mainline activity. The former SP station on Weber Avenue, along the UP double track, has been beautifully restored and is used by ACE passengers.

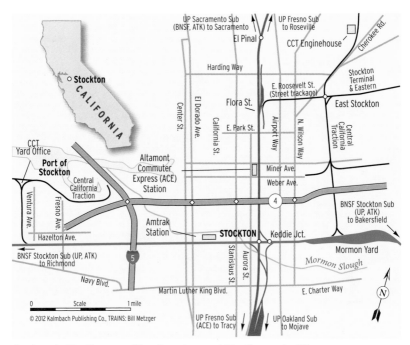

Stockton is 80 miles east of San Francisco and 50 miles south of Sacramento.

Several active and inactive drawbridges are located near public roads branching off Highway 4. Street running still exists for both CCT (B Street) and ST&E (Roosevelt Street). CCT's Lodi Turn, shortly after leaving Stockton, turns north through picturesque Morada. Highway 99 to Morada Lane (east) takes you there.

SAFETY: Stockton has seen a rise in crime, including the downtown rail corridors (including the BNSF-UP crossing), so be aware of your surroundings.

RAILROAD FREQUENCIES: UP: 161.550 (road), 160.680 (Fresno yardmaster); BNSF: 160.650 (road); CCT: 160.305, 161.415; ST&E 160.455, 161.235

TO DO: Stockton's waterfront is home to many restaurants, boating and fishing, and the Stockton Ports minor league baseball franchise. Haggin Museum at Victory Park is full of local history.

NEARBY: Three railroad museums are less than an hour's drive from Stockton: the Western Railway, the California State Railroad Museum in Sacramento, and CSRM's Railtown 1897.

DIRECTIONS: Take either Highway 5 or Highway 99 into Stockton. Then take Highway 4, which passes over the UP double track, just north of the interlocking plant. Exit at Stanislaus Street or Wilson Way and look for the tracks.

Tehachapi

Tom Danneman

The Tehachapi Mountains are nature's way of defining central and Southern California. For the Union Pacific and BNSF, it's miles of tough mountain railroading as the loop gains 77 feet in elevation as the track climbs a 2 percent grade. For railfans, however, the 60-odd miles between Mojave, on the south, and Bakersfield, on the north, is almost heaven on earth, with more than 60 trains daily. All the great rail photographers came here to capture trains fighting nature in all its glory.

ACTIVITY: The rails through the Tehachapi Mountains are owned by the Union Pacific, with the BNSF throwing in just as many trains via trackage rights. From the UP comes a smorgasbord of trains stitching together the western and southwestern areas of its vast system. The same for the BNSF. It is hot property. One of the few regular industries between Bakersfield and Mojave is a cement plant at Monolith on the Mojave side of the mountain. Served by a local, it is one of the few smaller train movements you'll see here.

TRAIN-WATCHING SPOTS: Take your choice. Attack Tehachapi from any direction and you quickly drive yourself crazy with seemingly unending train-watching and photographic possibilities. There are curves, bridges, tunnels, the famed Tehachapi Loop, mountains, cliffs, desert, more curves, more bridges, and more tunnels. Some excellent viewing locations are along Woodford-Tehachapi Road, either southeast from Keene or northwest of Old Towne Tehachapi.

The first instinct is to head to Tehachapi Loop and watch trains go round and round. But this is only a minute piece of the story. Arm yourself with a good local map, a full tank of gas, and a spirit of adventure and prowl the area.

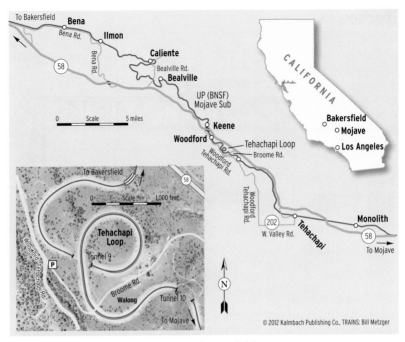

Tehachapi is located 35 miles southeast of Bakersfield.

You don't need anyone to tell you where the great areas are. Just when you think you've found the best one, another, seemingly better, comes into view. Explore the many side roads that lead you to places like Bealville and Caliente.

RAILROAD FREQUENCIES: UP: 160.320; BNSF: 161.190

SAFETY: Being aware of your environment is crucial in the Tehachapis. There are a multitude of places where trains can safely be seen from public access. The right-of-way is routinely patrolled and No Trespassing signs should be heeded.

TO DO: Tehachapi, the largest city in the mountains, features a walking tour of its historic downtown. You can also visit alpaca ranches, ostrich farms, and wind power plants. Edwards Air Force Base is southeast of Mojave and has numerous tours, including one by NASA.

NEARBY: Visit the Tehachapi Depot Railroad Museum (101 West Tehachapi Boulevard). Just east of Mojave is the local airport, home for dozens of decommissioned airliners.

DIRECTIONS: For this stretch of railroad, just follow Highway 58 between Bakersfield and Mojave.

Truckee

Dick Dorn

Truckee is in the heart of the Sierra Nevada Mountain Range and surrounded by mountains on all sides. The tracks run right through downtown Truckee, and Amtrak's *California Zephyr* stop at the historic ex-SP depot.

ACTIVITY: On average, there are about 20 UP freights in a 24-hour period. If you plan to do serious railfanning in the area, Altamont Press's California Railfan Timetable 20 is a real asset.

TRAIN-WATCHING SPOTS: The tracks are easily accessible in the immediate Truckee area from Donner Pass Road, the main drag through town. At the west end of town, check out the SP-style signal bridge and a nice curve looking east. You can hike west from here above the tracks for some nice elevation to take photos from.

If you are feeling adventurous, west of town at the Donner Pass Road Exit off I-80, you can go south up to Cold Stream Canyon. The gate past the gas stations and hotel is usually open in the summer. This is a rocky, gravel road but passable in a standard vehicle. The tracks make a big 5-mile loop through the canyon, and you have to park and hike to get to the tracks.

Go east out of town on Donner Pass Road and, just as you start to climb, turn right on Glenshire Drive. This road has several places from where you can photograph trains.

During winter, UP headquarters all snow removal operations in Truckee, and the spreaders and flangers can be seen from a public parking area east of the only grade crossing in town. Parking is limited in winter, especially after a snowstorm, so it is best to park your car and walk to photograph trains as they go through town.

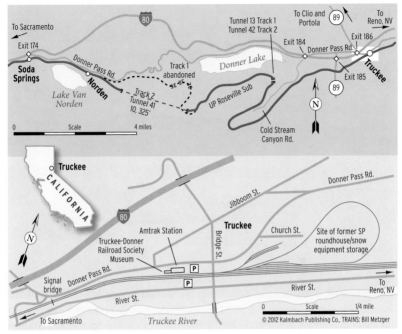

Truckee is located on Union Pacific's Roseville Subdivision 35 miles west of Reno, Nev., on I-80.

RAILROAD FREQUENCIES: UP: 160.320 (dispatcher)

TO DO: Just west of Truckee is Donner State Park, where you can view historical exhibits, hike, camp, and swim. Lake Tahoe is a short drive south on either Highway 267 or Highway 89. During winter, there are four ski resorts at the Donner Summit area.

NEARBY: The Portola Railroad Museum is located about 40 miles north of Truckee. You can explore railroad history in the Donner Summit area and check out the snow sheds along the old track. Make sure to view the support walls that were hand-built by Chinese laborers directly above the parking area at Rainbow Bridge.

DIRECTIONS: Take the central Truckee exit from either direction off I-80.

Denver

Mike Danneman

The Denver-Front Range region features many train-watching locations on the BNSF and UP lines radiating out of the metro area. The former Rio Grande main line heads west into the Front Range of the Rocky Mountains from North Yard. Spectacular scenery awaits the train watcher, and the line hosts Amtrak's *California Zephyr* for those wanting a beautiful train ride. A busy, mostly coal-hauling main line known as the Joint Line heads south featuring both UP and BNSF trains. The busiest route out of Denver heads east: the BNSF main to Brush, which sees freight, coal, and passenger traffic. Other rail lines include the former Colorado & Southern main, now also BNSF, through Boulder to Cheyenne, Wyo. Parallel to the east is UP's Denver to Cheyenne route through Greeley. UP's former Kansas Pacific line also traverses eastward out of Denver to Salina, Kans.

ACTIVITY: There are 10–15 trains a day on the Moffat Line, which includes BNSF freights and Amtrak. The busy Joint Line sees 30–40 trains per day. The Brush Sub sees 40–45 trains in 24 hours. BNSF's former C&S line to Cheyenne sees about 6 trains per day. Additional ballast trains and stack trains can be seen, but not daily. UP's Denver to Cheyenne route has about 10–12 trains per day, not including locals.

TRAIN-WATCHING SPOTS: Coal Creek Canyon and Big 10 curves are a great place to watch trains climb a 2 percent grade combined with 10 degree curves. UP trains, along with a pair each of BNSF and Amtrak trains, give the line some variety. Both locations can be reached via Highway 72 west of Denver. Open space provides some access to the Big 10 area, but only on foot. A good location to watch trains traversing the loop at Coal Creek Canyon is from Blue

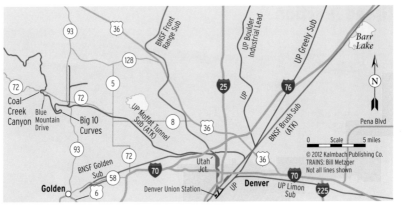

Denver is nestled at the eastern edge of the Rocky Mountains in north-central Colorado.

Mountain Drive, south off Highway 72. Another location for BNSF traffic is at Barr. Certain times of the year, Barr Lake provides a nice reflection of passing trains for photographers. Also, several overpasses in downtown Denver provide safe places to watch trains headed over the Joint Line.

RAILROAD FREQUENCIES: BNSF: 160.920 (Moffat Sub, Denver to Arvada), 160.455 (Moffat Sub, Arvada to Dotsero), 160.650 (Joint Line), 161.100 (Brush Sub), 161.160 (Front Range Sub); UP: 161.145 (Greeley Sub), 160.920 (Joint Line)

TO DO: Downtown Denver provides many activities. Check out a Rockies game at Coors Field, which is built on the site of a former UP yard.

NEARBY: The Colorado Railroad Museum in nearby Golden has 15 acres of Colorado railroad history on display. It is only 12 miles west of downtown Denver off I-70.

DIRECTIONS: Denver is at the crossroads of I-70 and I-25, with I-76 coming in from Nebraska.

Grand Junction

Mike Danneman

Once the midpoint of bridge carrier Denver & Rio Grande Western, Grand Junction still retains much of its railroad heritage. Named for the confluence of the Colorado (formerly the Grand) and Gunnison Rivers, Grand Junction was the location of a hump yard that Rio Grande used to sort tonnage for departing trains, but it was torn out in the Southern Pacific era. East Yard is used for marshaling coal trains serving a heavy coal-hauling branch line that heads south of town along the Gunnison River to the mines near Somerset. The rail lines in the area are now operated by Union Pacific, and they include the intermountain main line between Denver and Salt Lake City and the North Fork Branch to the coal mines.

ACTIVITY: Train frequency for the main line through Grand Junction is 6–10 trains per day, including BNSF trackage-rights trains and Amtrak's daily *California Zephyr*. Several coal trains arrive and depart on the North Fork Sub each day, and these train counts can vary dramatically.

TRAIN-WATCHING SPOTS: Several area grade crossings and overpasses provide spots to watch trains. The biggest hurdle while waiting at a location is the somewhat sporadic train frequency, so using a scanner can help locate trains. Also, both UP and BNSF operate locals that run west of town (BNSF only to a tank car loading facility on the west side of town). The *California Zephyr* makes a service stop at the Grand Junction station (339 South First Street). For those willing to wander farther, near the Utah state line, you'll find remarkable Ruby Canyon. Four-wheel drive is needed to reach an overlook at Dodges Bluff near Utaline.

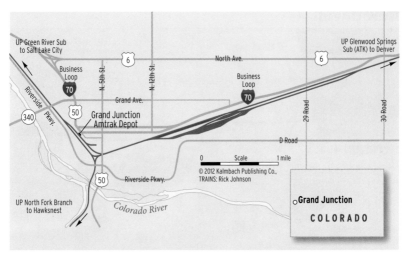

Grand Junction is located in far west-central Colorado off I-70.

SAFETY: If you decide to head west out into the Utah desert, make sure you have enough supplies and water to make it a safe trip.

RAILROAD FREQUENCIES: UP: 160.470 (Laramie Sub), 161.145 (Greeley Sub); BNSF: 161.160 (Front Range Sub)

TO DO: The area is ringed with national parks and forests. Colorado National Monument is one of the area's biggest outdoor attractions in the area. Towering sandstone monoliths, sheer-walled canyons, and beautiful valleys greet visitors to this U.S. National Park. The Grand Valley is also well known for producing high-quality wines and has several wineries that are open for wine-tasting.

NEARBY: Explore south of Grand Junction (about an hour) toward Montrose and Ridgway and you'll find remnants of Rio Grande's narrow gauge heritage.

DIRECTIONS: To reach Grand Junction from east or west, use I-70. The business loop will take you right downtown.

New Haven

Scott Hartley

The former New Haven Railroad Beaux-Arts Union Station, designed by noted architect Cass Gilbert and opened in 1920, stands at the junction of today's Boston-New York-Washington Northeast Corridor and Amtrak's 62-mile branch north to Springfield, Mass. This portion of the Corridor is operated by MTA Metro-North Railroad, and handles MN and Shore Line East commuter trains and Amtrak intercity runs.

ACTIVITY: Metro-North schedules 75 trains in and out of New Haven each weekday (less on weekends). Most use electric M.U. equipment. SLE has 26 weekday trains with some operating through to and from Stamford. Amtrak contributes 50 trains per day. Corridor trains, all electric-powered, include the high-speed *Acela Express* sets and conventional consists. The Springfield Line uses diesel-powered equipment. Although some through trains between Springfield and southern points and the *Vermonter* continue to make the swap from diesel to electric locomotives here, most Springfield service consists of two-car, push-pull diesel shuttles. CSX's weekday local freight train usually passes westbound through Union Station in the early morning, returning later in the day. Providence & Worcester runs aggregate trains west on the Corridor to reach Long Island and the Danbury area, mostly at nighttime during warmer months.

TRAIN-WATCHING SPOTS: Unlike many big-city stations, access to New Haven Union passenger platforms is not restricted to ticket holders. Platforms are reached via an under-track passageway. MTA, Amtrak, City of New Haven, and Connecticut State police all patrol Union Station, but train watching generally is allowed on platforms as long as it does not interfere with passenger access

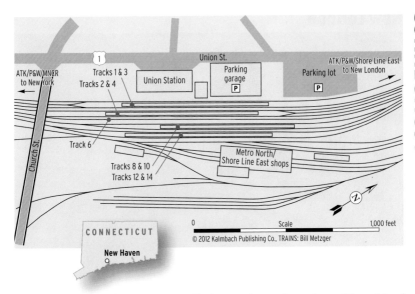

New Haven is located on New Haven Harbor on the northern shore of Long Island Sound.

and safety. Other public access to main lines is very limited along main lines in the region. MN, AMTK, and SLE shops can be seen from the station platforms, but are not open to the public.

SAFETY: All platforms are high-level to facilitate passenger boarding. Train movements through the terminal are constant and many move swiftly. Mind the yellow platform edge stripe, and do not attempt to pass the gates at the ends of each platform.

RAILROAD FREQUENCIES: MN: 160.545 (road), 160.950 (yard); Amtrak: 160.920 (Northeast Corridor, Springfield Line); CSX: 161.070 (Cedar Hill Yard)

TO DO: New Haven is home to numerous restaurants, the beautiful Yale University campus, which was founded in 1701, and the Yale Peabody Museum of Natural History.

NEARBY: The Shore Line Trolley Museum, located about 10 miles east, features 90 pieces of historic equipment and a 2-mile round trip through tidal marshes.

DIRECTIONS: From either I-91 or I-95, use the Route 34 Exit to downtown and follow the signs to Union Station (50 Union Avenue). A large public parking lot is connected to the station at its east end.

New London

Tom Nanos

The Whaling City hosts four railroads within its borders: the New England Central, Providence & Worcester, Amtrak, and the Shore Line East. There are a number of areas where these can be viewed within the city limits. In between trains, there's plenty else to see—the Thames River hosts a number of commercial, Coast Guard, and U.S. Navy vessels.

ACTIVITY: The bulk of train movements consist of passenger and commuter runs, with Amtrak holding the most activity with electric-powered Northeast regionals and *Acelas*. Shore Line East has 1 early morning and 4 evening runs to New London using diesel power. For more diesels under the wires, the P&W has a turn job (symbol NR-2) that passes through town westbound midmorning and back east early to midafternoon. The NECR visits town on an as-needed basis, but when it does, it spends some time working the yard near the State Pier.

TRAIN-WATCHING SPOTS: New London's Waterfront Park is a great spot to watch Amtrak, Shore Line East, and the Providence & Worcester pass by. The linear park parallels the tracks, following the shore of the Thames River starting at the Amtrak station (27 Water Street) and continuing south to the Shaw's Cove swing bridge. Another location is on the south side of Shaw's Cove near Fort Trumbull, where a walking path offers views of the swing bridge. For the New England Central, things are a bit tighter: the fencing put in around the State Pier and New London's partial closure of Riverside Park has hindered many views. Glances of operations can be seen from State Pier Road and from the nearby boat launch. At the end of Thomas Griffin Road, some views of the wooden Winthrop Cove trestle are possible.

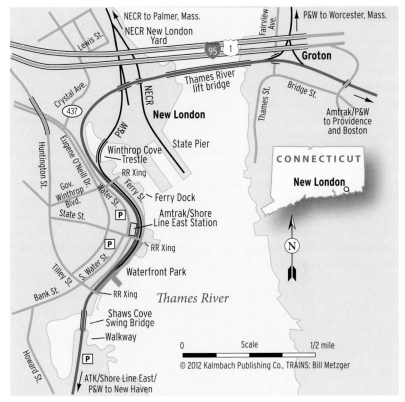

New London is on the Thames River in southeastern Connecticut.

SAFETY: Two crossings at either end of Waterfront Park provide safe crossing.

RAILROAD FREQUENCIES: Amtrak: 160.920; PW: 160.650; NECR: 161.205, 161.415

TO DO: There are many restaurants within walking distance of the waterfront area. The Mohegan Sun Casino is about 15 minutes north, and the Foxwoods Casino is about 30 minutes east.

NEARBY: The Essex Steam Train is about a 20-minute drive west and 40 minutes north is the Connecticut Eastern Railroad Museum in Willimantic.

DIRECTIONS: To Waterfront Park, take I-95 to downtown New London. Follow Eugene O'Neill Drive to Atlantic Street. Go left on Atlantic and park in the Water Street Garage (fees apply). Shaw's Cove path is off Howard Street. There is a parking lot at the end of Nameaug Street. Walk north toward the water to get to the foot path.

Jacksonville

Jacksonville is home to three railroad headquarters: CSX, Rail America, and Florida East Coast. CSX enters the city from the north via its former Atlantic Coast Line route from Georgia, from the south from Orlando, and from the west from Baldwin. The highest concentration of traffic for CSX is on the northern route from Jacksonville to Folkston, Ga., with roughly 30–40 trains per day. Its two main yards are Moncrief just north of downtown and Duval Intermodal Ramp just west of town.

The Florida East Coast's northern operation is at Bowden Yard on the city's south side. FEC operates roughly 10 scheduled trains a day with extras being possible on its route to Miami. Jacksonville is also served by Norfolk Southern via its route from Valdosta, Ga., with roughly 8 trains per day. Amtrak serves the city as well with 4 daily trains, and the Auto Train makes a daily appearance. The FEC bridge downtown is a good train-watching spot, where all carriers traverse to interchange with each other. Be careful railfanning around Beaver Street as the area is a high crime location.

St. Augustine

St. Augustine is the oldest city in continental United States, having been founded in 1565 by Spanish settlers. It was home to the Florida East Coast headquarters from 1895 until 2008. The FEC main line enters from the north and parallels US Highway 1 from Jacksonville. The FEC operates roughly 10 trains per day through the city, plus extras. A triweekly local from Bowden Yard in Jacksonville serves the industrial park west of downtown.

Near downtown, the main line makes a series of sharp turns that provide multiple locations for viewing and photographing trains. Be sure to check out the former FEC headquarters near the main line off US 1. It's now restored and in use as the appropriately named Flagler College, named for Henry Morrison Flagler, who started the FEC. You can also check out Memorial Presbyterian Church, where Flagler is entombed with his family.

Callahan

Eric Hendrickson

Callahan was the home of two railroads until the Atlantic Coast Line and Seaboard Air Line merger in 1967. Prior to the merger, the ACL crossed the SAL main line near downtown Callahan. After the merger, the new Seaboard Coast Line choose the former ACL main line for its route between Jacksonville and Richmond. The former SAL main line was kept from the crossing of the ACL main to Baldwin and farther south toward the Tampa area. East of the crossing was abandoned from Callahan to Yulee. Today, the main line is part of CSX's Nahunta Subdivision with the former SAL being part of the Callahan Subdivision.

ACTIVITY: North of Callahan, train traffic is heavy with 30–40 per day, along with 4 Amtrak scheduled trains and 2 Amtrak Auto Trains. The Callahan Sub hosts about 18 trains per day.

TRAIN-WATCHING SPOTS: Callahan has numerous locations for viewing or photography. The split of the Nahunta Sub with the Callahan Sub is just north of Brandies Avenue. From here, you can take excellent photos of southbound trains in the morning and afternoon light all year. Northbound trains can be a little tougher, with the afternoon offering the best light in summer. Just south of the mainline split is the Highway 301 overpass that follows the Callahan Sub to Baldwin. This vantage point offers an excellent view of southbound and northbound trains passing through Callahan. The bridge has walkways on both sides and traffic is minimal.

SAFETY: Be sure to stay off CSX property as the local police and CSX police regularly patrol the area.

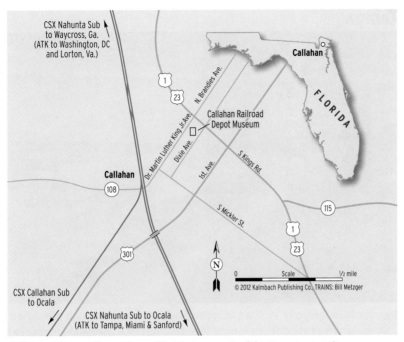

Callahan is located in northeast Florida, just south of the Georgia state line.

RAILROAD FREQUENCIES: CSX: 160.590, 160.320. CSX and Amtrak trains call signals out over the radio, so this is a handy tool for finding trains.

TO DO: Every March, the city of Callahan hosts an annual Railroad Days festival featuring a parade and numerous other activities. The West Nassau Historical Society has restored the former Callahan Depot which has a museum of railroad and historical items. A few miles east of Callahan is Amelia Island, a barrier island worth visiting. There are numerous golf courses and sightseeing locations within easy reach of Callahan.

NEARBY: Be sure to travel a few miles north to Folkston, Ga., and see the funnel where CSX's main line splits toward Waycross and Savannah. A few miles west is the Crawford crossing of NS main line from Valdosta, Ga., to Jacksonville. Jacksonville is only 20 miles south and offers additional train-watching locations.

DIRECTIONS: From Jacksonville, take US Highway 1 north to Callahan. Turn left onto Brandies Avenue and travel a quarter-mile west to the grade crossing of the Nahunta and Callahan Subs.

Tampa

Scott Hartley

Metropolitan Tampa offers a lot of railroading spread out through the region. CSX continues to use both its former Atlantic Coast Line Lakeland Subdivision (known locally as the A Line) and the ex-Seaboard Air Line Yeoman Subdivision (the S Line) for freight running between Tampa and the north. The two cross on a diamond at Plant City, 21 miles east (timetable north) of downtown Tampa. Amtrak's *Silver Star* operates here as well.

ACTIVITY: Most manifest freight trains and the Tropicana Juice Train between Tampa and the north use the S Line. Intermodal hotshots usually favor the A Line. Four Amtrak movements pass Plant City each day, but you will only see 2 trains as both the southbound and northbound *Silver Stars* make their Tampa stops as a detour from their trips between New York and Miami.

TRAIN-WATCHING SPOTS: Perhaps the best place to see the most trains is at the Plant City diamond, where 25–30 trains cross daily. Phosphate trains operating between the inland Bone Valley mining area and northern locations on the Yeoman Sub will join or leave via the Plant City Subdivision, just south of the diamond. CSX phosphate trains leave the Yeoman Sub 11 railroad timetable miles south of Plant City at Valrico Junction, so most of these heavy trains must be viewed closer to Tampa.

Favored locations are at Valrico Junction, where the Yeoman and Valrico subs split, and at the north end Yeoman Yard in Tampa, where CSX crosses a concrete trestle over the Tampa Bypass Canal at 78th Street just north of Highway 60.

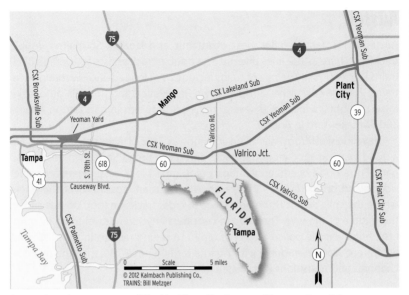

Located on the west coast of Florida, Plant City is east of Tampa along I-4.

All CSX train crews call signal aspects over the radio as they travel in automatic block signal and control point signaled territories such as the Yeoman and Lakeland Subs. The CSX dispatcher in Jacksonville provides track warrants on the radio to most trains operating through this region.

SAFETY: Highway congestion makes train chasing by car nearly impossible through most of the area.

RAILROAD FREQUENCIES: CSX: 160.230 (dispatcher), 160.590, 161.100, 161.370 (road and yard)

TO DO: Ybor City and Channelside, former industrial and marine areas on the east side of Tampa, now form an entertainment district with restaurants, clubs, and shops, all served by the TECO streetcar system that crosses CSX's line into Tampa Union Station on a diamond.

NEARBY: Florida Railroad Museum at Parrish operates tourist trains over a 5-mile segment of the former Seaboard Air Line route to Sarasota.

DIRECTIONS: Plant City is located at the intersection of US 92 and Highway 39, from I-4 Exit 21. Tampa locations and Valrico Junction can be reached from Highway 60.

Austell

Austell is located 10 miles west of Atlanta, and Norfolk Southern's double track ends here as the lines diverge. The double track boasts an average of 60 trains per 24 hours. The mix of trains includes 3–4 loaded BNSF Wyoming coal trains, 2 Amtrak *Crescents*, 2 Triple Crown RoadRailers, intermodals, auto racks, mixed freights, a local, and several transfers between Inman Yard in Atlanta and Whitaker Yard in Austell.

Traveling west from Atlanta on US Highway 78/278 takes you to Austell. For a good viewing spot, cross the tracks and go to Broad Street, where you can park. For a good overhead vantage point, go 1 block east, where a double-sidewalked bridge crosses the tracks. A pedestrian crossing over the tracks where the split begins is the best place to cross tracks on foot. Do not park in the middle of the wye. The railroad considers anything gravel to be its property; however, the police are accustomed to seeing railfans in town. NS uses a different scanner frequency for Atlanta terminal, 160.740, than the mainline channels and transitions it at Austell.

Cartersville

Cartersville is located near the Etowah River Basin and lower reaches of the Appalachians in northwest Georgia, an area rich in Native American and Civil War history. From I-75, Highway 113 (Main Street) takes you west to the tracks in downtown. You can park at the welcome center (a former Western & Atlantic depot built in 1854). Cartersville averages about 40 trains per 24 hours, including several loaded coal trains traveling to a coal-fired power plant.

A few blocks north, you'll find the Junta wye, which is a good train-watching location, as well as a small yard and office. Locomotives for yard and local switching are usually seen there. A branch line to the west serves Georgia Power Plant Bowen. The line continues west to Cedartown and is served by a daily local from Cartersville that usually departs in the morning and returns late afternoon.

Cordele

Known as the Watermelon Capital of the World, Cordele is located in Crisp County right off I-75 in the heart of Georgia. Between Eighth and Ninth Streets, west of the I-75 interchange, you'll find an at-grade junction of CSX's ex-ACL Fitzgerald Subdivision, Norfolk Southern's GS&F Macon District, and the Heart of Georgia Railroad's ex-SA&M main line (HOG or SAM short line). The tracks are surrounded on all sides by safe public parking. CSX averages 25–30 trains daily with NS running about 20–25. Both lines host numerous intermodals, mixed freights, locals, and bulk unit trains (coal, rock, grain, sulfur, and ethanol). HOG locals pass through town on weekdays as needed for local industries.

The HOG once hosted SAM excursions in downtown Cordele, but those passenger trains now board farther west of town at the Georgia Veterans State Park. Cordele exemplifies a Georgia town that grew because of the railroads and was named after Cordelia Hawkins, daughter of Savannah, Americus & Montgomery Railroad president Colonel Samuel Hugh Hawkins. It is typically very safe with plenty of amenities for the visitor in the form of food, fuel, and overnight accommodations.

Jesup

Jesup is located on CSX's A Line in Wayne County along US Highway 301. CSX's Nahunta Subdivision from Jacksonville and the Jesup Subdivision, which branches off toward Waycross in downtown Jesup, provide the majority of traffic. Six Amtrak trains also pass by, including the Auto Train, with the *Silver Meteor* having a scheduled stop. Norfolk Southern's main line from Brunswick/Macon also passes over CSX north of the junction and Amtrak station.

Traffic is generally brisk throughout the day, and it's easy to catch 25–30 trains as they make their way in and out of Florida. Many of these won't be seen in the more popular destination of Folkston as their journey generally begins or ends in Waycross. Jesup features a railfan platform on Cherry Street with views of the main line and Amtrak station. There is plenty of public parking and right-of-way available to see the train action. Like most small towns on the route, there is local lodging, eating, and shopping nearby.

Atlanta

Woody Harrison

Atlanta's railroad history and location make it a transportation hub of the Southeast. For years, a portion of Atlanta railroad traffic served the Ford and General Motors plants, but their closures and loss of traffic has been replaced by new intermodal yards, auto distribution centers, and ethanol facilities.

ACTIVITY: There are easily more than 100 train movements through Atlanta per day and roughly 60 percent are Norfolk Southern. Amtrak's *Crescent* stops at Peachtree Street's Brookwood Station southbound mornings and northbound evenings. BNSF hauls coal via NS from Wyoming to one of the largest coal-fired power plants in the country just south of Atlanta, which receives 3–4 loaded trains per day. UP and BNSF haul several intermodal trains into a yard, and KCS hauls the daily Transcon train from the west coast on NS. NS runs a daily Triple Crown RoadRailer southbound usually late mornings and northbound in the evenings. A yard in East Point handles the Triple Crown trains.

TRAIN-WATCHING SPOTS: There are not a lot of safe, legal and quality spots downtown. The bridges over the yards offer the best and safest locations. A parking lot at King Plow Art Center offers the safest views of Howell Interlocking, which sees the most train movements in the state. The Brickworks off Marietta Street is a fun eatery with parking on the roof that overlooks King Plow, just south of Howell Interlocking. Marietta Street runs just northwest of downtown following the rail lines to both NS Inman Yard and CSX Tilford Yard. Downtown bridges to photograph from are Techwood Drive, Peters Street, and Jones Avenue, but parking can be difficult.

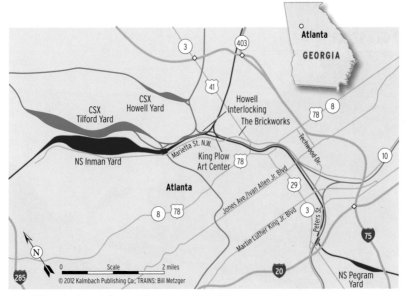

GEORGIA

Howell Interlocking is located just northwest of downtown Atlanta.

SAFETY: Atlanta auto traffic can be a challenge. Some areas are best traveled in the company of a friend. Atlanta is a high-security zone for the railroads due to ethanol trains, so railroad police can be tough. The suburbs offer somewhat friendlier conditions.

RAILROAD FREQUENCIES: NS: 160.740 (Atlanta terminal), 160.950 (road), 160.245 (dispatcher to train), 160.830 (train to dispatcher); CSX 161.370, 161.520, 161.100, 160.230; GNRR: 154.600

TO DO: The aquarium and High Museum of Art are great points of interest. At Stone Mountain Park, there is a tourist railroad running several vintage EMD locomotives and many other activities.

NEARBY: West of town is the Fulton County Railway, which serves Fulton Industrial Park. The Southern Museum of Civil War and Locomotive History hosts the famous *General* locomotive.

DIRECTIONS: To Howell Interlocking, take I-75/I-85 to 10th Street. Go west on 10th Street to Brady Avenue and turn left. Go to Marietta Street and turn right. Go a half-mile on until just past King Plow. There is a parking lot on the right. Another mile puts you at the south end of both the NS and CSX yards. Turn right onto Marietta Road.

Folkston

Kevin Andrusia

Folkston sees the blending of the Nahunta and Jesup Subdivisions in the Jacksonville Division, forming the Florida Funnel (or Folkston Funnel) for 20 miles to Callahan, Fla., making for an abundant mix of trains from all over the country. The Nahunta Subdivision follows CSX's A Line. The Jesup Subdivision actually diverges from the Nahunta Subdivision at Jesup, continuing southwest to Waycross and Rice Yard (the second-largest classification yard on CSX) and bending back to the southeast toward Folkston.

ACTIVITY: Folkston can see an average of 50–60 trains per day. This includes Amtrak's *Silver Meteor*, *Silver Star*, and Auto Train and the famous Tropicana Juice Train, which generally operates five days each week. Intermodal traffic is very heavy along both subdivisions, while multilevel (auto racks) favor the Jesup Sub side. With CSX's Bone Valley to the south in Central Florida, there is also a steady stream of bulk unit trains carrying coal southbound and phosphate northbound, with respective empty trains. Unit rock trains from points north head into Florida and return north after they've been unloaded. Unit ethanol trains are also seen once a week on average, heading to Winter Haven in central Florida.

TRAIN-WATCHING SPOTS: Folkston is an ideal spot for watching or photographing trains. It is safe, with ample public parking and routine law enforcement. The highway crossing pattern and public right-of-way is graded for an unobstructed view all day long. In downtown, a viewing platform is situated on the east side of the tracks and generally has a public scanner operating 24/7, so you can hear what is coming if you don't have a scanner of your own. Numerous defect detectors on all sides of town will alert you along with signal

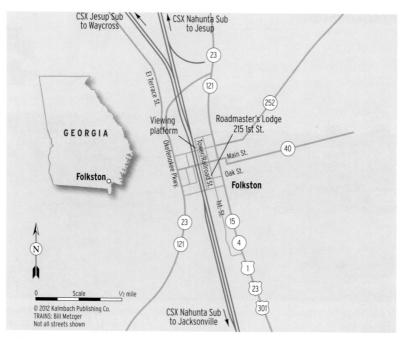

Folkston, Gateway to the Okeefenokee, is located in Charlton County approximately 21 miles west of Kingsland.

calls. The platform also has an adjacent restroom and grill, and food, fuel, and lodging is within walking distance. You can also watch trains from across the tracks at the restored depot and train museum. For a preview, a webcam is in operation that shows activity along the Folkston Funnel (search the Internet for latest website).

RAILROAD FREQUENCIES: CSX: 160.590, 161.100 (road), 160.320 (dispatcher to train)

TO DO: While there is ample traditional lodging, the most noteworthy place to stay in Folkston is Railside Lodging, a historic roadmaster's office and restored bay window caboose, both serving as trackside overnight accommodations.

NEARBY: For the adventurous seeking sights beyond the rails, the Okefenokee Swamp is a mere 32 miles north on US Highway 1. The drive is more than enough reason to take a peek at the city of Waycross, itself a huge piece of CSX history.

DIRECTIONS: Just north of the Florida state line, Folkston can be reached by taking Highway 40 west off I-95.

Manchester

Casey Thomason

Manchester is a bustling CSX town located at the junction of three vital subdivisions. The Manchester and Lineville Subs of the Atlanta Division merge from the north and flow south as the Fitzgerald Sub of the Jacksonville Division. The Lineville Sub hosts trains from the Midwest through Birmingham, Ala., some 170 miles northwest, while trains off the Manchester Sub run via Atlanta, 70 miles northeast. The main line to the south has seen extensive upgrades during the past 15 years, creating many double-track sections for the 200-mile run south to Waycross, Georgia's Rice Yard. An additional 75 miles beyond Rice is Florida's busy Jacksonville terminal. This is all former Atlantic Coast Line trackage. Manchester used to have a fairly large yard for local businesses, but it has been reduced to a few pickups and setoffs and is now primarily a crew change point.

ACTIVITY: CSX runs 30–40 trains per 24 hours, and just about anything can be seen passing through town: unit coal, grain, aggregates, chemical, auto racks, intermodal, and general freight, as well as an occasional office car train heading to or from its home base in Jacksonville.

TRAIN-WATCHING SPOTS: The City of Manchester has built a covered viewing platform at the north end of the small yard, complete with electricity, scanner, and picnic tables. The platform has plenty of free parking, and is adjacent to the Highway 85 overpass, which also offers a wide array of great vantage points from its sidewalks.

SAFETY: All the action can be viewed safely from the viewing platform, the parking lot, or the bridge.

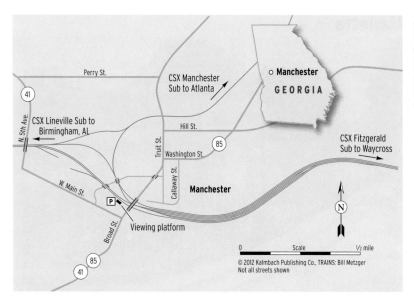

Manchester is located in west-central Georgia, 70 miles south of Atlanta, along the fall line of the Appalachian Mountains.

RAILROAD FREQUENCIES: CSX: 160.590 (Lineville Sub), 161.520 (Lineville Sub dispatcher), 161.100 and 160.230 (Manchester Sub), 160.590 (Fitzgerald Sub), 160.410 (Fitzgerald Sub dispatcher)

TO DO: Every third weekend in October, the city hosts Manchester Railroad Days with items displayed from the Manchester Railroad Museum. President Franklin Delano Roosevelt's Little White House is located 5 miles west in Warm Springs. Nearby Pine Mountain offers camping and outdoor activities, along with Callaway Gardens, which features an enclosed butterfly habitat, gardens, and other attractions. There are several local restaurants, motels, grocery stores, and gas stations in town, and all the amenities of a big city can be found 40 miles south in Columbus.

NEARBY: Junction City, 22 miles south, hosts the Fitzgerald Sub as it crosses over Norfolk Southern's Birmingham-Macon main line (6 NS trains per day). LaGrange, 30 miles west, hosts the Lineville Sub as well as CSX's A&WP Sub (Atlanta-Montgomery).

DIRECTIONS: From Atlanta, take Route 85 south for 70 miles. From Columbus, take Route 85 north for 40 miles.

Marietta

Woody Harrison

Western & Atlantic's historic Civil War route between Atlanta and Chattanooga was the stage for the Great Locomotive Chase, which began in Marietta. Still owned by the State of Georgia, today the line is leased to CSX, which has double-tracked much of the line from Elizabeth, just north of Marietta, and south to the south end of Smyrna near Atlanta. The west main rail is mounted on concrete ties, and the east main rail is on conventional wooden ties. This was a short-term test project for CSX. At Elizabeth, a connection is made with the Georgia Northeastern Railroad, the former L&N Hook & Eye route.

ACTIVITY: Averaging about 40 trains per 24 hours, Marietta offers some classic railroad action on CSX's busiest main line in the metro Atlanta area. The mix includes loaded and empty coal trains, auto racks, mixed freight, and hot intermodals. A local freight runs between Cartersville and Atlanta as train A703. This train will usually pick up or set out at the Elizabeth yard. GNRR has a yard office there and usually a good mix of vintage EMD power. On CSX, the dispatcher for the W&A takes over at north Elizabeth as this is the northern limit for the Atlanta terminal.

TRAIN-WATCHING SPOTS: The best and most leisurely spot in town to watch the train action is the park and gazebo just south of downtown near the overpass at the Highway 120 South Loop and West Atlanta Street, adjacent to the cemetery. The Kennesaw House, next to the depot in downtown, is full of history and offers a good trackside location. About a half-mile south of town, Atlanta Road crosses over the main lines next to Dobbins Air Base. This offers a nice view of trains and planes in action, and parking is within walking distance of the bridge.

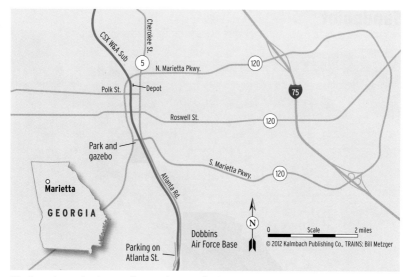

Marietta is a suburb 10 miles northwest of Atlanta and just west of I-75 in northwest Georgia.

RAILROAD FREQUENCIES: CSX: 161.370, 161.520, 161.100, 160.230; GNRR: 154.600, 160.560

TO DO: Marietta has many Civil War historical locations. The most well known, Kennesaw Mountain Battlefield Park is just west of town. The National Cemetery is just 4 blocks east of town. The Southern Museum of Civil War and Locomotive History features the *General*, best known for the Great Locomotive Chase.

NEARBY: The Georgia Northeastern Railroad in Elizabeth, just north of town, operates the old L&N Hook & Eye line to Tate. Watch for occasional Goldkist grain trains routed to customers on its line via CSX. Just a few mile south, downtown Atlanta offers railroading on a large scale, but it can be frustrating to tackle.

DIRECTIONS: From I-75 northwest of Atlanta, exit on South Highway 120 Loop and travel west toward downtown Marietta. Just before you go under the CSX main line, turn left onto Atlanta Road, go to the first right and cross over the main line, and turn back right again onto West Atlanta Street.

Sandpoint

Tom Danneman

Sandpoint features the main line of BNSF's Kootenai River Subdivision, the busy northern transcontinental route, as well as Union Pacific's Spokane Subdivision to Eastport. Sandpoint Junction (just east of the depot) is where the Montana Rail Link officially begins. At the junction, MRL's 4th Subdivision heads east toward Missoula, Mont. To the west, the BNSF main heads toward Spokane and points west. Montana Rail Link has trackage rights on BNSF to Spokane.

ACTIVITY: Amtrak's *Empire Builder* makes a nighttime stop at the Sandpoint depot on its journey between Chicago and Portland or Seattle. Short line Pend Oreille Valley Railroad operates from Newport, Wash., to Dover, and over trackage rights (with UP) to BNSF's Boyer Yard. The BNSF line between Sandpoint and Spokane usually hosts more than 40 trains a day. Just about any type of train can be seen on the BNSF including intermodal, manifests, coal, and grain. On the Montana Rail Link, it is mostly coal, grain, and manifest trains. Union Pacific's Spokane Subdivision features mostly freight, potash, and grain trains.

TRAIN-WATCHING SPOTS: The biggest attraction is BNSF's massive bridge over Lake Pend Oreille. Viewing areas for the bridge are located off Bottle Bay Road, which can be reached from Highway 95 south of town, and from the sidewalk/bike path along Highway 95 itself as it leaves town to the south. The BNSF bridge across Sand Creek Slough can be seen from the parking lot of the visitor center right off Highway 2/95 just north of downtown. Union Pacific can be seen along Highway 200 north of town or at numerous grade crossings in town. An interesting steel and concrete trestle can be viewed right from Highway 2/95 right after Highway 200 splits off toward the east.

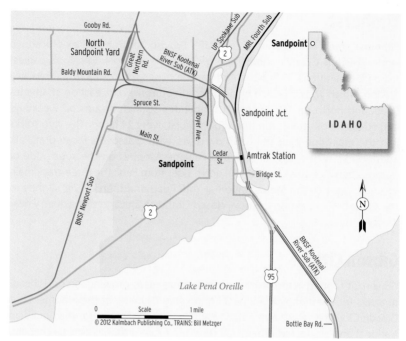

Sandpoint is located in north-central Idaho on Lake Pend Oreille.

SAFETY: The Sand Creek Byway construction project is seemingly perpetual, so you can expect less-than-great ambiance and construction delays near downtown Sandpoint.

RAILROAD FREQUENCIES: BNSF: 161.250 (Boyer west), 160.920 (Boyer east); UP: 160.740 (Spokane Sub); MRL: 160.950 (4th Subdivision), 161.415 and 160.305 (Pend Oreille Valley)

TO DO: Sandpoint is a thriving arts community and a tourist hot spot. Downtown Sandpoint includes many fine restaurants and places to shop. Lake Pend Oreille offers water sports and—of course—beach time. Sandpoint's City Beach is within sight of BNSF's main line.

NEARBY: Schweitzer Mountain Resort, located 11 miles from Sandpoint, is a great place to ski, hike, and mountain bike. Silverwood, the Northwest's largest theme park, is only 26 miles south of Sandpoint near Athol. Silverwood offers a day full of riding roller coasters, getting soaked in a water park, and riding behind a steam locomotive.

DIRECTIONS: Sandpoint is located where US 2 from Spokane and US 95 from Coeur d'Alene converge. It is about a 90-minute drive from Spokane.

ILLINOIS

Elmhurst

Elmhurst starts at the west end of UP's Proviso Yard on the ex-Chicago & North Western Geneva Subdivision (or Metra West Line), Chicago's earliest railroad. Operations at Proviso Yard can be observed from Metra's Berkeley Station, which you can reach by going south on York Road, east on St. Charles Road, and north on Taft Avenue. UP operates 58 Metra trains on weekdays and 60–80 freight trains run through Elmhurst every 24 hours. The yard tracks join the main line near the I-294 overpass, with crossovers located at Park interlocking, with access at Park and Fairlane Avenues on the south side or from Golden Meadows Park on the north side. From Park, the three-track main proceeds west to the Metra station at York Road and then curves slightly to the south before passing the now-closed Elmhurst-Chicago stone quarry near West Avenue.

Gibson City

Gibson City, found in the heart of central Illinois' grain-growing region, is head-quarters for the Bloomer Shippers Connecting Railroad, or the Bloomer Line. Gibson City also serves as a junction and interchange point for the Canadian National and Norfolk Southern. CN runs 1–2 locals a day, as well as coal and grain extras, while NS runs a local, as well as 2–3 daily run-through trains. Bloomer operates a major yard at its shop on the northwest end of town and another on the west side. CN maintains an interchange yard with Bloomer on the southwest side and a centrally located yard. NS shares a small interchange with Bloomer on the west end of town. Bloomer's shops, yards, and trackage are all highly accessible. Gibson City interlocking (minus its tower) is a wide-open spot to see all three railroads, and Illinois Routes 9, 47, and 54 parallel the NS, Bloomer, and CN, respectively, into and out of town. Frequencies include CN: 161.190; NS: 160.440, 161.250; and Bloomer: 160.365, 161.355.

Hinsdale

Hinsdale, 3 miles west of La Grange on BNSF's ex-Burlington triple-track main line, has three Metra stations with crossovers at Highlands and West Hinsdale. Highlands, the easternmost of these stations, is famed for the single-lane, wooden rainbow bridge that carries Oak Avenue over the tracks. The bridge, slated for replacement by 2015, provides one of the few overhead vantage points on the eastern half of the "race track," and the gingerbread passenger station was recently renovated. A pair of crossovers sits west of the bridge. The main station in downtown Hinsdale is adjacent to a park, while the West Hinsdale Station, where the other pair of crossovers can be found, is in a residential area. There are many public access points along the tracks in Hinsdale, and signals are plentiful to help predict train movements.

Homewood

Located in Chicago's railroad heartland on the far south side, Homewood contains Canadian National's ex-Illinois Central Markham Yard and Woodcrest locomotive shops, as well as the CN/IC main line to New Orleans. Amtrak, CN, Metra, and NS and UP run-throughs and transfers keep the rails humming all day long. Eight busy tracks split Homewood's quaint downtown and offer train counts approaching 100 a day during the week, including Metra's Electric District (an IC legacy and a heavy traction system unique west of the Allegheny Mountains) running at near-streetcar frequencies during rush hours. Homewood has embraced its status as a railroad hub and features a scanner-equipped viewing platform ideally situated just south of the busy throat of Markham Yard (Harwood and Kroner Avenues). A restored Illinois Central GP10 locomotive and long-porch Centralia caboose reside next to the still-in-use vintage 1923 southwestern style depot.

Kankakee

Kankakee is located about 40 miles southeast of Joliet. Kankakee's current and historic railroad landscape is dominated by Canadian National's ex-Illinois Central Chicago-New Orleans main line. Norfolk Southern and short line Kankakee, Beaverville & Southern also contribute to the activity. The Kankakee Amtrak station (199 South East Avenue), built by Illinois Central in 1898, is today beautifully restored and an excellent place to watch trains on CN's main line. Daily, you'll see 6 Amtrak (*City of New Orleans*, *Illini*, *Saluki*), 4 NS Chicago-Decatur, and a mix of 12–15 CN intermodal, merchandise, and bulk commodity trains. There is ample public parking at the depot, which also houses the Kankakee Railroad Museum. Two-thirds of a mile north of the depot, NS's east-west Kankakee Line crosses the CN at grade and KB&S's former New York Central line connects from the southeast. NS operates 3–4 trains daily over the Kankakee Line, notably 1 train each way connecting with BNSF at Streator. KB&S runs into Kankakee as needed, usually weekdays only.

Matteson

At Matteson, about 30 miles south of downtown Chicago, Canadian National's Chicago Sub (ex-Illinois Central) crosses over CN's Matteson Sub (ex-Elgin, Joliet & Eastern), a short distance south of the Metra Electric station. Using the turnouts at Swede (adjacent to the Metra platform on the IC track elevation) and Lowe (east of Main Street on the EJ&E), trains can move in any combination of directions except north on IC to east on EJ&E, but that maneuver can be made over the Harris connection in the southeast quadrant. From the sidewalk east of the Main Street crossing, you can see how the EJ&E main was shifted to the south, through what used to be an interchange yard, to make room for the new Swede-Lowe connection. Grading has been completed for a railfan platform east of the Metra station.

Centralia

Scott Muskopf

In Centralia, main lines of Norfolk Southern, Canadian National, and BNSF cross at grade. Amtrak operates over CN's former Illinois Central Chicago-New Orleans main line. Canadian National maintains a yard, shops, and crew change point just south of Centralia in the town of Wamac. (Some CN trains bypass Centralia on the parallel Edgewood Cutoff 25 miles to the east.) BNSF has a crew change and yard on the north side of town on a former CB&Q secondary main line to Paducah, Ky. Norfolk Southern bases a local next to the BNSF yard. The NS is the former Southern Railway's St. Louis Line. Both NS and BNSF have trackage rights over CN southward—NS to Fulton, Ky., and BNSF to Memphis.

ACTIVITY: Over a 24-hour period, you can see 12–15 NS freights, 5–8 BNSF trains, and 10–12 from the CN. Traffic includes coal, grain, mixed freight, and intermodals. In addition, Amtrak's *City of New Orleans*, *Saluki*, and *Illini* run daily both southbound and northbound.

TRAIN-WATCHING SPOTS: All three lines travel through downtown Centralia, where you can watch from many public locations. Several grade crossings and parallel streets allow for wide-open scenes. BNSF's yard on the north side of town is visible from the north end of Chestnut Street. Amtrak has a small station and platform (110 South Oak Street).

RAILROAD FREQUENCIES: CN: 161.190; NS: 160.950; BNSF: 161.100

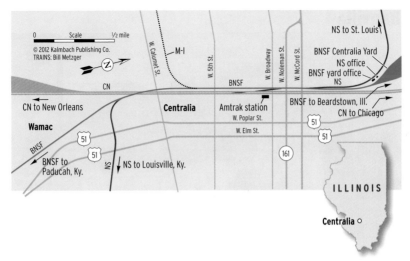

Centralia is located in southern Illinois, east of St. Louis, 10 miles west of I-57 and 12 miles north of I-64.

TO DO: Illinois Central 4-8-2 locomotive No. 2500 is displayed at Fairview Park, along with a Republic F-105 Thunderchief, a rare supersonic fighter-bomber. The Centralia Area Historical Society Museum (240 South Locust Street) features railroad, coal mining, and oil industry artifacts. The Crooked Creek Winery is located 4 miles west of town off Route 161.

NEARBY: Mount Vernon, 25 miles southeast, is a busy junction, where Union Pacific's Chicago-Little Rock main line crosses at grade the same NS main line that goes through Centralia, along with the Evansville Western Railway. At Salem, 15 miles northeast of Centralia, there is a junction of UP's main and CSX's former B&O main line between St. Louis and Cincinnati. The CSX and CN main lines cross at grade in the tiny town of Odin, 5 miles west of Salem.

DIRECTIONS: Centralia is equally accessible from I-57, I-64, or I-70.

Danville

Mike Blaszak

Four railroads converge at the eastern Illinois city of Danville, and trains of a fifth are also seen. Danville's primary players are CSX, operating the former Chicago & Eastern Illinois line to Evansville, Ind., and Norfolk Southern, which runs the old Wabash main line from Detroit to Kansas City. The two lines cross at Danville Junction, northeast of downtown. Indiana Rail Road unit coke trains operate over CSX from Terre Haute, Ind., to Chicago. Class III roads Kankakee, Beaverville & Southern and Vermilion Valley enter Danville from the east. Vermilion Valley connects with CSX at CP Daisy Lane.

ACTIVITY: CSX's single-track Woodland Subdivision main line hosts 25–30 train movements every 24 hours through Danville. Virtually any type of traffic, from double-stack intermodal trains to unit coal trains serving Duke Energy's Cayuga Generating Station in nearby Cayuga, Ind., can be seen. As CSX has a runner track from Cory to Brewer Yard, south of the crossing, you'll frequently see a southbound and a northbound bang the NS diamonds in rapid succession. North Yard, just north of the junction, is where CSX and NS interchange. NS's single-track Lafayette District hosts about the same number of trains as CSX, carrying motor vehicle, grain, and coal traffic, along with RoadRailers. As NS has two tracks from its yard in Tilton northeast through Danville to Eldan, dispatchers often time trains to pass in town. KB&S operates as needed to a connection with NS at Newell, northeast of Danville.

TRAIN-WATCHING SPOTS: The NS-CSX crossing was renamed Danville Junction by NS several years ago. The crossing is railroad property but can be viewed from the west end of May Street or the parking lot in the southwest quadrant off Fairchild Avenue (stay on the upper level, avoiding the Fairchild under-

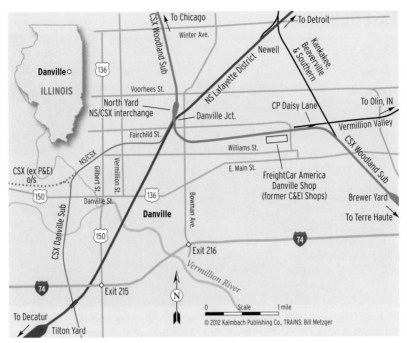

Danville is the seat of Vermilion County, a few miles west of the Indiana state line and north of I-74.

pass). Daisy Lane crosses CSX, Vermilion Valley, and KB&S in succession. NS crosses over KB&S on a bridge at Newell (Newell Road and Winter Avenue). The south end of CSX's Brewer Yard (including the locomotive facility) can be viewed from Jones Road, immediately north of I-74. NS's yard in nearby Tilton can be observed from the Glendale Avenue overpass.

RAILROAD FREQUENCIES: NS: 160.440; CSX: 161.370 and 161.520 (road), 160.290 (yard); KB&S: 160.215, 161.490

NEARBY: Monticello Railway Museum operates former Southern Railway 2-8-0 steam locomotive 401 on summer weekends and historic diesels at other times. The museum is 57 miles west of Danville.

DIRECTIONS: From Vermilion and Main Streets in downtown Danville, proceed east on Main Street , north on Bowman Avenue, and west on Fairchild Avenue to reach North Yard/Danville Junction. Continue east on Main Street from Bowman to Daisy Lane and then turn north to reach CP Daisy Lane.

East Dubuque

Nick Tharalson

At East Dubuque, the Canadian National's IC subsidiary crosses the BNSF's Aurora Sub at the Mississippi River into Dubuque, where it crosses CP's DM&E. The single-track rail bridge first opened in 1868 and was rebuilt in the 1890s. The truss bridge has five spans and a swing span. At one time, an interlocking called East Cabin controlled the Illinois side, but it was closed after signal upgrades in the '90s, although the structure still stands.

ACTIVITY: All BNSF traffic, intermodal, manifest, unit taconite, and unit oil between Savanna and the Twin Cities, up to 20 in daylight, pass through here. CN traffic includes manifest 337 before noon, and 338 early morning, a local switcher for industrial work, and occasional unit grain and coal trains. DM&E runs manifests, unit grain, and ethanol trains randomly, no more than 6 per day.

TRAIN-WATCHING SPOTS: In East Dubuque, you can park by the former, now derelict, CB&Q depot at the north end of the downtown district, near the east end of the CN tunnel through the bluff. There is a small parking lot next to East Cabin for a local bank, and there are some grade crossings where you can safely cross the BNSF tracks to get to the west side in the afternoon. Dubuque, however, is much more difficult. While the DM&E facilities are somewhat open, they are away from the main traveled areas and parking is poor. A highway project several years ago wiped out the old IC depot and freight house, and parking anywhere along the tracks downtown is not allowed. There are some streets to the harbor attractions where parking is available, and best used when you know something's coming.

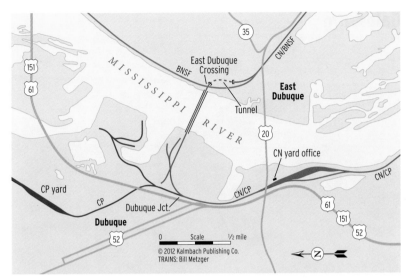

East Dubuque and Dubuque are located on the Mississippi River, where Iowa, Illinois, and Wisconsin come together.

RAILROAD FREQUENCIES: BNSF: 161.100; CN: 161.190; DM&E: 161.370. The scanner works best for the DM&E, which calls the CN dispatcher in Homewood to get permission to run between Dubuque Junction and Wood, a junction south of Dubuque that is difficult to access.

TO DO: Dubuque features a variety of chain motels, as well as fast food and sit-down restaurants, while East Dubuque has few such facilities. The Dubuque Greyhound Park and Casino is located near the US 61 bridge over the Mississippi. In Dubuque, near the CN yard office, families can enjoy the National Mississippi River Museum & Aquarium, take a ride on an authentic paddle wheeler, or walk along the Mississippi Riverwalk.

DIRECTIONS: The best way to the area is by US 20, US 61, or US 151, which are four lanes either side of Dubuque.

Galesburg

Drew Halverson

Galesburg, located in the northwest region of the state, is the hub of seven BNSF lines and is home to the railroad's second largest classification yard. The Mendota, Barstow, Ottumwa, Brookfield, and Peoria Subdivisions all originate in Galesburg, while the Chillicothe Subdivision passes through on its way from Chicago to Fort Madison, Iowa.

ACTIVITY: It's not uncommon to see more than 100 trains a day rumble through Galesburg. Nearly 20 merchandise trains, on average, are assembled in the yard, while much of the traffic through town is comprised of intermodal, coal, general merchandise, grain, and ore. Amtrak's *Southwest Chief*, *California Zephyr*, *Illinois Zephyr*, and *Carl Sandburg* all stop at Galesburg.

TRAIN-WATCHING SPOTS: Peck Park, where the Mendota Sub crosses above the Chillicothe Sub, is one of the most popular hot spots in Galesburg. You'll see an average of 4 trains per hour here, including Union Pacific run-through trains, in addition to the primary flow of intermodal, coal, and manifest traffic. Thirwell Bridge, a popular two-lane structure with extra-wide parking lanes on each side of the span, crosses over the middle of Galesburg Yard and provides ample room for stopping. Here, you'll get a good view of the entire complex, engine facilities, and hump yard. You can't get bored here! The Galesburg Amtrak station (225 South Seminary Street) is also a good place to relax and watch trains roll by. In addition to the Amtrak trains that stop here, BNSF keeps freights rolling into and out of the yard. Cameron, located southwest of the city, provides perfect heartland scenery and is home to the Cameron Connection, where the Chillicothe and Ottumwa Subdivisions connect. If you're looking for a brief escape from the traffic-heavy city center, this is the spot.

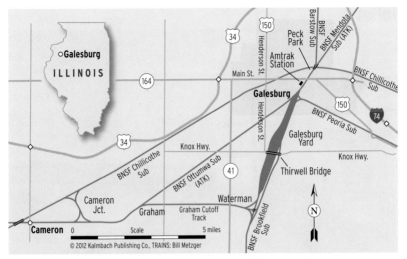

Galesburg lies halfway between Davenport, Iowa, and Peoria on I-74.

SAFETY: When stopping on Thirwell Bridge, show extra caution due to sometimes heavy traffic volumes.

RAILROAD FREQUENCIES: BNSF: 160.875 (yard), 160.380 (Chillicothe Sub), 160.695 (Ottumwa Sub), 160.815 (Brookfield Sub), 161.415 (Barstow Sub), 161.385 (Mendota and Peoria Subs)

TO DO: Since Galesburg is a rather large city, it provides many opportunities for dining, shopping, and fun. The city is home to Galesburg Railroad Days, a very popular event in June, Stearman Fly-In Days, a vintage World War II air show on Labor Day weekend, as well as many other festivals, including the Chocolate Festival in February and the Black Earth Film Festival in September.

NEARBY: Burlington, Iowa, home to the former Chicago, Burlington & Quincy Railroad, sits 50 miles to the west of Galesburg, via Highway 34. Located on the Mississippi River, this location features a newly constructed lift bridge, not to mention more 30 freights a day and Amtrak's *California Zephyr*.

DIRECTIONS: If traveling west from Chicago, I-80 and I-88 connect with I-74, leaving only a short southward journey on I-74 to Galesburg.

Joliet

Chris Guss

Joliet features rail action from BNSF, UP, CN, CSX, Iowa Interstate Railroad (IAIS), Amtrak, and Metra. Joliet also has a manned tower (UD Tower) at the crossing of the BNSF and UP main lines with Metra's Joliet Sub District. Many of the rail lines feature trains from other railroad using trackage rights to reach various yards or rail lines around the Chicago area, so the variety is great.

ACTIVITY: Action is heavy in Joliet, with BNSF providing 50–60 trains daily, CN operating 15–20, UP 8–12, IAIS 2–3, and CSX 2. Amtrak provides 10 trains daily including the *Texas Eagle* and four pairs of Illinois service trains. Metra offers 29 trains with service on both the Heritage and Rock Island District corridors. Intermodal, freight, coal, automotive, and unit trains pass through the city daily.

TRAIN-WATCHING SPOTS: Constructed in 1921, Joliet Union Station (50 East Jefferson Street) is the best place to watch trains in Joliet. Located on the northwest corner of the diamonds where Santa Fe and GM&O trains once crossed the Rock Island main line, this location is the busiest place in town. The US 6 overpass on the northeast side of town gives a great vantage point of the CN yard.

SAFETY: Joliet Union Station is bordered by busy mainline tracks with fast-moving trains.

RADIO FREQUENCIES: BNSF: 160.650 (road); CN: 160.920 (road), 161.475 (dispatcher to train); Metra: 161.340; UP: 161.280 (Joliet Sub); CSX: 160.230 (road), 160.290 (dispatcher to train)

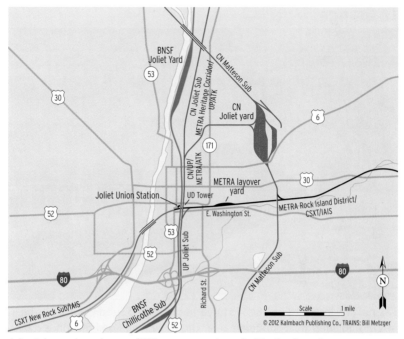

Joliet is located southwest of Chicago, approximately 45 miles from downtown.

TO DO: Silver Cross Field is located immediately east of Union Station and is where the Joliet Slammers baseball team (independent Frontier League) plays. Also nearby are two casinos and for racing fans, the Route 66 Raceway and Chicagoland Speedway.

NEARBY: While railfanning hot spots in Chicago abound, the rail crossing at Blue Island is only 30 miles east of Joliet and is another great place to watch trains.

DIRECTIONS: From I-55, take Exit 253 and go east on West Jefferson Street to Joliet Union Station which will be on the south side just before the railroad overpass. To reach the US 6 overpass, continue east on West Jefferson which turns into North Collins Street. Go east of East Jackson street to the overpass. From I-80, take Exit 132 northbound (South Chicago Street) to the station.

La Grange

Marshall Beecher

La Grange is located along BNSF's three-track Chicago Subdivision in the heart of Chicagoland's west suburban area. The La Grange Road Station is a busy stop along Metra's Chicago-Aurora commuter service. Approximately a half-mile east of La Grange Road Station, Indiana Harbor Belt's busy three-track main line passes beneath BNSF's Chicago Subdivision, and a half-mile west of La Grange Road is another, less-busy Metra station, La Grange Stone Avenue.

ACTIVITY: Depending on the day of the week (more activity Thursday-Saturday), BNSF operates approximately 45–50 trains per day, mostly inter-modal, coal, and merchandise, along with several Union Pacific trains operating via trackage rights. This line is one of Metra's busiest on weekdays, with approximately 100 moves, and most are concentrated during the morning and afternoon rush hours. Amtrak also has a major presence on this BNSF line. The *Carl Sandburg* and *Illinois Zephyr* stop at La Grange Road daily while the *California Zephyr* and *Southwest Chief* roll through nonstop each afternoon. Nearby Indiana Harbor Belt has one of the region's busiest main lines, with constant run-through and transfer activity.

TRAIN-WATCHING SPOTS: The La Grange Road and Stone Avenue Stations offer ample room on public property to photograph or simply watch the passing parade on BNSF. The Indiana Harbor Belt main line is more difficult to access, although the Shawmut Avenue grade crossing north of BNSF is a popular viewing location at CP LaGrange, a set of crossovers and signals. A sidewalk on the south side of the Ogden Avenue Bridge over IHB provides for overhead viewing.

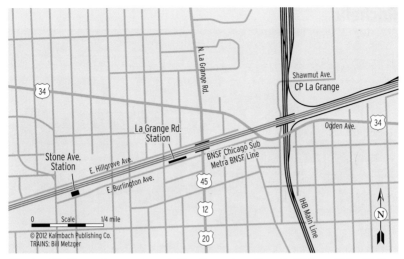

The city of La Grange is approximately 14 miles west-southwest of Chicago Union Station.

RAILROAD FREQUENCIES: BNSF: 161.100; Indiana Harbor Belt: 160.980

TO DO: For family fun, the Brookfield Zoo is just three Metra stops east of La Grange Road at the Hollywood Station. A trip to downtown Chicago via Metra takes approximately 35 minutes on weekends. La Grange and other nearby villages on the BNSF line have vibrant downtown districts with dining and shopping options.

NEARBY: Chicagoland is the railroad capital of the world. The Highlands and Hinsdale Stations on BNSF, west of La Grange Road, are popular train-watching places. The Elmhurst Station on Union Pacific's busy ex-Chicago & North Western Geneva Sub, at the west end of Proviso Yard, is 11 miles away by car and the west end of Canadian Pacific's Bensenville Yard is a mere 4 miles north of Elmhurst.

DIRECTIONS: La Grange Road Station is located at 25 West Burlington Avenue in downtown La Grange. Take I-294 to the Ogden Avenue Exit, go east 2 miles to LaGrange Road, and then south to the tracks; the station is on your right.

Rochelle

Rob McGonigal

Main lines of the Union Pacific and BNSF cross each other at grade on the west side of town. UP's route was the main line of the Chicago & North Western. This portion of BNSF's Chicago-Twin Cities Line is often called the C&I, for the Chicago & Iowa, a CB&Q predecessor. Both lines are under Centralized Traffic Control, operated by UP dispatchers in Omaha, and BNSF dispatchers in Fort Worth. Once controlled by an on-site interlocking tower, the crossing is now an automatic interlocking, meaning it is "first-come, first-served" for the right-of-way for any approaching train, regardless of railroad or direction. Although the BNSF line is mostly single track, both lines are double track through town.

ACTIVITY: As many as 120 freight trains (but no passenger trains) cross the Rochelle diamonds every day. UP's traffic here is largely coal and intermodal; BNSF's is mostly intermodal. Both roads also haul trains of trilevel auto rack cars. Many UP trains enter or leave the Global III intermodal terminal, located 1 mile west of the diamonds. The city-owned Rochelle Railroad provides switching service in the industrial park southeast of town. BNSF has a small yard in this area and keeps a locomotive for local work at the site of the old CB&Q depot on North Washington Street.

TRAIN-WATCHING SPOTS: The Rochelle Railroad Park, built by the city just east of the diamonds in 1998, is one of the top train-watching locations in the country. It's open 24 hours a day and provides a safe, elevated vantage point. A pavilion with benches and tables offers shelter from the weather.

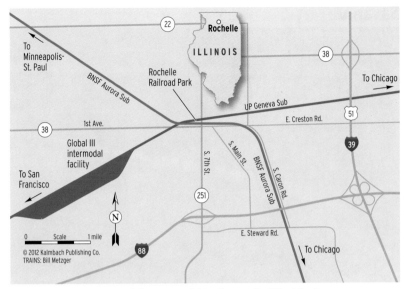

Rochelle is 80 miles west of Chicago and 30 miles south of Rockford.

TRAINS magazine's Rochelle webcam is mounted on its roof, and a computer monitor that shows the locations of UP and BNSF trains. For more information, go to www.rochellerailroadpark.org.

SAFETY: Trains can move in either direction on any of the four tracks through town.

RAILROAD RADIO FREQUENCIES: BNSF: 161.160; UP: 161.040

TO DO: Rochelle is a classic Midwestern small town, with an active business district along Lincoln Highway, named for the coast-to-coast route established in 1913. The Rochelle Diamond Lodge (215 North Ninth Street), next to the UP tracks, caters to railfans.

NEARBY: The Illinois Railway Museum is 48 miles to the northeast in Union, the Lincoln Highway Association National Headquarters is 16 miles west in Franklin Grove, and the Flagg Township Museum is in downtown Rochelle.

DIRECTIONS: From east, west, or south, take I-88 to the Highway 251 Exit and then take 251 north into town. From the north, take I-39 to the Highway 38 Exit, and then 38 west into town. The railroad park is located at 124 North Ninth Street between Lincoln and First Avenues.

Savanna

Nick Tharalson

Located along the Mississippi River in northwest Illinois, Savanna is at the crossing of BNSF and CP rail lines.

ACTIVITY: The BNSF combines lines from Chicago and Galesburg to the double-track line to the Twin Cities. This trackage sees all types of trains except unit coal, with up to 20 per day. The CP line is now operated by CP's DM&E subsidiary. Across the river, the line splits to Kansas City and the Twin Cities. This trackage can see up to 10 trains per day.

TRAIN-WATCHING SPOTS: There are several good spots in Savanna for watching and photographing trains. The diamonds themselves are a popular morning spot, with the city wastewater treatment plant a block north being a good place for watching in the afternoon. North of Savanna, Lookout Point in Palisades State Park offers views high above the trains both mornings and afternoons. Across the river, the end of CP's Mississippi River bridge is easily accessible in Sabula, Iowa, while trackage north of Sabula Junction can be viewed from an access road.

East of Savanna, the two roads parallel each other. Wacker Road leads to an overhead of the BNSF in the middle of the interlocking, and later, to a nice crossing of CP on a curve. Watch for Big Cut Road, which takes you to a CP grade crossing and an overhead of the BNSF tracks a mile farther on. At the north edge of the city's airport, Airport Road off Highway 84 takes you east to East Burke grade crossing of the BNSF. Lookout Point has a nice platform with railings and benches.

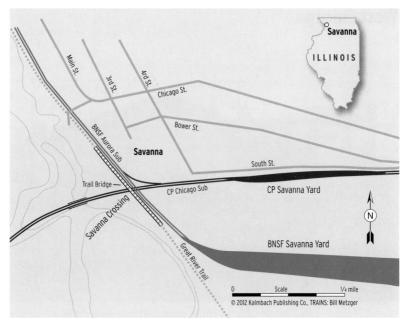

Savanna sits near the Mississippi River at the junction of US 52 and Highway 84.

FREQUENCIES: BNSF: 161.100, 161.160, 161.415; CP: 161.370, 161.085

TO DO: Savanna is just south of Mississippi Palisades State Park and offers hiking, biking, and rock climbing. It is also a mecca for motorcyclists.

NEARBY: Other train-watching spots within a 30-minute drive are Clinton, Iowa, a UP crew change point where CP's DM&E crosses the UP at grade, and East Dubuque.

DIRECTIONS: To get to Savanna from the east, take I-88 to US 30 to Highway 84 and then north. From the west, take US 30 to Highway 84 and then north. From the north, take either US 52 or Highway 84.

West Chicago

Dave Kuntz

West Chicago is well known for its triple diamond mainline crossing. To the west of the diamonds is West Chicago Yard, a mid-sized interchange for switching with an automobile unloading ramp. Kress Road passes over the yard's west end. North of the tower, the CN track splits two ways. One track loops around to West Chicago Yard, and the other track continues on to a north yard, which is accessible only from a bike trail overpass. From that yard, a UP branch goes to Belvidere, and the CN main line continues to Waukegan. A short walk south of the tower reveals an abandoned right-of-way that once reached the UP line. Although this looks like an industrial spur, It is actually the birthplace of the BNSF. In 1850, the first Aurora Branch Railroad train ran from Batavia, 6 miles west, to West Chicago, where, for several years, the trains then used Galena & Chicago Union Railroad trackage (later C&NW, now UP) to reach Chicago. In 1864, the Aurora Branch Railroad became the Chicago, Burlington & Quincy and ultimately the Burlington Northern and then BNSF.

ACTIVITY: It's common for up to 100 Canadian National, Union Pacific, and Metra trains to pass through each day.

TRAIN-WATCHING SPOTS: Visible from the Metra station (508 West Main Street) is UP's Larry Provo Training Center, home to unusual locomotives and rolling stock. The parking lot behind the public library, west of the station, offers views of UP and Metra trains running left-handed under C&NW-style signals. The diamonds are a short walk west of the train station. The former Elgin, Joliet & Eastern interlocking tower, now operational under CN, is adjacent to the diamonds.

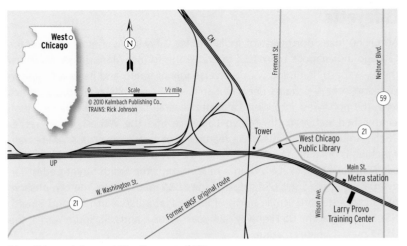

West Chicago is located 28 miles west of Chicago.

RAILROAD FREQUENCIES: CN: 161.475; UP: 160.890 (road), 161.175 (yard)

SAFETY: Washington Street, the main thoroughfare, crosses both railroads within feet of the junction, and traffic backups often extend through the downtown.

TO DO: The West Chicago City Museum is on Main Street. Four miles away in Wheaton, Cantigny Park features 29 acres of gardens to explore. It is also home to the McCormick Museum, centered on *Chicago Tribune* publisher Robert R. McCormick, and the First Division Museum and its tank park.

NEARBY: The Illinois Railway Museum is an hour north in Union, and downtown Chicago is always a Metra ride away.

DIRECTIONS: The easiest way to get to West Chicago is to take Metra's UP West Line from downtown Chicago. By car, West Chicago is north of I-88 off the Route 59 Exit.

Lafayette

About 60 miles northwest of Indianapolis, Lafayette is a stop on Amtrak's Chicago-Indianapolis train. CSX operates the former Monon line, NS keeps the ex-Wabash humming with a diverse mix of traffic, and its ex-NKP line to Frankfort sees 4–6 trains per day. Kankakee, Beaverville & Southern comes from the northwest into West Lafayette several days per week. Riehle Plaza, sandwiched between downtown Lafayette and the Wabash River, serves as the Amtrak station. The plaza features a pedestrian overpass where train watching is great all day. About 10 trains a day use CSX's single track, and 30 use NS's double track. Less than a mile south is the Smith Street pedestrian overpass that straddles CSX, NS, and the KB&S interchange. You can observe CSX's Lafayette Yard 1 mile north of Riehle Plaza (200 North Second Street), NS's East Yard at the US Highway 52 bypass bridge, and NS's South Yard at the US 52 bypass grade crossing.

Michigan City

Michigan City sits on the shores of Lake Michigan 60 miles east of Chicago. Rail lines that converge on the city belong to Chicago South Shore & South Bend, Amtrak, and CSX. The biggest show in town is the South Shore, the last remaining interurban railroad in the country, which hosts 32 weekday and 20 weekend electric passenger trains to and from Chicago. These trains are operated by NICTD, the state-sponsored commuter agency. The South Shore Freight short line provides freight service with 5–7 weekday and 1–2 weekend freight trains. Downtown also affords views of Amtrak's Michigan Line that hosts 8 daily passenger trains and an occasional NS or South Shore Freight local. CSX's lightly trafficked ex-Pere Marquette line runs south of town and sees 2 daily Amtrak trains. Things to see include the railroad shops at Carroll Avenue east of downtown and street-running trackage on 10th and 11th Streets.

Porter

Porter is a busy junction of Norfolk Southern, CSX, and Amtrak lines in northwest Indiana, about 40 miles from downtown Chicago. Approximately 90–100 trains pass this location every 24 hours, most on NS's ex-Conrail Chicago Line, including Amtrak's *Lake Shore Limited* and *Capital Limited* and an array of NS and Canadian Pacific intermodal, merchandise, coal, and steel traffic. The Amtrak main line from Kalamazoo joins the Chicago Line at Porter, which is used by the Wolverine and Blue Water services from Detroit and Port Huron, Mich., respectively—a total of 10 trains per day. CSX's main line also connects with the Chicago Line here and sees 2–4 freights daily plus Amtrak's *Pere Marquette*. Another freight-only line, the Porter Branch, connects from the southwest and sees 8–10 run-through trains per day. The best viewing sites with parking include 15th Street (east of the junction) and Lincoln Street (just north).

Princeton

Princeton is located in southwest Indiana at the junction of Route 41 with Routes 64/65 about 25 miles north of Evansville. One place to watch trains from is Gibson County visitor center on West Broadway. The former depot is also home to the Princeton Railway Museum. The CSX Nashville Division's CED Subdivision crosses Norfolk Southern's Southern-West District (Illinois Division) at grade. The CSX line (running north-south) is the busier of the two railroads and sees intermodal, automobile, manifest, coal, grain, and hopper trains. In addition to the long-distance intermodals, automobile, and mixed freights, Norfolk Southern moves a great deal of coal from nearby mines to a substantial Duke Power generation plant located about 10 miles west of town along the eastern banks of the Wabash River. The lines parallel each other for nearly 2 miles north of the diamond before the NS main resumes its westbound trajectory. Princeton is a crew change point on the former Southern Railway's St. Louis Line and features a small yard from which local freights operate. A huge Toyota assembly plant just south of town is served by both railroads.

Terre Haute

Terre Haute, about 60 miles south of Danville via I-74 and Route 63, is where two CSX routes cross: the CE&D Subdivision from Danville to Evansville and the St. Louis Line. Haley Tower, which is preserved near its original site by the Wabash Valley Railroaders Museum, features a railfan observation platform. Roughly 50–60 trains pass the site every 24 hours, including Schneider Intermodal trains Q106 and Q107, running through to Kansas City usually behind Kansas City Southern power, and Indiana Rail Road haulage trains. INRD's Chicago Subdivision enters Terre Haute from the south, crossing CSX at Spring Hill and proceeding around the east edge of town to Van Yard, south of the connection with the St. Louis Line at Preston. INRD's belt line continues north from Preston across the CE&D Sub at Dewey to the Wabash River Generating Station at Fayette, carrying mostly coal trains.

Wellsboro

Wellsboro is the crossing of CSX's ex-Baltimore & Ohio main line from Chicago to the East with Canadian National's Grand Trunk Western main line from Chicago to Detroit and Port Huron, Mich. CSX operates 55–65 trains per 24 hours, while CN contributes 20–25 movements. A gravel parking lot west of the crossing is a good place to watch the action, although trains also may be observed at nearby public crossings. The Chesapeake & Indiana appears sporadically, moving grain and fertilizer in season. To reach Wellsboro, drive about 40 miles east on US 6 from the I-65 interchange in Gary to Long Lane and then south about 2 miles to the CSX crossing.

Hammond

Mike Blaszak

Hammond, at the northwest apex of Indiana, has been described as one giant railroad yard. Even though rationalization has claimed some rail lines since the 1970s, it's still an apt description. Main lines of Canadian National, CSX, and Norfolk Southern parallel the Lake Michigan shoreline. About 3 miles south, Baltimore & Ohio Chicago Terminal and Chicago South Shore & South Bend traverse the town east to west, and about a half-mile farther, NS's ex-Nickel Plate Road crosses the Indiana Harbor Belt.

ACTIVITY: Every 24 hours, Amtrak operates 14 trains over the NS Lakefront Line, while South Shore runs 37 weekday passenger trains. Freight activity over the NS Lakefront Line and IHB is heavy and constant. CSX and Canadian Pacific trains use NS, and CSX and NS trains can be seen on IHB along with BNSF and UP power. Gibson Yard, east of downtown, flat switches trains of auto racks for Chicago's Class I railroads. The former Nickel Plate, hosting auto trains serving the Ford mixing center in Chicago, sees 20–25 train movements every 24 hours, while B&OCT runs 55–65. The ex-B&O lakefront line is used primarily by South Chicago & Indiana Harbor to deliver coal to the Arcelor-Mittal steel mills in east Chicago.

TRAIN-WATCHING SPOTS: The Amtrak station (404 NW Railroad Avenue) is a prime location for viewing action on the lakefront lines and the east end of NS's Colehour Yard. The South Shore station is at Hohman Avenue and the tracks, and B&OCT skirts the south edge of the parking lot. Farther south, Hohman Avenue passes over the Nickel Plate-IHB crossing on a bridge with sidewalks on both sides. Willow Court parallels IHB through town.

Hammond is southeast of Chicago on the NS main line in Lake County, Indiana.

SAFETY: Avoid the State Line crossing of the Nickel Plate, IHB, and B&OCT lines, as it is on railroad property and patrolled by the police.

RAILROAD FREQUENCIES: NS: 160.800 (Lakefront), 161.250 (Nickel Plate); CSX/B&OCT: 160.230, 160.320; IHB: 160.980 and 161.070 (road), 160.485 (Gibson Yard); CSS&SB: 161.355; CN 160.350

TO DO: Gambling is the primary tourist attraction in northwest Indiana, with the Horseshoe Casino immediately north of the Amtrak station and others along the lakefront eastward to New Buffalo, Mich. Indiana Dunes National Lakeshore is between Gary and Michigan City.

NEARBY: IHB's Gibson roundhouse is one of the few survivors in the Chicago area; it can be viewed from McCook Avenue and Gibson Transfer Road off Kennedy Avenue.

DIRECTIONS: From Chicago, take I-90 to the Indianapolis Boulevard Exit. Drive southeast on Indianapolis Boulevard to Calumet Avenue and turn left to the Amtrak station. To reach the South Shore station and Hohman Avenue crossing, take Calumet Avenue south to Sheffield and then continue south on Hohman.

Muncie

Don Nickel

Muncie plays host to the double-track main line of CSX's former Conrail Bee Line and Norfolk Southern's New Castle District and Frankfort District main lines. The CSX and NS New Castle mains cross just east of Walnut Street. The Frankfort District line splits from the New Castle District northeast of the diamond. A connection west of Walnut Street creates a wye for NS that allows trains on the Frankfort District to continue south on the New Castle District. NS handles local switching at East Yard, located approximately 1 mile east of the diamond. And a new addition to the Muncie rail scene is Progress Rail's 740,000-square-foot facility for locomotive manufacturing.

ACTIVITY: The CSX double track sees approximately 25 trains a day, with a mix of manifest, intermodal, and seasonal unit grain shipments. CSX activity tends to favor more trains in the morning and late afternoon. Norfolk Southern adds 20–25 trains a day on the New Castle District and another 4–6 trains on the Frankfort District. Norfolk Southern traffic includes manifest, intermodal, and Triple Crown RoadRailer service. Locals also mix in with the mainline action on both lines. Run-through power is not uncommon, making it possible to view power from BNSF, UP, KCS, and CN.

TRAIN-WATCHING SPOTS: The diamonds are easily viewed from a parking lot on the north side of the tracks. This location offers a central location for all lines. The former Big Four freight house still stands west of the diamonds and can add a photographic backdrop. The building now processes recycling, and parking there is not recommended.

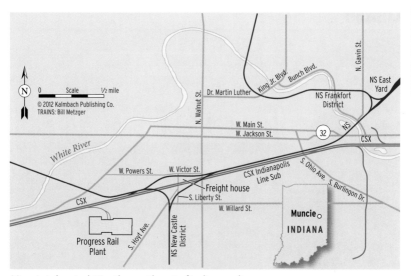

Muncie is located 50 miles northeast of Indianapolis.

The CSX line parallels State Road 32 west of town, which opens up additional opportunities for photography outside of town. The NS line to Fort Wayne crosses the White River at three locations in Muncie, and all of these bridges are easily accessed.

SAFETY: Nighttime in downtown Muncie can be an issue.

RAILROAD FREQUENCIES: CSX: 160.800 (road); NS: 160.440 (road), 161.250 and 161.190 (yard, locals), 161.115 (EOT)

TO DO: Muncie is home to Ball State University. Its campus provides an opportunity to explore a scenic Midwestern college. Also, walking and biking enthusiasts will enjoy the trail that occupies the former C&O of Indiana right-of-way through Muncie.

NEARBY: The Indiana Transportation Museum is 40 miles west in Noblesville, and the Whitewater Valley Railroad is located 50 miles southeast in Connersville.

DIRECTIONS: From Indianapolis, take I-69 north about 40 miles to the Highway 32 Exit. Proceed east another 11 miles to Muncie. Continue to Walnut Street, turn right, and proceed south to the track. The diamonds are east of Walnut Street.

Clinton

Nick Tharalson

Clinton is the first crew change point on the Union Pacific's main line west from Chicago. Crossing at grade is the DM&E/CP's line to Kansas City, over which BNSF has trackage rights southward to Davenport.

ACTIVITY: The UP runs everything through here as this is a primary Chicago-West Coast route, and you can see more than 50 trains per day. Because this is a crew change point, there can be congestion at the UP's Clinton Yard office. DM&E runs manifests and grain trains across the UP, while BNSF now runs a Clinton-Galesburg job.

TRAIN-WATCHING SPOTS: The City of Clinton has undergone a massive renewal project in the area east of UP's Clinton Yard, which has eliminated several longtime photo spots and landmarks, most notably the grain elevator with the Planter's Peanut logo painted on it. However, you can still shoot at the east end of the former CNW Clinton depot, and can get to Second Street, where there's a turnoff to the UP's Clinton Swing Bridge. You can park off the street and away from the tracks here, while the bridge itself is off limits. On the DM&E, there are several grade crossings north of the UP that can be accessed for photos.

RAILROAD FREQUENCIES: The UP's main channel, 161.040, is usually busy as dispatchers coordinate crew changes. Since the DM&E uses track warrants, their 161.370 frequency is also busy, and DM&E crews can talk to the UP dispatcher when they approach the Fifth Street interlocking. BNSF operates on the DM&E frequency.

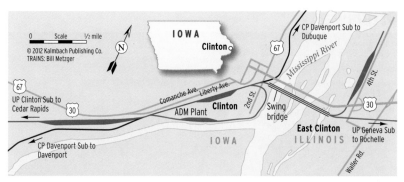

Clinton is located on the Mississippi River in east-central Iowa along the Illinois border on US 30.

TO DO: The big attraction is the *Mississippi Belle II* Riverboat Casino, which cruises the river during summer. Also in summer, you can watch the LumberKings, a class-A minor league baseball team. There are also numerous activities, from hiking to theater, available in Riverview Park.

NEARBY: From Clinton, you can access Savanna, Ill., another fine hot spot, which is about 30 minutes north on Highway 84 that intersects US 30 just east of Clinton.

DIRECTIONS: The best route to Clinton is US 30, which will take you across the river next to the UP tracks. US 67 runs north and south through the town.

Ottumwa

Nick Trimburger

The City of Bridges once hosted trains of the Chicago, Burlington & Quincy, Milwaukee Road, Rock Island, and Wabash. Today, the Rock Island and Wabash lines are gone, the Milwaukee Road is part of Canadian Pacific's line to Kansas City, and the CB&Q main line across southern Iowa is a key part of BNSF Railway's coal distribution network. Amtrak's *California Zephyr* runs on the BNSF and includes a station stop in Ottumwa, and the Burlington Junction Railway has a switching operation in the BNSF yard on the east side of Ottumwa.

ACTIVITY: Approximately 35 trains roll through Ottumwa on the BNSF daily. The majority of these trains are coal loads or empties with a daily manifest and intermodal in each direction. The Canadian Pacific has 2 daily trains in each direction plus grain extras. The BJRY primarily operates in the morning.

TRAIN-WATCHING SPOTS: The BNSF and CP interlocking (referred to as Lawler on the CP and IC&E RRX on the BNSF) can easily be viewed by parking on Clay Street or Gateway Drive. Parking can also be found at or near the restored CB&Q depot that functions as the Amtrak station (210 West Main Street) and contains the Wapello County Historical Museum. East of Ottumwa, the bridge on Old Agency Road provides a nice vantage point for coal trains battling the Des Moines River Valley. On the CP, Rutledge Hill is a steep northbound climb that can be viewed from Rutledge Road.

SAFETY: There are many one-way streets in downtown Ottumwa, so a little extra caution may be needed while driving.

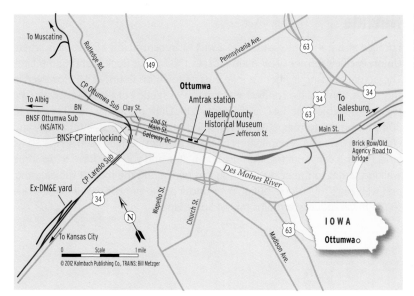

Ottumwa is located in southern Iowa, and the Des Moines River runs through it, split-ting the city in halves.

RAILROAD FREQUENCIES: BNSF: 160.695 (road, east of Ottumwa), 161.100 (road, west of Ottumwa); CP: 160.770 (road)

TO DO: The Greater Ottumwa Park along Highway 34 offers space to relax and picnic. The Antique Airfield museum is home to a collection of antique aircraft. You can visit the setting for Grant Woods' American Gothic painting, which is southeast of Ottumwa in nearby Eldon.

NEARBY: The former Rock Island depot in Eldon has been restored into a rail-road museum. A restored CB&Q steam engine is on display near the Ottumwa depot. In Albia, a former Milwaukee Road FM diesel has been restored near the town square, and Relco has a locomotive facility that can be viewed from public roads.

DIRECTIONS: Take Highway 34 west into Ottumwa and head north on South Jefferson Street. Take a left on Second Street and head west to Clay Street. The depot is just south of Second Street off Washington Street. To get to Rutledge Hill, continue west along Second Street and take a right on Caldwell Street, which becomes Rutledge Road. To get to Agency Hill, take a right when exiting Highway 34 and take a right onto 73rd Street. Head east and Old Agency Road will be the first road on the right after crossing Highway 34.

Nevada

Located about 4 miles east of I-35 Exit 111 in central Iowa, Nevada is where Union Pacific's former CNW main crosses the former Rock Island Spine Line. The actual crossing is about a mile east of town on County E41. However, in the 1980s, CNW built a connector along the west edge of Nevada between the two lines, visible from E41, and County S14. During the day, you'll see up to 30 trains on the former CNW evenly split between manifest, intermodal, and coal. Up to 6 trains, predominately coal and manifest, can be seen on the Spine Line. Parking can be difficult on the connector, and you may have to do some walking to get to the best spots. You can park along the road at the crossing, and walk onto the bridge, but an over-under photograph is problematical due to the low frequency of trains on the Spine Line.

Hutchinson

About 40 miles northwest of Wichita on the Arkansas River, Hutchinson is the crossing and junction of BNSF's La Junta Subdivision and Union Pacific's Herington Subdivision, along with junctions with the Kansas & Oklahoma and the Hutchinson & Northern. UP operates more than 20 trains through Hutchinson and has a daylight road-switcher based here. BNSF operates 4–6 trains a day including yard jobs to handle local switching. K&O operates a daily yard job to serve local customers and a local between Hutchinson and Wichita. The UP, BNSF, and Kansas & Oklahoma pass through downtown, where there are numerous locations to watch and photograph trains, including the Amtrak and UP depots, which are both located just off Main Street. Highway 61 parallels the UP from McPherson into Hutchinson, and southwest of town, it parallels both the UP and BNSF lines to Partridge. Highway 96 follows the K&O northwest out of town past Yaggy Yard. For an interesting space adventure, you can take in the Kansas Cosmosphere and Space Center (www.cosmo.org). Frequencies are BNSF: 160.935, UP: 161.550, and K&O: 161.085.

Topeka

Located 65 miles west of Kansas City, Topeka has had a long history with railroading. Today, Topeka is served by two railroads: the BNSF and the Union Pacific, with each following opposite banks of the Kansas River. Along the north bank, three UP lines converge from the west, flowing together as a high-traffic, double-track main line with locals, manifests, and unit grain trains. On the south side of the river, the single-track BNSF Topeka Sub hosts a small number of daily locals, coal trains, and Amtrak's *Southwest Chief*. Topeka is also home to a large BNSF diesel shop and the railroad's business car fleet, located just north of the Amtrak depot. Business cars are often sent out as complete trains or occasionally on the local or with Amtrak. Porubsky's Curve in North Topeka, where the BNSF interchanges with the UP, is a good viewing location with ample parking on either side of the tracks. The line turns north-south here, so photography is pretty good in both the morning and afternoon. To get here, exit I-70W at Fourth Street, go north on Kansas Avenue, and then head east to the tracks on Gordon Street.

Emporia

Dan Munson

This is the heart of BNSF's (former ATSF) Emporia Subdivision between Kansas City and Wellington on the southern Transcon. Two and three CTC main lines stretch between NR Junction in Emporia on the east end to the Ellinor on the west end. NR Junction is where the west end of BNSF's Topeka Subdivision connects to the Emporia Subdivision. At Ellinor, the La Junta Subdivision starts and heads west to Newton and Dodge City.

ACTIVITY: BNSF operates more than 50 trains a day through this location, the majority being intermodal, manifest, and grain. UP operates more than 8 trains a day on trackage rights from the Chicago area to Hutchinson. All UP trains are intermodal or auto trains. Ellinor is the east end of single directional trackage (Mulvane is the west end). Most BNSF westbounds operate over the Emporia Sub, turning southwest out of Ellinor. Most eastbounds come off the La Junta Sub into Ellinor. Watch for the Topeka Sub to be used to take trains off a busy Emporia Sub. Trains may fleet one direction due to limited sidings on the Topeka Sub. Emporia Yard keeps a single yard job on days and afternoons to service local customers and work in the yard. Manifest trains may be shuttled to Emporia from Kansas City to wait for additional locomotives.

TRAIN-WATCHING SPOTS: Emporia offers several photo locations from public streets through downtown with historic buildings and the east end of yard as backdrops. Look for large signal bridges at each end of town. West of Emporia, the County Road G crossing is a great place to watch westbounds throttle out of town.

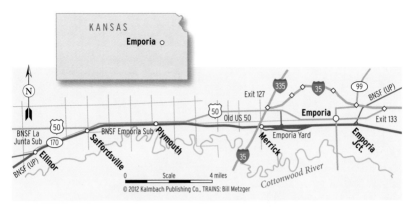

Emporia lies between Wichita and Topeka in east-central Kansas.

The south main separates and rises slightly from the other mains west of Merrick to Ellinor. You can use County Road 170 and Highway 50 to follow the tracks between Merrick and Ellinor, and there are several grade crossings to shoot from. At Saffordville, Old Highway 50 branches off to the southwest and follows the tracks to Ellinor.

SAFETY: Watch for fast trains at grade crossings; the track speed is 70 mph west of Emporia.

RAILROAD FREQUENCIES: BNSF: 160.650 (Emporia Sub), 160.935 (La Junta Sub), 161.145 (Topeka Sub)

TO DO: Take US Highway 50 west to the Flint Hills Scenic Byway (Highway 177) and explore the grasslands of the Great Plains. The single-track section of the Emporia Sub offers several beautiful photo locations.

NEARBY: Operating passenger excursions, Midland Railway is about 75 miles northeast at Baldwin City off I-35.

DIRECTIONS: Take I-35 southwest out of Kansas City to Emporia, exit at Highway 50, and follow it into town.

Mulvane

Bruce Barrett

Mulvane is the junction of BNSF's Emporia and Arkansas City Subdivisions. The subdivisions form a large X at Mulvane. The Emporia Sub, between Kansas City and Wellington, runs northeast to southwest. The Arkansas City Sub (Ark City), between Newton and Arkansas City, runs northwest to southeast. The Emporia Sub has a long siding that branches off at East Junction, down into the town of Mulvane, connecting with the Arkansas City, while the main stays elevated east of town. Just south of the former ATSF depot, a wye on the Ark City Sub allows trains to operate in all directions. BNSF numbers both subdivisions as Main 1 through 4 in Mulvane. Main 1 is the northwestern-most track, connecting the Ark City Sub to the Emporia Sub at West Junction. Main 2 parallels Main 1 on same route. Main 3 starts at East Junction and runs through downtown Mulvane onto the Ark City Sub. Main 4 runs directly from East Junction to West Junction.

ACTIVITY: BNSF operates more than 50 trains a day throught this location; the majority are intermodal, manifest, and grain. Mulvane is the west end of single-track directional trackage (Ellinor is the east end). Most BNSF westbounds operate over the Emporia Sub, staying on Main 4 east of town. Most eastbounds come off the Emporia and Ark City Subs into Mulvane and head north through Wichita to Newton, where they turn back east. Most trains from Kansas City going to Oklahoma and Texas turn south at Augusta, down the more-direct Douglas Sub, but don't be surprised to see a Texas-bound train through Mulvane. Also watch for northbound trains heading up the Ark City Sub to Wichita and Newton. UP has rights over the BNSF from Wichita to Fort Worth that it uses periodically. South Kansas & Oklahoma has rights over BNSF from Winfield to Wichita and runs a daily local.

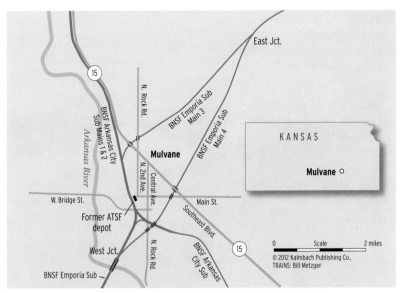

Mulvane is about 25 miles south of Wichita.

TRAIN-WATCHING SPOTS: Mulvane offers several viewing locations from public streets through downtown with the former ATSF depot as a backdrop, and the north end of the wye can be photographed from the West Bridge Street crossing. Going northwest to the 95th Street crossing, you'll see the lines split at East Junction, with the main passing through a tunnel.

RAILROAD FREQUENCIES: BNSF: 161.190 (Emporia Sub), 161.055 (Arkansas City Sub); UP and SKOL trains will use BNSF channels.

TO DO: The former ATSF depot in Mulvane houses the Mulvane Historical Museum (300 West Main Street), with its displays of local history.

NEARBY: The Great Plains Transportation Museum in Wichita (700 East Douglas Avenue) offers another location for watching trains on the Ark City Sub as well as UP trains.

DIRECTIONS: Take Exit 33 off I-35 and head east on Highway 53 straight into Mulvane.

Paola

Dan Munson

At Paola, the Union Pacific's (former MP) Coffeyville Subdivision, the BNSF's (former BN, Frisco) Fort Scott Subdivision, and the north end of the UP's Parsons Subdivision (former MKT) cross at grade. The UP has trackage rights over the BNSF from Kansas City to Paola via old MKT rights. The UP lines split just south of the diamonds, the former MP line heads south to Osawatomie, and the former MKT heads south to Parsons. Both roads have CTC trackage with BNSF's Ustick dispatcher controlling the crossing, except the Parsons Sub which is TWC/ABS.

ACTIVITY: BNSF operates more than 20 trains a day through Paola, with a mix of coal, manifest, intermodal, and grain. UP operates more than 30 trains daily, most being coal, manifest, and grain. UP operates mostly directionally at Paola, with southbounds coming off the BNSF trackage rights and onto the Parsons Sub and northbounds running up the former MP trackage.

TRAIN-WATCHING SPOTS: There are several locations to watch and photograph trains from the West Peoria Street crossing just north of the diamonds. Watch for UP trains using the "long track" to connect off the BNSF to their own tracks. There are several good photo locations on all lines both north and south of Paola. A good local map will assist in finding these spots.

FREQUENCIES: UP: 160.875 (Parsons Sub), 161.265 (Coffeyville Sub, north of Paola), 160.410 (Coffeyville Sub, south of Paola); BNSF: 161.235, 161.410

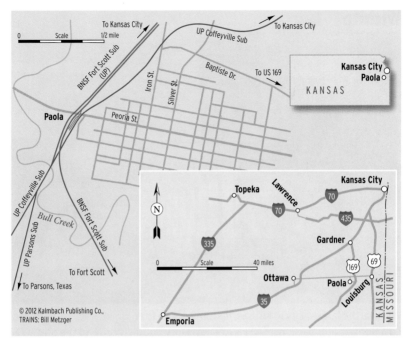

Paola is about 40 miles south of downtown Kansas City on US 169.

TO DO: All Kansas City attractions are 45 minutes to the north. Midland Railway operates excursions at Baldwin City, which is approximately 30 miles northwest.

NEARBY: You can catch BNSF action in several other locations. Both BNSF's Fort Scott Sub and Emporia Sub pass through Olathe, 20 miles north. BNSF Emporia Sub is 20 miles to the west at Ottawa.

DIRECTIONS: Take US 169 south from Kansas City and exit at Baptiste Drive. Go west into Paola to North Silver Street, turn left, go 8 blocks to West Peoria Street, turn right, and go to the tracks.

Wichita

Bruce Barrett

Wichita, the largest city in Kansas, features action from Union Pacific's Enid and Lost Springs Subdivisions, BNSF's Arkansas City Subdivision, and the Kansas & Oklahoma short line. Traffic funnels into a common right-of-way through the downtown district that is owned by the Wichita Union Terminal (UP and BNSF each own 50 percent of this railroad). For decades, a portion of the downtown right-of-way was elevated over four city streets. BNSF embarked on a major project between 2004 and 2009 to elevate the right-of-way farther north over three additional city streets that allowed train speeds to increase from 10 mph to 30 mph through town.

ACTIVITY: BNSF is the dominant railroad with 20–30 trains daily, with Union Pacific providing 6–10 trains per day. Kansas & Oklahoma Railroad provides a handful of trains per day, with both road freights and transfers to and from BNSF and UP. BNSF traffic can vary from day to day with primarily eastbound traffic routed via Wichita off the parallel Emporia Subdivision (located 20 miles east of Wichita) as traffic levels dictate. Intermodal, automotive, grain, manifest, and coal trains are seen here along with the chance to catch BNSF's unique airplane fuselage movements from Wichita to Seattle that originate just south of town.

TRAIN-WATCHING SPOTS: The best location to view trains downtown on the elevated trackage is at the former Wichita Union Station, which is now the Great Plains Transportation Museum (700 East Douglas Avenue). The north end of elevated trackage can be accessed at East 17th Street North and the south end at East Gilbert Street crossing. Kansas & Oklahoma's facilities are just west of downtown along Orient Avenue while BNSF's are just north of

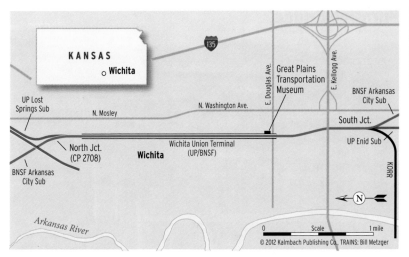

Wichita is located in south-central Kansas, about 200 miles southwest of Kansas City.

downtown on North Broadway. UP's yard is a few blocks east of BNSF's yard along North New York Street.

FREQUENCIES: BNSF: 161.055 (Arkansas City); UP: 160.470 (Enid), 161.550 (Lost Springs); Kansas & Oklahoma: 161.085

TO DO: The downtown district offers many shops and places to dine, including the Old Mill Tasty Shop, a block west of the station, which is an original Old Town soda fountain. In addition to the Great Plains Transportation Museum, Wichita boasts more than 30 additional museums. At the confluence of the Big Arkansas and Little Arkansas Rivers, you can photograph the iconic Keeper of the Plains sculpture.

NEARBY: Just south of Wichita is the town of Mulvane, where BNSF's Arkansas City Subdivision crosses under the busy Emporia Subdivision.

DIRECTIONS: Take I-35 to Kellogg Avenue (Exit 50) and head west to Washington Street. Take Washington Street north to Douglas and then go west several blocks to Wichita Union Station and the museum.

Burnside Bridge

Steve Forrest

Burnside is located about halfway between Cincinnati and Chattanooga on Norfolk Southern's famed CNO&TP main line. Burnside is now the only crew change point on the NS between Cincinnati and Chattanooga. The crews may run four different directions from here to Cincinnati, Louisville, Knoxville, or Chattanooga.

ACTIVITY: Approximately 40–50 trains may pass here in 24 hours, and with all trains stopping to change crews, there can be congestion. You will see all types of freight traffic here including intermodals, RoadRailers, general freights, and unit trains of coal, sulfur, phosphate, grain, and ethanol. Foreign power is also seen here, sometimes in the lead, usually UP and BNSF but occasionally CN and KCS will appear.

TRAIN-WATCHING SPOTS: The new NS depot (159 East French Avenue), the railroad crossing, and trains may be viewed from the road. Most trains will change crews right at the depot, but occasionally, they will swap out crews at either end of the holding yard. The south end of the holding yard is known as General and the north end, Burnside. Both locations can be viewed from public roadways.

In addition, south of the Burnside and Tateville areas, several county and state roads cross over the tracks and offer excellent high vantage points. (A good topographical map or atlas is recommended.) Less than a half-mile north of the depot is the often-photographed double-track bridge over the Cumberland River (Lake Cumberland).

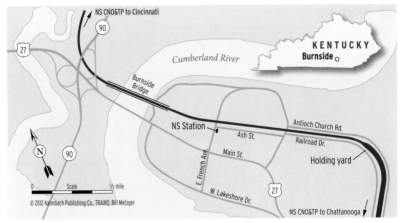

Burnside is 80 miles south of Lexington on US 27.

SAFETY: To photograph the bridge, you will need to find a safe place to park and then walk around to the dead end of the north end of the fence (installed with the new road to keep animals off the highway). Follow the fence southward back around to the bluff, carefully walking along the edge to the desired photo location. There is more than one vantage point to view the bridge from but exercise extreme caution as there are no safety barriers along the bluff.

RAILROAD FREQUENCIES: NS: 160.950, 160.245 (dispatcher to train), 160.830 (train to dispatcher)

TO DO: Lake Cumberland is a major area attraction for boating and fishing. Also country music lovers may find the shows at nearby Renfro Valley (Mount Vernon) of interest. During summer, motel rooms may be in short supply due to vacationing boaters.

NEARBY: The Big South Fork Scenic Railroad operates Alco S2 powered excursion trains out of Stearns, about 25 miles south of Burnside. The CSX main line between Cincinnati and Atlanta is about 45 miles to the east, and there is a major CSX yard at Corbin.

DIRECTIONS: The depot is located just east of US 27. To get to the Burnside Bridge overlook, take US 27 north of the Burnside area. The bridge can be easily seen from the highway.

La Grange

Ron Flanary

La Grange was a way station on the Louisville, Cincinnati & Lexington (LC&L), a predecessor company of the former Louisville & Nashville. Before the Civil War, trains operated between Louisville and Frankfort via La Grange. By 1869, however, a branch was completed north from La Grange to Cincinnati (actually Newport, Ky., on the south bank of the Ohio River). The LC&L was known as the Short Line, a moniker that endures to this very day. In a throwback to an earlier time, today's CSX LCL Subdivision goes right down the main street of La Grange for nearly a quarter-mile of street running.

ACTIVITY: La Grange typically sees 18–22 daily CSX freights. Traffic is a mix of general freight and auto rack trains, and movements are usually spaced throughout the day. The line is CTC controlled, and there's an 8,330-foot passing siding immediately north of the business district. The former L&N passenger station is also located just north of the business district, but it's no longer in railroad use. Crews verbally acknowledge signal indications on the radio—a particularly helpful practice in predicting approaching trains. There are no scheduled passenger trains.

TRAIN-WATCHING SPOTS: Railroad photography doesn't get any easier than in La Grange—you just hang around Main Street, enjoy some specialty shops (including several quaint restaurants and sandwich shops) between trains, and they come to you. CSX freights are required to reduce speed to 10 mph until the engines pass through town, when they can increase to 20 mph.

SAFETY: While LaGrange is a reduced-speed operation, given the density of trains, you should expect something in either direction at any time.

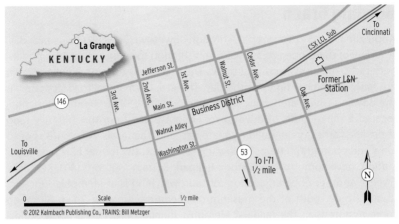

La Grange is 25 miles northeast of Louisville near the Indiana border.

RAILROAD FREQUENCIES: CSX: 161.370 (road), 161.520 (dispatcher)

TO DO: La Grange is the county seat of Oldham County. The best locations for dining are downtown, right beside the main line. Camping and RV facilities are within easy reach. There are several bed and breakfasts nearby but not on the railroad. Lodging and dining options increase the closer you get to Louisville. La Grange has held several Railroad Festivals in fall. Look for this continuing event.

NEARBY: The Kentucky Railway Museum at New Haven is 70 miles south of La Grange via I-71, I-264 (Louisville), and I-65. Louisville is just 26 miles to the south and Cincinnati 82 miles to the north, both via I-71.

DIRECTIONS: La Grange is located off Exit 22 from I-71. From there, it's less than a half-mile northeast to downtown, where the CSX main line is located. Route 146 north and south of La Grange are within range of the CSX main, but the real appeal is La Grange itself, for its classic street running, and the slow speed of trains as they pass through.

Bowling Green

Approximately 15–18 trains pass through downtown Bowling Green each day. A variety of trains operate over CSX rails through town including intermodals, auto racks, manifests, and coal trains. The CSX tracks through Bowling Green are fairly busy most times of the day. The R. J. Corman Railroad operates in the Bowling Green area daily, interchanging with CSX at Memphis Junction, located 5 miles south of downtown. Freight traffic from the 100-mile-long short line carries grain, building materials, and chemicals. A favorite spot to view and photograph trains in Bowling Green is at the former L&N passenger station, now home to the Historic Railpark & Train Museum (401 Kentucky Street). Another popular location for train watching is at Memphis Junction, about a mile south of the museum on Memphis Junction Road. Although more remote than the railpark, Memphis Junction provides a good opportunity for photographing CSX freights and the daily R. J. Corman train that arrive on the former L&N Memphis Line. There are several areas to park in the area. Frequencies are CSX: 161.370 (road), 161.520 (dispatcher); R. J. Corman: 160.845.

Corbin

In southeastern Kentucky, Corbin is a busy junction for CSX on its Cincinnati-Atlanta main line (former Louisville & Nashville). The coal-producing Cumberland Valley Subdivision brings bituminous (mostly southbound from Corbin) from the east. Corbin sees several scheduled through north-south general freights, along with some grain, intermodal, and other commodities, but coal still dominates the traffic mix. Density is 40–45 movements per day, with trains on all three subdivisions. Crews change here for all trains in all directions. There are actually two yards (East and West), with the locomotive shop and servicing facilities between them (not accessible by public roads). Safe photo locations include the south end of the yard near Bacon Creek, where the Corbin bypass (Route 3041) crosses the south throat of both yards. Public grade crossings and an overhead bridge (Old Corbin Pike Road) located 2 miles south just off Route 26 provide excellent vantage points. Action on the north end can be safely photographed around Center Street as well as from some overhead bridges immediately north of town. The Cumberland Valley Subdivision can be photographed from public grade crossings and the Route 3041 overpass just east of Corbin.

New Orleans

Spanning the Mississippi River, the Huey P. Long Bridge is located in Jefferson Parish, several miles west of New Orleans. Owned by the New Orleans Public Belt Railroad, the combined rail/highway structure is the longest (4.35 miles) and highest steel railroad bridge in the United States. The double-tracked bridge is a vital gateway between Eastern and Western railroads. It sees an average of 25–30 trains per day, including Amtrak's *Sunset Limited* and transfer trains between CSX and NS and BNSF and UP. Most are manifest and intermodal trains, but coal and grain trains make rare appearances. Local trains from the New Orleans Public Belt also travel over the bridge. Due to the height of the bridge, it can be seen from many public areas. There are numerous locations on the east side of the river for viewing trains on the bridge. The adjacent South Clearview Parkway in Elmwood offers a wide-open view. One of the best viewing locations is Central Avenue, which is at the eastern approach to the bridge. The area is a mixture of residential and business neighborhoods that are generally safe.

Blanchard

Mike Harbour

Technically in the tiny town of Blanchard, Texas Junction is where Kansas City Southern's active north-south and east-west main lines meet; just south of the junction in Shreveport sits Deramus Yard, the railroad's operating hub and main locomotive shop, which means constant rail movements that should accommodate most any railfan.

ACTIVITY: Although Texas Junction is a one-railroad show, 40-plus trains daily move through the interlocking. Be prepared for plenty of unit trains (coal, grain, and aggregates), but intermodal and manifest runs roll past here as well.

TRAIN-WATCHING SPOTS: Texas Junction is a wye that diverges from KCS's original Kansas City-Port Arthur, Texas, main and heads, logically, into Texas. All three legs are active, but there's no place to watch the entire complex due to the surrounding dense pine forest. Thankfully, several good vantage points of the north switch exist, including the Dollar General parking lot (often used by the company's crew shuttle to drop and pick up crews). There's an area near the south switch suitable for parking.

When the action slows at the junction, head south to Deramus; just remember most of this expansive facility is fenced, so stay on public property and look for higher vantage points to shoot from such as highway shoulders. You can drive all the way around the yard, too, but the east side is more photogenic (the impressive yard tower, though, is on the west side). Don't forget downtown Shreveport, either, where you can find Union Pacific running through town on ex-Southern Pacific tracks, as well as KCS's eastbound main to Meridian, Miss., via a large, through-truss bridge over the Red River.

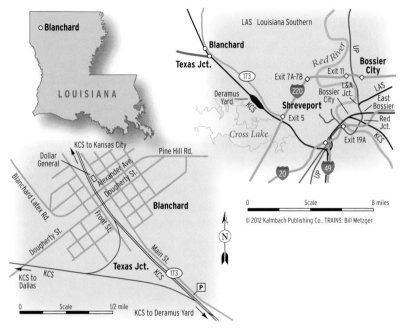

Blanchard is in the northwest corner of the state.

SAFETY: Blanchard is relatively safe, but be aware of your surroundings near Deramus Yard and downtown Shreveport.

RAILROAD FREQUENCIES: KCS: 160.260, 160.350, 160.89, 160.305

TO DO: With only gas and food available in Blanchard, visitors will need to rely on Shreveport and neighboring Bossier City across the river for places to stay and play. Scenic Cross Lake, which KCS traverses on a long, concrete pier bridge, sits between Blanchard and Shreveport and has several eateries.

NEARBY: Casino resorts abound in Shreveport-Bossier, as locals call the area, and there are many hotel and motel options both downtown and along I-20. There's also plenty of shopping, an alligator park, several zoos, galleries, and museums. The Louisiana State Fair takes place each fall in Shreveport.

DIRECTIONS: From downtown Shreveport, take Spring Street/US Highway 71 north to I-220 and then go west on this loop to Highway 173 (also known as the Shreveport-Blanchard Highway). Go north, and Deramus Yard will soon appear on your left; a few more miles past the KCS general office is Blanchard.

Brownville Junction

Brownville Junction is located 50 miles north of Bangor in the 100-Mile Wilderness of the Appalachian Trail. It is where the Montreal, Maine & Atlantic and New Brunswick Southern interchange. The railroads have a rich history, and the configuration of the rails has MMA traffic running south of Brownville Junction to a wye at Brownville, where trains can go farther south or turn to head back north. This has eastbound and westbound Montreal traffic passing Brownville Junction twice. Traffic usually consists of the MMA road trains 1 and 2, operating every other day respectively, along with a local from Northern Maine Junction and/or Derby plus the NBSR interchange, which tends to operate on the days Job 2 is headed east into Millinocket. In mid-2011, NBSR took over operations of the MMA's line north of Millinocket to the Canadian border under the Maine Northern moniker, which increased its activity in the area. Most of the action is visible from public right-of-way on Highway 11.

Hyattsville

Hyattsville is located in suburban Washington, D.C., 6 miles northeast of Amtrak's Union Station. It is home to a wye that connects CSX Baltimore Division's busy Alexandria Subdivision with the even busier Capitol Subdivision. The majority of trains on the former are intermodal or manifest trains traveling to and from the RF&P Subdivision south of the Potomac River, whereas the latter sees automobile, manifest freight, crushed stone, grain, coal, and hopper trains totaling up to 30–35 scheduled movements per day, especially near the end of the workweek. In addition to CSX operations, the Capitol Subdivision also hosts MARC's Camden Line commuter trains between Washington, D.C., and Baltimore, Monday through Friday. Both Hyattsville and Bladensburg (just to the south) offer a plethora of places for photographing the action from public property. Let the time of day and the angle of sunlight be your guide. Fast food and fuel is easy to find in nearby Riverdale to the north.

Cumberland

Alex Mayes

Cumberland features a major CSX classification yard, diesel shops, and a junction between the Cumberland Terminal Subdivision and the Mountain Subdivision, both former B&O lines. The two lines join at Viaduct Junction in downtown Cumberland, where the Cumberland Terminal Subdivision ends and the Keystone Subdivision begins and heads west over Sand Patch Grade. The Mountain Subdivision also begins here and heads southwest to Grafton, W.Va., over Cranberry and Seventeen Mile Grades and then points south and west.

ACTIVITY: About 25–30 scheduled CSX trains and Amtrak's *Capitol Limited* pass through Cumberland in 24 hours. Additionally, there are loaded and empty coal, grain, and ethanol trains. Traffic on the Mountain Subdivision is all eastbound loaded coal trains and westbound empty coal trains, except for 2 scheduled freights, trains Q316 and Q317, that run between Cumberland and Russell, Ky.

TRAIN-WATCHING SPOTS: The Amtrak station is located downtown just east of Baltimore Street (201 East Harrison Street) and is a popular train-watching spot. East of downtown, CSX's massive yard runs parallel to Route 51 for 3 miles, with good views from this road. The shops, turntable, and servicing facilities are on Virginia Avenue. (Watch trains here from public streets and not from the CSX employee parking lot or other CSX property.) The east end of the yard can be viewed from Mexico Farm Road, which crosses over the east throat over the yard.

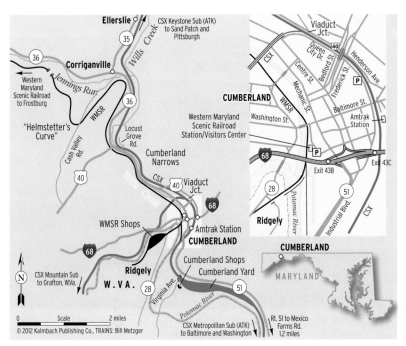

Cumberland is in the northwestern part of the state near the Pennsylvania border.

West of the Amtrak station on Front Street are several grade crossings that provide good photo locations, especially Knox Street. Just east of Knox Street is Viaduct Junction, a great afternoon photo location for westbounds on either line. Park at the animal supply store and walk to the edge of the lot.

FREQUENCIES: CSX: 160.230, 160.320, 161.520, 160.410, 160.290

TO DO: The Western Maryland Scenic Railroad operates steam-powered excursions to Frostburg. The trips depart from the old former Western Maryland Railway passenger station in downtown Cumberland. Adjacent to the station is the beginning of the C&O Canal with walkways and interpretive signs.

NEARBY: Go west on Alternate 40, and you will enter Cumberland Narrows, a narrow gap between Wills and Haystack Mountains, with the CSX main on the right and the former Western Maryland Railway on the left. Near Corriganville is Cash Valley Road, which leads to famed Helmstetter's Curve. Go west about 3 miles, and Helmstetter's Curve is on the right as you cross the tracks. An outstanding view of the curve is available from the ledge above the tracks in the adjacent cemetery. Sand Patch Grade is northwest of Cumberland.

DIRECTIONS: From I-68, take Exit 43D and turn right on Park Street. A left on East Harrison Street will take you to the Amtrak station.

Perryville

David Warner

The area features two impressive bridges. The Amtrak Susquehanna River Bridge (officially the Susquehanna River Movable Bridge) is a double-track, steel truss bridge more than a half-mile long with a swing span about 800 feet from the Havre de Grace end. The current bridge was built in 1904-1906, and piers that supported two previous bridges still stand south of the current bridge. Nearly a mile upstream is the mile-long, single-track CSX bridge. Built between 1908 and 1910, its deck trusses carry the railroad tracks over portions of the river, and above Garrett Island in the middle of the river, with two fixed through trusses spanning the navigable parts of the river.

ACTIVITY: More than 70 Amtrak NEC and intercity trains run on weekdays, with slightly fewer on weekends. On weekdays, 4 MARC trains depart Perryville in the early morning and 4 arrive in the evening. You'll also see 8–10 Norfolk Southern freights but mostly at night.

TRAIN-WATCHING SPOTS: Public locations are plentiful on both sides of the river, which provide good photo angles all day. Track-level access is available at the Perryville station platform (650 Broad Street). The Perryville station, built in 1905 by PRR subsidiary Philadelphia, Baltimore & Washington (PB&W), sits in the center of a wye connection to the former PB&W Columbia and Port Deposit Branch (now part of Norfolk Southern).

SAFETY: Track speed is 90 mph across the bridge. The railroad is on an elevated structure in Havre de Grace with no access.

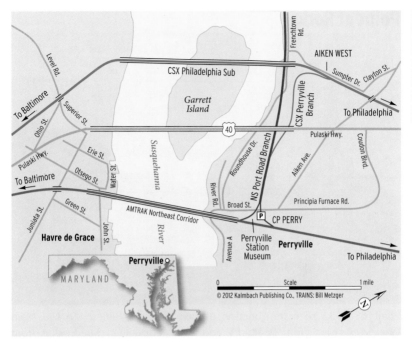

Perryville and Havre de Grace are halfway between Baltimore and Wilmington, Del., separated by the Susquehanna River.

RADIO FREQUENCIES: Amtrak: 160.920 (road); NS: 161.070 (port road); CSX: 160.230 (road)

TO DO: The Perryville Chapter of the National Railway Historical Society operates a small museum and model railroad in the Perryville station.

NEARBY: If you'd like to spend some money, the Hollywood Casino, the first casino in the state, is located in Perryville. In Havre de Grace, you can visit the Concord Point Lighthouse, stroll along the boardwalk, take in the decoy museum, or engage in maritime activities.

DIRECTIONS: To reach the Amtrak bridge, take I-95 to Exit 93. Take Route 222 south 2 miles into Perryville. Turn right on Route 7 and continue until you pass under the Amtrak bridge at Perry Point. US Route 40 takes you between Perryville and Havre de Grace.

Point of Rocks

Alex Mayes

Point of Rocks sees the junction of two CSX main lines: the Old Main Line Subdivision from Baltimore and the Metropolitan Subdivision from Washington, D.C., both former B&O lines. The Metropolitan Sub is also known as MARC's Brunswick Line. Situated between the two lines is the historic and picturesque Point of Rocks Station, built in 1873 by noted architect E. Francis Baldwin. The station is a stop for most MARC trains en route to Brunswick or Martinsburg, W.Va. The town gets its name from a rock formation on the nearby Catoctin Mountains that is visible only from the adjacent Potomac River or from the Virginia shore.

ACTIVITY: About 25–30 scheduled CSX trains, 6 morning eastbound and 7 afternoon westbound MARC commuter trains, and Amtrak's *Capitol Limited* pass by the station in a day. MARC trains to and from Frederick pass behind the station on a connection between the Old Main Line and the Metropolitan Sub. Three morning and 3 afternoon MARC trains to or from Frederick use the connection. MARC trains run only on weekdays. Additionally, you'll see loaded and empty coal, grain, and ethanol trains. Most CSX freights use the Metropolitan Sub.

TRAIN-WATCHING SPOTS: The classic shot with trains passing the front of the station can be taken in the afternoon from the platforms or from adjacent areas just west of the station. There are many westbound afternoon shots available, with or without the signals. Morning shots of eastbound trains can be taken from the platforms of trains splitting signals or diverging onto the Old Main Line. Morning MARC trains have cab-control cars leading, with diesels pushing on the rear.

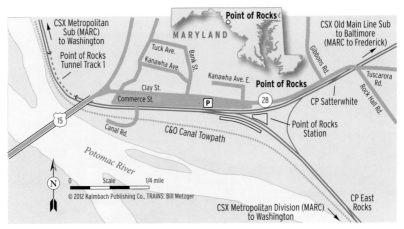

Point of Rocks is in the northeast corner of the state on the Potomac River.

Photos can also be taken from the open field behind the station. The signals at the station display red indications until trains are approaching, which provide ample time to set up for photos.

SAFETY: Both lines see trains running at 40 mph or higher, and trains pass by the station on both lines.

FREQUENCIES: CSX: 160.230, 160.320, 161.520, 160.410, 160.290

TO DO: The Potomac River and the historic Chesapeake & Ohio Canal run parallel to the Metropolitan Sub east and west of the station. Access to hiking and biking on the canal towpath is via a road across the tracks 200 yards west of the station.

NEARBY: CSX's yard and MARC servicing facilities are in Brunswick, 5 miles west. Two other hot spots are Harpers Ferry, W.Va., 12 miles to the west, and Shenandoah Junction, W.Va., 19 miles to the west.

DIRECTIONS: From I-70 west of Frederick, take Exit 52 and go west on US Route 340 for 6 miles, take Exit 10, and go south on US Route 15 for 7 miles. Turn left on Route 28 and then turn right into the MARC parking lot.

Palmer

Scott Hartley

Three rail routes intersect in Palmer's pleasant downtown area. CSX's Boston-Selkirk, N.Y., route (acquired from Conrail in 1999, originally New York Central's Boston & Albany) is New England's busiest freight line and also hosts Amtrak's *Lake Shore Limited*. The onetime Central Vermont Railway, now RailAmerica's New England Central, crosses CSX at a diamond by the former Union Station, now a popular restaurant. The 26-mile Massachusetts Central short line leaves town northward alongside the NECR to serve a onetime B&A branch.

ACTIVITY: CSX runs approximately 20 freights every 24 hours, in addition to 2 Amtrak round trips it hosts. NECR runs a road freight in and out of Palmer in each direction, plus a local switcher, daily. MCER usually runs only on weekdays. The three freight lines all interchange in CSX's yard, just east of the diamond. NECR has its own yard south of the diamond, and MCER's offices and locomotive servicing area are about 1 mile north of town. CSX is largely a single-track railroad, although a 4-mile signaled siding begins at CP 83 just east of the CSX/NECR diamond, and meets frequently occur here. CSX train crews call each interlocking signal, and a scanner picks up westbounds calling CP 79, the east end of the two-track section. A defect detector 8 miles west in Wilbraham announces eastbounds.

Amtrak's *Vermonter* uses CSX between Springfield and Palmer, and NECR north to St. Albans, Vt. These trains reverse direction at Palmer, so they usually have a locomotive at each end. (In the future, the *Vermonter* may be rerouted north of Springfield over Pan Am Southern's former Boston & Maine Connecticut River Line.)

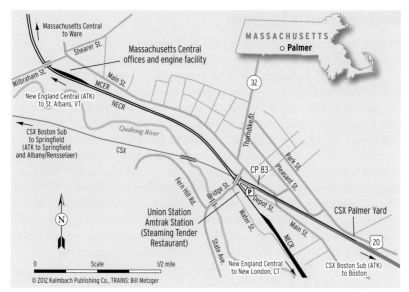

Palmer is in the south-central portion of the state near Springfield.

TRAIN-WATCHING SPOTS: The long driveway to the station restaurant (28 Depot Street) offers parking, and all four railroads can be safely viewed and photographed from this elevated location along the south side of the CSX main.

SAFETY: Trains from several railroads often move simultaneously. Top speed on CSX is 60 mph, and visibility of approaching trains is limited.

RAILROAD FREQUENCIES: CSX: 160.800 (road), 161.070 (yard), 160.560 (dispatcher); NECR: 161.415, 161.205, 160.935; MCER: 160.470

TO DO: The historic station, designed by noted architect H. H. Richardson, now houses the Steaming Tender Restaurant, where you can dine as trains from four railroads pass on two sides. An ancient New Haven Railroad wooden coach along NECR serves weekend brunch.

NEARBY: Springfield Union Station (66 Lyman Street), 15 miles west, hosts Amtrak's New Haven-Springfield trains and is a stop for the *Lake Shore Limited*. Connecticut Southern and Pan Am Southern freights can be seen in addition to the parade of CSX trains.

DIRECTIONS: Take Exit 8 off the Massachusetts Turnpike (I-90) to Route 32 and continue south until intersects with Route 20.

Boston, South Station

Boston's South Station opened in 1899, replacing four separate stations that served a multitude of New Haven Railroad and New York Central/Boston & Albany routes to the south and west. Today, South Station's 13 tracks serve Massachusetts Bay Transportation Authority commuter trains over nine different lines as well as Amtrak Northeast Corridor trains and the Boston-Chicago *Lake Shore Limited*. The surviving main station building, situated at the corner of Atlantic Avenue and Summer Street, is busier than ever, converted to a customer-friendly terminal with restaurants and stores facing the passenger platforms. Amtrak's electric-powered trains, including high-speed *Acela* services, normally use the center tracks while the outer tracks keep busy with a constant parade of MBTA diesel commuter runs that arrive and depart from a variety of points in Massachusetts and Rhode Island. About a mile to the north, but not connected directly by rail, is North Station, the terminus for T trains to the north and northwest and Amtrak's *Downeaster* service to Maine.

Springfield

Springfield, situated at the intersection of Amtrak's Springfield Line (north-south) and CSX's Boston Line (east-west), sees action from four railroads: Amtrak, CSX, Connecticut Southern, and PanAm Railways. The best train-watching spot is from the platforms of the Amtrak Station (66 Lyman Street), which is located at the intersection of the two lines. The platforms are situated along a straight section of CSX's Boston Line tracks and provide plenty of warning of approaching trains. While there, you can expect to see at least 30 trains within a 24-hour period. These include Amtrak's *Vermonter* and *Lake Shore Limited* and New Haven shuttles for passenger runs. You will also see general mixed freight, intermodal, and auto rack traffic, with the bulk belonging to CSX. CSOR typically has one turn job from Hartford to West Springfield, and PAR will visit town 2–3 times a week as the trains pass between East Deerfield and Plainville, Conn.

Detroit

The CSX line from Grand Rapids and the Norfolk Southern from Fort Wayne join at Delray Tower and cross the Conrail-Detroit Shared Assets Detroit Line and continue to the old NS Boat Yard in Detroit near downtown. CSX mans the tower but NS, Canadian National, and Canadian Pacific trains also operate through this crossing. During the day, there are usually 20 or so movements and 15 or so at night. Weekends usually see 15 or so train movements. CP provides the most trains daily, usually 5 each way along with extra ethanol and grain trains. CN operates a RoadRailer train between NS Oakwood Yard and Toronto, eastbound Sunday-Friday and westbound Monday-Saturday. You can view trains from the street. Dearborn Avenue goes through this crossing. However, there is no parking on Dearborn Avenue, but you can park off the driveway for St. Marys Cement and on Carbon Street. Dearborn Avenue and St. Marys Cement are very busy with heavy truck traffic. It is best to not go to this area alone, and when the shadows get long, you should be long gone. Do not go by the tower and stay out of the triangle area between the tracks.

Durand

Greg McDonnell

This historic mid-Michigan crossing of Canadian National's former Grand Trunk Western Railroad is best known for its large, distinctive brick station, which stands at the junction of CN's Chicago-Port Huron and Durand-Detroit main lines. In addition to CN trains, Durand also is served by Amtrak and short lines Huron & Eastern (HESR), which operates the ex-GTW line to Saginaw, and Great Lakes Central (GLC), which operates on the ex-GTW line to the north via Owosso and Cadillac and the former Ann Arbor to the south.

ACTIVITY: The fast, heavy-duty CTC-controlled CN single-track main line features local interchange switching performed by HESR and GLC. Approximate train frequency is 40 freights per day on CN, 2 daily Amtrak trains, and at least 1-per-day service from HESR and GLC. Amtrak's Chicago-Port Huron *Blue Water* makes a morning departure westbound for Chicago, and the eastbound train from Chicago has a late-evening arrival.

TRAIN-WATCHING SPOTS: Although there are plenty of public locations for viewing trains around Durand, especially at grade crossings, the best and safest option is to go to the station (200 South Railroad Street), which was built in 1903 in the Chateau Romanesque style. Ample parking is available on the east side of the structure. Concrete station platforms along the west and north edges of the building provide good places to see trains on all the railroads operating through town. Generous eaves and a platform roof at the front of the depot are a respite from wet weather. A secure metal fence aside the tracks makes this a hassle-free train-watching location.

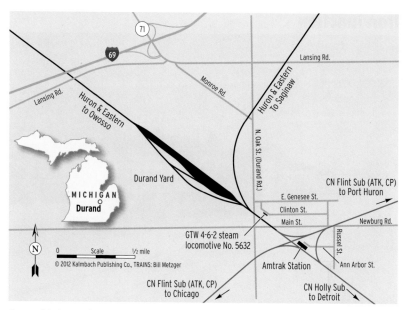

Durand is located on I-69, approximately 20 miles west of Flint and 40 miles east of Lansing.

RAILROAD FREQUENCIES: CN: 160.590; HESR: 160.440; GLC: 160.575 (road), 161.000 (yard)

TO DO: Durand has a variety of locally owned eateries, some with a railroad theme, most in the downtown area just north of the depot. The main attraction in town, Union Station, also houses the Michigan Railroad History Museum. The large waiting and dining rooms of the old station are full of railroad exhibits, mostly from the steam age, which encompass a variety of subjects from passenger trains to local railroaders.

NEARBY: The busy CN main line is always a good subject for photography, and it can be photographed from numerous locations in the picturesque farmland around Durand.

DIRECTIONS: Durand is located just south of Exit 118 on I-69 at the intersection of M-71. To reach the depot, follow the signs to downtown Durand and head east on Main Street to Russell Road. Turn right on Russell, cross the CN tracks, and head south 1 block to Ann Arbor Street. Turn right and head west another block to the train station.

Iron Junction

Steve Glischinski

Iron Junction is a wye in the northwoods of Minnesota's Arrowhead Region where two busy iron ore-hauling Canadian National main lines split. At a series of junctions immediately north of Iron, several CN routes converge. One arrives from the Canadian border crossing at Ranier, Minn.; the others split to serve two iron ore processing plants (Minorca and Minntac) and a mine (Thunderbird North). Traffic arriving from the north takes one of two routings at Iron. Some trains run eastward on the Iron Range Subdivision to the ore docks at Two Harbors. Others continue down the Missabe Subdivision to reach the United Taconite plant at Forbes, an ore dock at Duluth, and the CN main line to Chicago.

ACTIVITY: You'll see 4–5 daily "core" trains, freight and intermodal trains moving between Canada and the Midwest, each way. Taconite trains include 5–6 daily moves to and from Minntac, plus 1 to and from Minorca. You'll see occasional BNSF haulage-rights trains to Minntac, plus occasional CSX and Norfolk Southern run-through trains in winter, when shipping on the Great Lakes ceases. Thunderbird Mine trains (T-birds) make several daily round trips most days through Iron on their roughly 10-mile journey from the mine to the United Taconite plant. CN and BNSF haulage-rights locals pass through Iron on their way to the taconite plants. CN's locals also deliver coal to the Laskin Energy Center at Aurora, and mete out cars to a handful of smaller shippers in the area.

TRAIN-WATCHING SPOTS: Main Street and Iron Junction Road (County Road 452) cross east-west near the south edge of the wye, with Merritt Avenue (County Road 127) closely following much of the wye's west leg. These are quiet roads,

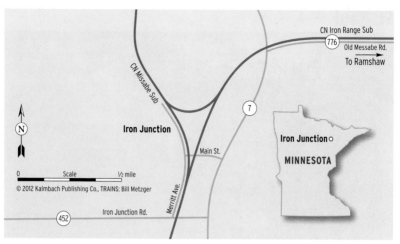

Iron Junction is located in northeast Minnesota, about 50 miles north of Duluth.

and it's easy to pull off and watch the action. County Road 7 crosses the Iron Range Subdivision to the east. For some variety, take County Road 776 east a mile to Ramshaw, where you'll find more CN core trains on the former Duluth, Winnipeg & Pacific main line crossing the Iron Range Subdivision at grade.

RAILROAD FREQUENCIES: CN: 160.350, 160.860, 160.800, 160.230

TO DO: Mineview in the Sky near Virginia offers overhead views of Thunderbird Mine. Farther west, the Minnesota Discovery Center at Chisholm tells the story of iron mining and sometimes offers tours of a working taconite plant during summer. Both fast food and sit-down restaurants can be found in Eveleth, 7 miles away; Eveleth is also home to the United States Hockey Hall of Fame Museum.

DIRECTIONS: From Duluth, take US 53 north for about 50 miles and then turn left onto Route 37. Go two miles to County Road 7, take a right, go 1 mile, and turn left onto Iron Junction Road.

St. Paul

Steve Glischinski

Minnesota's capital, St. Paul, is laced with mainline railroading. Traversing the city are the main lines of three BNSF Railway predecessors: the Chicago, Burlington & Quincy, the Great Northern, and the Northern Pacific. Canadian Pacific's former Milwaukee Road and Soo Line routes also pass through. At Westminster Junction near downtown St. Paul, UP's line from Chicago joins BNSF's Midway Subdivision. The UP has a wye at the BNSF connection. Tunneling under all these lines is the double-track former Northern Pacific route from Minneapolis, now BNSF's St. Paul Subdivision.

ACTIVITY: BNSF, CP, and UP trains all use the St. Paul Sub, totaling about 50 trains a day. The Midway Sub also sees trains of the three Class I railroads, and BNSF intermodal trains are regulars on the Midway Sub since the railroad's Midway Intermodal Terminal is 4 miles west of the junction. Minnesota Commercial has rights through Westminster Junction, and it uses the Midway Sub from St. Anthony interlocking to Westminster. These trains run about twice a week. On weekdays, Twin Cities & Western occasionally uses the St. Paul Sub to reach CP's St. Paul Yard.

TRAIN-WATCHING SPOTS: Phalen Boulevard passes over Westminster Junction. A new bridge over the tracks features a viewing platform. Photography from the platform is best in the morning for eastbound trains. By walking a short distance west, you can also photograph eastbound trains on the Midway Sub. In the afternoon, the next bridge over the tracks to the south, Lafayette Road, offers a view of eastbound trains popping out of the tunnel under Westminster Junction. The Midway Sub also runs under this bridge, and trains can be seen dropping downgrade from Westminster toward downtown.

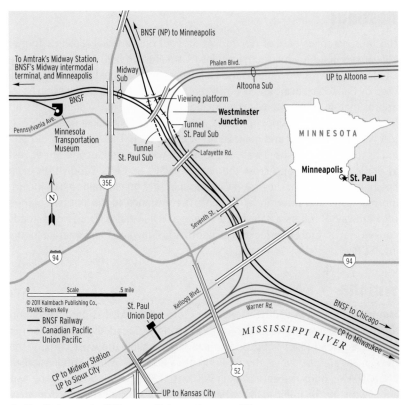

St. Paul is just east of Minneapolis in southeastern Minnesota.

Another nice location is the Kellogg Boulevard Bridge, east of the junction near St. Paul Union Depot. In the afternoon, the bridge offers excellent views of westbound trains rounding a big curve with the Mississippi River as a backdrop.

RAILROAD FREQUENCIES: BNSF: 161.250, 160.335, 161.160 (yard); CP: 160.770, 161.370, 161.520 (yard); UP: 160.890, 161.175 (yard); Minnesota Commercial: 160.560, 160.740; Twin Cities & Western: 161.460

TO DO: Downtown St. Paul is home to the Fitzgerald Theatre, Minnesota Children's Museum, and Science Museum of Minnesota.

NEARBY: The Minnesota Transportation Museum's ex-Great Northern Jackson Street Roundhouse is less than a half-mile from Westminster Junction. Union Depot (214 East Fourth Street) is being renovated, but the building's head-house is open.

DIRECTIONS: The downtown area is north of the Mississippi River and easily accessible from I-94.

Hastings

Hastings, 19 miles east of downtown St. Paul on Canadian Pacific's former Milwaukee Road main line, still retains its small-town feel. At the foot of the city's main downtown street is the ex-Milwaukee Road passenger depot, still used by Canadian Pacific and recently refurbished. CP's River Subdivision hosts approximately 25–30 trains a day, including Amtrak's *Empire Builder*. CP's lift bridge over the Mississippi River, still wearing huge Milwaukee Road logos, is just west of the depot and makes a great photo prop. There is plenty of parking in town within a short walk of the tracks, which cross Second Street East at grade by the depot. Across the river is BNSF's St. Croix Subdivision main line between the Twin Cities and Chicago that sees 40–50 trains a day, including manifests and intermodal Z trains. The entrance to King's Cove Marina off Highway 61 offers a safe place to watch BNSF trains. The two railroads converge at St. Croix interlocking just north of Highway 61 and operate jointly into St. Paul.

Winona

Winona is located in southeastern Minnesota on the Mississippi River, along the border between Minnesota and Wisconsin. Canadian Pacific's former Milwaukee Road River Subdivision main line parallels the west bank of the river in Minnesota, while the ex-Burlington Route St. Croix Subdivision of BNSF Railway hugs the east bank in Wisconsin. BNSF is the busier of the two lines, with 40–50 trains daily, while Canadian Pacific hosts approximately 25–30 trains a day, including Amtrak's *Empire Builder*. Winona's Amtrak depot (65 East Mark Street) provides a peaceful, safe place for watching trains. If you want scenic views, traveling on Highway 61 north or south of Winona will yield vistas of CP and Amtrak trains along the Father of Waters, while Wisconsin Route 35 parallels BNSF. Union Pacific has a small yard in the north side of Winona along Riverview Drive; the railroad reaches Winona from Adams, Wis., via trackage rights over CP from Tunnel City, Wis. At Goodview, 3 miles from downtown Winona, Canadian Pacific's Dakota, Minnesota & Eastern Waseca Subdivision main line joins the CP.

Jackson

Jackson is located at the crossing of the former Illinois Central Chicago-New Orleans main line that is now the southern leg of the Canadian National and the Kansas City Southern's Meridian Speedway, which can also trace its roots to the Illinois Central. You can expect 15–20 trains a day through Jackson. The predominant east-west traffic on the KCS main line is intermodals from the west coast and grain trains. CN traffic includes occasional unit coal trains through town that divert onto the Beaumont Subdivision toward Hattiesburg. Amtrak's *City of New Orleans* can be seen northbound and southbound during the daylight hours. One popular spot for catching the action is the Switch Tender, just 2 blocks south of the Amtrak station downtown. This is the point where the KCS crosses the elevated CN main line at grade. Switch Tender is best viewed from the parking area below the tracks. Another great spot for watching is the east end of KCS's High Oak Yard in Pearl, which is 5 miles east of Jackson.

Meridian

Mick Nussbaum

In Meridian, the former Southern Railway Washington, D.C.-New Orleans main line, which is now part of the Norfolk Southern Crescent Corridor, meets the Kansas City Southern Meridian Speedway. Meridian also is home to two short line railroads that run south out of the city: the Meridian & Bigbee, which is owned by Genesee & Wyoming, and the independently owned Meridian Southern (MDS). All four railroads and Amtrak use Meridian as crew bases for all their operations.

ACTIVITY: There are 20–25 trains a day either passing through or originating in Meridian. In addition to regular manifest trains, a large part of the traffic on the KCS is intermodal traffic from the West Coast. NS also runs a number of rock trains and twice-weekly unit coal trains through town. You can catch the Amtrak *Crescent* at Union Station passing through in each direction during daylight hours.

TRAIN-WATCHING SPOTS: In downtown, Union Station (1901 Front Street) is a great spot to watch the action, and plenty of free parking is available. The station's second-story observation deck is open to the public, and from there, you can see all KCS and NS traffic as well as M&B interchange traffic. Both the KCS and NS yards are accessible from public roads, and the NS-KCS diamond is accessible by way of a gravel parking lot behind the old warehouse off 11th Avenue just east of Union Station.

SAFETY: Union Station has 24-hour security and is very safe; however, most other locations adjacent to the railroad throughout town should be avoided after dark.

Meridian is located in east-central Mississippi at the point where I-20 and I-59 merge, 20 miles west of the Alabama state line.

RAILROAD FREQUENCIES: NS: 160.950 (road), 160.245 (dispatcher to train), 160.830 (train to dispatcher); KCS: 160.454 (road west), 161.085 (road north), 160.215 (yard); M&B: 160.350 (road); MDS: 161.310 (road)

TO DO: You can visit the Jimmie Rodgers Memorial Museum at Highland Park, which also includes some railroad displays. You could also enjoy a meal, followed by some world famous Black Bottom Pie, at Weidmann's restaurant near Union Station, which was founded in 1870.

NEARBY: The Meridian Railroad Museum is located adjacent to Union Station in the old 1907 Railway Express Agency building and features a display of rolling stock alongside the station platforms.

DIRECTIONS: Take Exit 153 off I-20 at 22nd Avenue and proceed north until you cross over the NS and KCS main lines. Turn right at the bottom of the bridge on Front Street, and Union Station is on your right 2 blocks down.

Eureka

Eureka is situated in an area of rolling hills about 30 miles southwest of St. Louis, at the edge of the metropolitan area. The 7 miles between Eureka and Pacific feature the generally parallel main lines of both Union Pacific and BNSF. Along these lines, you can see 35–45 UP trains, 8–9 BNSF trains, and Amtrak's *Missouri River Runner*. There are plenty of train-watching spots throughout the area on public streets and county roads that feature grade crossings and the Highway 109 bridge. Remnants of famed Route 66 still exist between Allenton and Pacific for you to explore. Frequencies are UP: 161.220 and BNSF: 161.160.

Kansas City, Union Station

Kansas City has one of the most magnificently preserved train stations in the nation, and it is also a great place to watch trains from. The triple-track BNSF Railway Transcon main line passes just outside Union Station (30 West Pershing Road), and a footbridge over the tracks provides an excellent vantage point. Signals on either side of the bridge indicate when trains are coming, changing from red to green minutes before the next move. The bridge is about a half-mile east of Santa Fe Junction, where BNSF trains may take the flyover to and from Argentine Yard. Kansas City Southern occasionally puts in an appearance hauling grain cars over the UP High Line to elevators in the Fairfax industrial district on the Kansas side of the Missouri River. Amtrak's *Southwest Chief* is easily visible from the bridge, and after the *Missouri River Runner* drops off passengers, the train deadheads to Santa Fe Junction to turn around. Inside Union Station, you can visit the KC Rail Experience and grab an excellent chocolate malt at the Harvey House Diner.

La Plata

La Plata is located in north-central Missouri where US 65 crosses the BNSF Transcon between Kirksville and Macon, the key Chicago-Los Angeles route of the BNSF. This former Santa Fe trackage sees more than 50 trains per day. The majority are intermodal, double-stack, double-stack/piggyback, and a few solid piggyback trains. Some manifests and grain trains are also in the mix. Amtrak visits twice daily as the *Southwestern Chief* goes east at mid-morning and the westbound edition usually passes through after sunset. The grade crossing east of the restored art deco Amtrak station (535 North Owensby Street) is the most popular train-watching spot. Another is the old US 65 bridge just to the east, which features light traffic and a sidewalk. You can safely park in the Amtrak station lot or on any of the public streets. The Depot Inn (1245 North Brown Street) provides a photo platform on the north side of the tracks within easy walking distance of the motel, and it is next to the Exhibition of Amtrak History, which is displayed in an ex-Amtrak mail-handling car.

Neosho

In the southwest corner of Missouri, Neosho is where the BNSF's Cherokee Subdivision crosses the KCS's Pittsburg Sub. With about 15 trains a day on each railroad, the action at Neosho can keep you busy. The KCS has the passing track of Dalby just north of the interlocker, and the BNSF's Jeff siding is east of the interlocker. The interlocker, just northeast of town, is not easy to get to, but numerous crossings nearby provide easy access to both railroads. On the KCS, you'll see 1 intermodal train with the rest being general merchandise or coal trains. You'll see distributed power on the merchandise trains and all the coal trains running with distributed power. On the BNSF side, a majority of the trains are intermodal with some mixed freight and empty coal trains. On the KCS between Neosho and Siloam Springs, Ark., there are many good photo opportunities, but they do require some searching. For the BNSF, good viewing locations exist to the east along Shoal Creek. Going to the west is more accessible but less scenic.

Scott City (Thebes Bridge)

Located in southern Missouri, Scott City is a place where you can view the massive Thebes Bridge. The bridge takes the busy Union Pacific Chester Subdivision from Illinois across the Mississippi into Missouri. This former Missouri Pacific main line once hosted its own trains as well as Southern Pacific/Cotton Belt trains. Today, UP trains dominate with approximately 40 trains daily, with a single BNSF trackage-rights train operating northbound most days. On the west side of the bridge, Scott City has both overpasses and grade crossings with open views. A great place to watch trains is the parking lot on the southwest corner of Main and Oak Streets, near where the Cotton Belt caboose is on display. On the Illinois side, you can watch trains from the Route 3 overpass.

Birmingham

Zach Pumphery

The joint Norfolk Southern Kansas City District/BNSF Brookfield Subdivision and the joint Union Pacific Trenton Sub/Canadian Pacific Kansas City Sub cross at grade in Birmingham. It also sees the junction of the NS's Claycomo Branch and Watco's Kearney Branch.

ACTIVITY: UP operates mostly southbound traffic on this line, featuring more than 10 trains a day (reroutes will increase this number). The traffic is mostly merchandise and grain, along with some auto and intermodal. NS operates more than 12 trains a day, which include jobs shuttling from North Kansas City and to its Voltz intermodal facilities, just east of crossing, and 2 jobs running to the Ford plant in Claycomo. Look for foreign power on jobs shuttling to Voltz. Most NS trains are intermodal, auto, or merchandise. BNSF operates more than 6 trains a day, mainly merchandise and coal loads to and empties from the Thomas Hill power plant. The BNSF Kearney Turn interchanges cars with Watco in the small yard and works industries just west of crossing. CP operates more than 6 merchandise and grain trains. Look for IC&E/DM&E power on these trains.

TRAIN-WATCHING SPOTS: Good train-watching and photo-taking locations include the crossing at grade at Milwaukee Street, the 40th Street crossing, and the North Arlington crossing. There are numerous photo locations between North Kansas City to Birmingham including cold storage caves just west of Birmingham.

SAFETY: There is limited access at the grade crossing and near the NS Voltz intermodal facility, which is regularly patrolled by special agents.

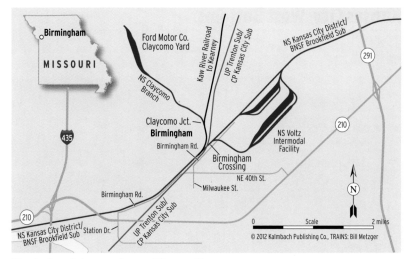

Birmingham is just northeast of Kansas City.

RAILROAD FREQUENCIES: NS: 160.380 (road); CPR: 160.770 (road); UP trains use CPR channel, and BNSF trains use NS channel. All trains on NS call all signals on the radio.

TO DO: Check out Kansas City Union Station (30 West Pershing Road) for train watching and family events. Dining and lodging options, including casinos, can be found along Highway 210 between Birmingham and North Kansas City. Worlds of Fun and Ocean of Fun theme parks are just north of Highway 210 off I-435.

NEARBY: The Harry S. Truman Bridge, a vertical lift drawbridge over the Missouri River, is just southwest of Birmingham. Used by the UP and CPR, access is limited, but it can be viewed off River Front Road. The joint BNSF Marceline Sub and UP River Sub are just south and east at Courtney.

DIRECTIONS: Take Highway 210 east from North Kansas City and turn left on Arlington Avenue. Then turn right onto Birmingham Road, which will become 40th Street. Turn left on Milwaukee Street and follow it to the crossing.

Kansas City, West Bottoms

Dan Munson

Kansas City Terminal Railway trackage and UP terminal trackage travels through a narrow passage between the Missouri River and the cliffs on the northeast side of downtown Kansas City called the gooseneck, which is the approach to the BNSF Hannibal Bridge on the east end, to a large junction with diamonds and two flyovers on the west end called Santa Fe Junction. This whole area is in the river bottoms on the west side of downtown Kansas City, hence the name the West Bottoms.

ACTIVITY: UP runs more than 30 trains a day along the Missouri River to the west. This trackage connects the former MP trackage to the original UP. BNSF operates more than 20 trains a day connecting from the former BN Murray Yard on the north end to the former ATSF Yard at Argentine on the west end. BNSF trains to and from Murray Yard to the Fort Scott Subdivision travel through here as well. Kansas City Southern regularly runs interchange trains to BNSF through the bottoms on the bluff track on the far east side. NS runs several transfer/through trains to both the UP and BNSF through the bottoms. KCS and KCT transfers are also seen.

TRAIN-WATCHING SPOTS: There are numerous train-watching locations in the Kansas City area. You can walk up on Woodswether Road Bridge (at Broadway) over the tracks to view trains coming off the Hannibal Bridge and those skirting the Missouri River. Look for KCT's three main lines running below grade in the "canyons" just east of Union Station.

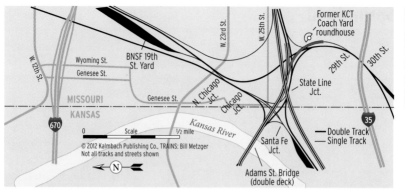

The West Bottoms are west of downtown Kansas City at the confluence of the Missouri and Kansas Rivers.

Beardsley Road on east side of bluffs is a great location for watching and photographing trains, but it has limited parking. Hickory Street in the bottoms offers a view from grade level with buildings as a backdrop. Views of Santa Fe Junction on the west end can be accessed at the grade crossing at corner of Genessee and 25th Streets.

SAFETY: Be sure to stay on public access, as it is easy to stray onto railroad or other private property.

RAILROAD FREQUENCIES: KCT: 161.010; UP: 160.980 (east of Broadway), 160.680 (west of Broadway); BNSF: 161.100 (Murray Yard to KCT trackage), 161.695 (south of Fort Scott Sub), 160.650 and 161.085 (Santa Fe Junction into Argentine)

TO DO: Kansas City's Union Station (30 West Pershing Road) is another train-watching location and offers family activities. For dining, shopping, and entertainment, the upscale Power and Light District is just south of downtown.

NEARBY: More train-watching action can be found northeast of the city in Birmingham and southwest of Birmingham is the Truman vertical lift drawbridge.

DIRECTIONS: Take I-670 west to the Wyoming/Genessee Streets Exit 1B. Head north to 12th Street for the gooseneck or go south to access Santa Fe Junction.

Springfield

Charlie Dischinger

Springfield was the headquarters of the former Frisco Railroad, and it sits at the crossroad of two main lines. One line runs from St. Louis to the southwest via Springfield and Tulsa, and the other heads south to the Dallas area. The other main line runs from Kansas City via Springfield to Memphis. It remains a busy place on the BNSF, where it is not uncommon to see more than 40 trains a day.

ACTIVITY: You'll see coal trains coming from the Powder River Basin along with merchandise trains and intermodal trains. Patterns have changed numerous times through the years on how coal trains are handled through Springfield, but the current routine for loaded coal trains is to run them in a 2x3 configuration of distributed power to make it up the hills on the Thayer Sub south of town. Also, it is not uncommon for empty coal trains to run west out of town.

TRAIN-WATCHING SPOTS: One favorite location is the Jefferson Avenue footbridge that crosses over 13 tracks. The bridge itself is photogenic, and from it, you can peer down the throat of the east end of the Springfield Yard as trains head east or south as they pass under the grain elevator. With the advent of remote control locomotives working the main Kansas Avenue Yard, and the subsequent security fencing to protect them, photographing yard activity is rather difficult. A little bit can be seen at the west end of the yard along Division Street, but visibility is limited. For afternoon photography, you can try one of the street crossings near Nichols Junction west of town where the lines split.

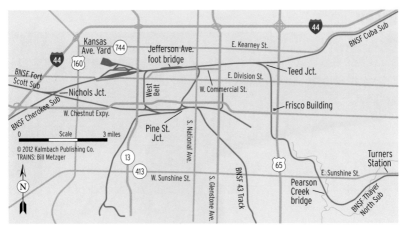

Springfield is in the southwest corner of the state off I-44.

On the east side of Springfield, there are numerous public access spots from where you can watch trains going south. Other places include the crossings at Chestnut Street, Catalpa Street, and Pearson Creek. While not as nice as it used to be, still one of the best spots near town is around Turners Station on Highway D.

TO DO: Springfield is home to the state's number-one tourist attraction, the original Bass Pro Shop. Just southwest of Springfield is Wilson Creek Battlefield National Park, where the second major Civil War battle took place.

NEARBY: Going southeast from Springfield, you'll find Thayer North and South Subs, a 300-mile, single-track railroad hosting more than 30 trains a day along numerous scenic locations, especially around Mammoth Spring, Ark.

DIRECTIONS: Located near Lafayette Park, the Jefferson Avenue footbridge connects Commercial Street with Chase Street.

Essex

Tom Danneman

BNSF's Hi Line Subdivision main line rolls through Essex and is located roughly on the southern border of Glacier National Park. Essex is the helper base for the line running over Marias Pass to the east.

ACTIVITY: An average of 35–40 BNSF trains can be seen anytime throughout the day. These trains can be intermodal, grain, coal, and manifest trains. Amtrak's daily *Empire Builder* passes through Essex, which is an Amtrak flag stop. Locomotives used as helpers are stationed here to assist eastbound trains to the summit of Marias Pass. Work trains during the summer and plow trains during the winter can be seen coming and going from the small yard in Essex.

TRAIN-WATCHING SPOTS: The pedestrian bridge, situated just a short walk from the Izaak Walton Inn, offers nice views of the BNSF main line in both directions. Other spectacular views can be had right from US Highway 2, both east and west of Essex. The area east between the summit of Marias Pass and East Glacier is quite easy to photograph right from the highway in many places.

SAFETY: During the summer months, grizzly bears can be seen in the area. Take the necessary precautions. On Highway 2, be sure to find locations where you can pull off the road completely. This can be tricky during the winter months.

RAILROAD FREQUENCIES: BNSF: 161.250 (Hi Line Sub)

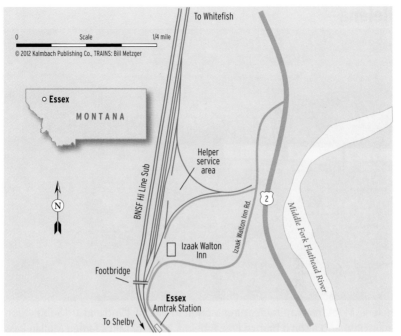

Essex is located just off US Highway 2 in the northwest part of Montana.

TO DO: The BNSF line passes within sight of the famous Izaak Walton Inn, which was built in 1939 to service railroad personnel. If sitting on the Izaak Walton's porch during the summer or by the fire in the Inn's front room during the winter, all while having a great view of the BNSF action sounds good to you, this place is for you. If you feel more adventurous, Glacier National Park is practically next door.

NEARBY: The east and west entrances to Glacier National Park are only a 30-minute drive from Essex. Endless outdoor activities such as hiking, fishing, horseback riding, rafting, and sightseeing, to name a few, abound in and around the park. Whitefish, located 53 miles west of Essex, boasts a quaint downtown area that offers shopping, dining, and other activities. Big Mountain, a world-class ski area, is located just outside of Whitefish.

DIRECTIONS: From Helena or Great Falls, take I-15 north to Shelby and US Highway 2 West. From Whitefish, take US Highway 93 south to Highway 40 East and continue to US Highway 2 East.

Helena

Tom Danneman

Helena, Montana's capital, features Montana Rail Link's 2nd and 3rd Subdivision main lines and a short branch line. A helper base for MRL's famed Mullan Pass is also located here.

ACTIVITY: Around 15 trains a day ply Montana Rail Link's main line through town. Mullan Pass to the west is a helper district, so light engine movements add to the train count. The run-through trains from the BNSF are mostly coal, manifest, and grain, but an occasional intermodal train is seen. Montana Rail Link also runs a short branch to Montana City to serve a cement plant. This branch is serviced on an as-needed basis.

TRAIN-WATCHING SPOTS: Montana Rail Link operations can be viewed from grade crossings in town. The park near the Roberts Street crossing just west of the former Northern Pacific depot is a good place to hang out. A former Northern Pacific steam locomotive is on display in the park. About 15 miles west of the city in Helana National Forest is the grade up spectacular Mullan Pass. Between Helena and Elliston, spectacular locations to view the railroad are endless. Birdseye Road follows the main for a short distance west of Helena before crossing the tracks. Continue west until you reach Austin Road. This dirt road leads to Austin, where you can view several levels of track climbing toward Mullan Tunnel. The dirt road continues over Mullan Pass and eventually meets up with US Highway 12 just west of Elliston. On the way, you'll go under the spectacular Austin Creek trestle.

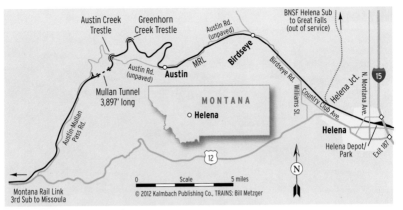

Helena is east of Missoula in the foothills of the Rockies off I-15.

SAFETY: Austin Road is usually closed due to snow pack beyond Austin Creek trestle during the winter months until late spring so be aware that this route could be impassable at times. Make sure you are on public property on Mullan Pass, as much of the land surrounding the railroad is private property.

RAILROAD FREQUENCIES: 160.335 (east of Helena), 160.950 (west of Helena)

TO DO: Downtown Helena features the Pedestrian Walking Mall, an outdoor area with historic sites, shops, and restaurants. Outdoor activities are endless during any season around the area. Four area lakes (Hauser, Helena, Holter, and Canyon Ferry) offer opportunities for swimming, boating, fishing, and camping.

NEARBY: Garrison, located 50 miles west of Helena, is where the BNSF from Butte connects with the MRL main line. Montana Rail Link interchanges with the BNSF here on a regular basis.

DIRECTIONS: I-15 runs north-south on the east side of Helena. Take the US Highway 12 Exit for access to the MRL in the Helena area. Highway 12 continues west toward Garrison and I-90 but does not follow the railroad over Mullan Pass.

Missoula

Tom Danneman

Montana Rail Link's 4th Subdivision main line rolls through Missoula just north of downtown. Missoula Yard is the terminus and origination point for the railroad's Laurel-Missoula and Missoula-Laurel manifest freights. The railroad's prized Gas Local originates in Missoula and runs a turn to Pipeline, just east of Thompson Falls. Missoula is also the home base for locals to Polson on MRL's 10th and 11th Subdivisions, as well as to Hamilton on MRL's 9th Subdivision (Darby Branch). All of BNSF's run-through trains operated by MRL pass through Missoula. Missoula is also a crew change point for the railroad.

ACTIVITY: BNSF trains can be seen anytime throughout the day. Montana Rail Link's Gas Local usually makes two turns to Pipeline every day. The train usually departs Missoula around 6 a.m. and again around 6 p.m. Both the local to Polson and to Hamilton on the Darby Branch are run as extras out of Missoula on Saturday (Darby) and Sunday (Polson). These trains are called on an as-needed basis and usually depart in the morning.

TRAIN-WATCHING SPOTS: Views of the yard are found along Railroad Street on the south and west portions of the yard. A pedestrian overpass is located just west of the former Northern Pacific depot and the Orange Street underpass. Montana Rail Link's locomotive servicing facility can be viewed from North Second Street and other nearby city streets. Numerous scenic locations are located both east and west of Missoula.

RAILROAD FREQUENCIES: MRL: 160.950 (4th Sub), 160.395 (Missoula Yard)

TO DO: Missoula is a college town with a dynamic arts and music scene. Shopping and restaurants are located downtown and throughout the Missoula area. Outdoor activities are never-ending in the Missoula area. The nation's largest training base for smoke jumpers is located adjacent to Missoula International Airport. A visitor center is located on West Broadway Street and features guided tours of the parachute loft and training facilities during summer. Fort Missoula, located southwest of downtown Missoula, is a former military post established by the U.S. Army in 1877. It features a free grounds tour, museum, exhibits, a World War II internment site, and educational tours. Skiing, hiking, biking, golf, and fishing are all nearby.

NEARBY: A trip up the 10th Subdivision to see the awe-inspiring Marent trestle, which soars to 200 feet tall, is a must. For the best photos, be there in the afternoon for good light. To get there, take I-90 west to the Wye Exit and continue north on Highway 93.

DIRECTIONS: Exit I-90 at Reserve Street and head south to access the west end of Missoula Yard. For access to the east end of the yard and the diesel service area, take the Van Buren Exit off 1-90.

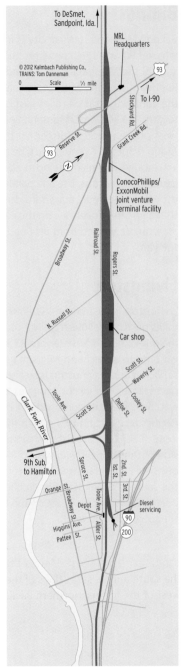

Missoula is located off I-90 in western Montana along the Clark Fork and Bitterroot Rivers.

Billings

Billings, Montana's largest city, is in the south-central part of the Treasure State where I-90 and I-94 converge. Huntley, located east of Billings is the official start of the Montana Rail Link and is where BNSF's Big Horn Subdivision from Sheridan joins the MRL. Most coal trains from the Big Horn Subdivision take the connector track 4 miles east of Huntley at Moran Junction and head east toward the Midwest. Montana Rail Link maintains a small yard in Billings just west of the restored former Northern Pacific depot (2310 Montana Avenue). Along Montana Avenue, you'll be able to watch the action. Montana Rail Link's 1st Subdivision main line hosts about 15 BNSF run-through trains and Billings-Laurel transfer runs. The line parallels I-90 15 miles to Laurel, where MRL's largest yard is located. Laurel Yard can easily be viewed along Main Street and at the Main Street overpass on the east end of the yard. The MRL diesel-servicing area can be viewed from BN Road off Railroad Street on the southeast side of the yard.

Livingston

Livingston is located on I-90 in the south-central part of the state, about 50 miles north of Yellowstone National Park. Montana Rail Link's 2nd Subdivision main line, which hosts about 15 trains a day, runs through town. Livingston is home to a yard and MRL's major locomotive shop, which includes a large servicing area. Livingston is also the base of the grade up Bozeman Hill, which necessitates helper locomotives to be stationed here. On Park Street, after watching the trains go by, check out the beautifully restored former Northern Pacific depot. It houses a nice museum and includes many railroad-related items. The Livingston shops can be viewed from Gallatin Street on the north side of the shops. Travel west of Livingston, and from several grade crossings off the I-90 frontage road, you can watch the trains tackle Bozeman Hill. Take the Jackson Creek Road interchange about 12 miles west of Livingston and head a short distance east on the frontage road to view Bozeman Tunnel near the top of the grade.

Hastings

Hastings is in central Nebraska, 23 miles south of I-80 Exit 312. The city is at the intersection of BNSF's former Burlington Route Hastings Subdivision main line from Lincoln to McCook and Union Pacific's Marysville Subdivision from Kansas City to Gibbon. The UP is the busier line, with a near constant parade of about 50–60 empty and loaded coal trains a day. At nearby Grand Island, the railroads once crossed at grade, but as traffic increased, a grade separation was built. UP constructed a 5.4-mile double-track bypass around Hastings that included elevating its line over BNSF. Good photo spots on the bypass include overpasses at North Showboat Boulevard, North Elm Avenue, and North Minnesota Avenue. The restored Burlington depot (501 West First Street) makes a great spot for watching trains on BNSF and is also a stop for Amtrak's *California Zephyr*, although it is scheduled to pass at night in both directions. Freight traffic on BNSF is relatively light, with approximately 10–20 trains a day. Two BNSF branch lines serve Hastings from Aurora and Superior.

Belmont

Tom Danneman

Belmont is located in the scenic Pine Ridge area of northwest Nebraska. Nearby Crawford Hill is part of BNSF's Butte Subdivision and includes a manned helper district that is based in Crawford. The Butte Subdivision is a busy artery for Powder River Basin coal traffic to the Midwest and South. The Canadian Pacific (formerly DM&E) line from Rapid City, S.D., connects with the BNSF in Crawford.

ACTIVITY: Up to 40 trains a day (sometimes more, depending on coal traffic) negotiate Crawford Hill, including several horseshoe curves, every day. Most of the trains are loaded coal trains from the Powder River Basin headed to the Midwest and South or empties returning. Some manifest traffic can also be seen on occasion. Keep an eye out for the Kansas City-Pasco, Wash., freights. Many times they will have Boeing 737 fuselages and other airplane parts behind the locomotives. The Canadian Pacific to Crawford is operated on an as-needed basis.

TRAIN-WATCHING SPOTS: The overpass in Belmont is the easiest location from which to view the action. Another spot that is easily accessible is the lower horseshoe area right off Sawlog Road. You can also find public spots to watch from in Crawford.

SAFETY: Bring plenty of food and beverages as conveniences are few and far between Crawford and Alliance. Rainy or snowy weather can make roads slippery and sometimes impassable.

RAILROAD FREQUENCIES: BNSF: 161.415

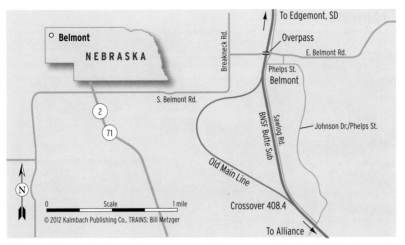

To Edgemont, SD

Overpass

E. Belmont Rd.

Breakneck Rd.

Phelps St.
Belmont

S. Belmont Rd.

BNSF Butte Sub

Sawlog Rd.

Johnson Dr./Phelps St.

2

71

Old Main Line

N

0   Scale   1 mile

© 2012 Kalmbach Publishing Co., TRAINS: Bill Metzger

Crossover 408.4

To Alliance

Belmont is located in the northwest corner of the state and Crawford is 10 miles north.

TO DO: Belmont is a tiny town with no conveniences, while Crawford is small with only a handful of stores and shops, so watching trains will be your main activity. However, the Pine Ridge area is known for its great hiking, biking, and horseback riding. If you stay in one of the cabins at the Ponderosa Ranch, you'll get unlimited access to the property, which surrounds the upper horseshoe curves. You just have to wrangle some cattle on this working ranch. You can also view the Belmont Tunnel, now abandoned, which was the only railroad tunnel built in the state.

NEARBY: Alliance, slightly more than 40 miles south of Belmont, boasts a major BNSF yard and maintenance facility. BNSF and UP's Powder River Basin Line is about 115 miles west. Check out Fort Robinson State Park just west of Crawford. Fort Robinson is a former U.S. Army fort, where Crazy Horse surrendered in 1877. You can also explore area ghost towns.

DIRECTIONS: Belmont is on a dirt road off Highway 2. From Alliance, take Highway 2 north about 42 miles to Belmont (Highway 2 joins Highway 71 west of Hemingford). From Scottsbluff, take Highway 71 north about 60 miles to Belmont. Continue north on Highway 71 to reach Crawford.

Fremont

Dan Munson

Fremont sees the crossing at grade of the Union Pacific's Columbus Subdivision and the BNSF (former BN and CB&Q) Sioux City Subdivision. The Main Street depot was the former connection between the UP and CNW. The BNSF depot still stands about a block south of the UP depot. This is still a crew change point for about half the UP trains that pass through. UP trackage is Centralized Traffic Control (CTC) through Fremont while BNSF is track warrant control.

ACTIVITY: UP operates more than 50 trains a day through Fremont from two different directions. The former CNW between Missouri Valley, Iowa, and Fremont via Blair is single-track CTC, over which the UP runs directionally westbound. The original UP runs southwest out of Fremont to Omaha and Council Bluffs, and the UP operates directionally eastbound over this route. There are a few scheduled exceptions to directional running. Maintenance work windows and service interruptions drive changes, so watch for trains on either route in either direction. Look for all types for trains on the UP. BNSF operates up to 16 trains a day through Fremont that are mostly grain, merchandise, and coal. Both roads operate road-switchers that are based in Fremont.

TRAIN-WATCHING SPOTS: There are numerous public crossings from which to watch and photograph trains. UP westbounds and BNSF northbounds (both are geographically west at depots) can be shot from Main Street passing their respective depots. Opposite-direction trains can be shot from the same location with grain elevators as a backdrop. The crossing at grade of the UP and BNSF can be photographed from M Street in the morning and Pierce Street in the afternoon. You can access the diamonds from the north end of North Morrell Street.

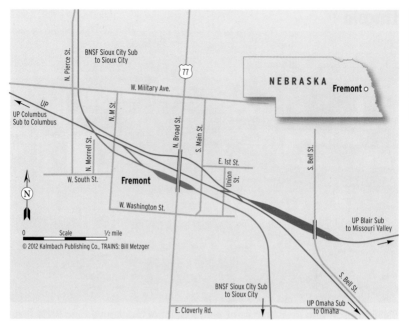

Fremont is about 35 miles northwest of Omaha along the Platte River.

RAILROAD FREQUENCIES: UP: 160.740; BNSF: 161.235; Fremont & Elkhorn Valley: 160.245; BNSF trains will call the UP dispatcher for signals over the UP and will hold out of town until cleared.

TO DO: The Fremont & Elkhorn Valley Railroad operates excursion trains from Fremont just north of the UP/BNSF crossing. There are plenty of dining and lodging options on old US 30 on the north side of Fremont. Filled with family activities, the annual John C. Fremont Days take place in July.

NEARBY: US 30 parallels the UP main west out of Fremont and provides great train watching all the way to North Platte. The BNSF Sioux City Sub can be closely followed on US 77 to Sioux City through rolling hills. Omaha and Council Bluffs attractions are only 45 minutes to the east.

DIRECTIONS: Take US 30 into Fremont and turn south on US 77. After you cross the tracks on a bridge, take a left on Washington Street and then another left on Main Street. You'll see the BNSF depot on your right first and then the UP depot.

Lincoln

Dan Munson

BNSF Hobson Yard in Lincoln is the center point of four converging BNSF main lines: Creston Sub from the east (Creston-Galesburg), St. Joseph Sub from the south (St. Joseph-Kansas City), Hastings Sub from the southwest (Hastings-Denver), and Ravenna Sub from the west (Alliance-Powder River Basin).

ACTIVITY: Lincoln sees more than 60 trains a day from these four routes, predominantly coal loads and empties, as well as grain, merchandise, and locals. Hobson has a medium-size diesel shop, and locomotives are swapped out, as required, on through trains. It also has a small hump yard that originates 10 or more merchandise trains and locals. UP operates a local out of Valley that makes a daily turn to Hobson Yard.

TRAIN-WATCHING SPOTS: There is public access to mains on the east end of the yard at the First Street crossing near the old Carling Tower. Carling is still the control operator for this section of railroad but is now located in the yard office. At Carling, Creston and St. Joseph Subs converge to head west into Hobson Yard. There is no public access to west end of the yard. Good photo locations are located west of Hobson on Ravenna Sub at Emerald and at Denton on Hastings Sub.

RAILROAD FREQUENCIES: BNSF: 161.415 (Creston Sub), 161.100 (Lincoln Yard), 160.920 (Hastings Sub), 160.695 (Ravenna Sub), 161.250 (St. Joseph Sub)

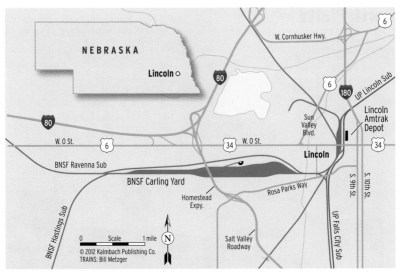

Lincoln is 55 miles southwest of Omaha off I-80 in eastern Nebraska.

TO DO: Plenty of food and drink is available on O Street on the north side of Hobson Yard. Avoid visiting Lincoln on Nebraska Cornhuskers football days as traffic will be backed up in all directions. Omaha and Council Bluffs attractions are 45 minutes to the east on I-80.

NEARBY: There are good photo locations on all four lines just outside of Lincoln. US 6 parallels the Creston Sub out to Ashland, which is the junction of the Sioux City and Omaha Subs into Creston. Head south on the St. Joseph Sub to watch trains climb up Firth Hill. BNSF's Havelock wheel shop is located on the northeast side of Lincoln in the Havelock neighborhood. This is the last railroad-owned wheel shop in the United States. The Omaha, Lincoln & Beatrice railroad has a small switching operation on the east side of town, off the Creston Sub.

DIRECTIONS: Follow US 6 into Lincoln. From the west, the highway follows the Ravenna Sub into Hobson, where it becomes O Street. Turn right on First Street to the east end of the yard. From the east, the highway follows the Creston Sub into Lincoln, passing near the Havelock shops, and becomes O Street on the west side of town.

North Platte

Andy Cummings

Bailey, the world's largest freight yard, located astride North America's busiest freight main line, stretches from downtown North Platte westward for 8 miles. Union Pacific's main lines, reaching eastward from Los Angeles, the San Francisco Bay Area, and the Pacific Northwest, enter western Nebraska as one main line. At O'Fallons, 14 miles west of North Platte, UP's busy route from the Powder River Basin coalfields of Wyoming adds its traffic to the now-triple-track main line. The triple-track extends through North Platte and 110 miles to the east, where main lines for Omaha and Kansas City diverge. At Bailey Yard, UP workers inspect and service all trains. Switch crews use Bailey's twin hump yards to break down inbound manifest trains, mating cars of common destinations in the bowl tracks. Trim crews then rebuild the cuts of cars into outbound trains. At the diesel shop, mechanics service and repair locomotives.

ACTIVITY: North Platte hosts 120–140 UP trains daily including coal, intermodal, manifest, and bulk trains.

TRAIN-WATCHING SPOTS: The Golden Spike Tower rises eight stories tall and offers a commanding view of Bailey's operations. The tower sits roughly 5 miles west of downtown North Platte, immediately adjacent to the yard's diesel shop and east hump. You can watch the show from the big windows of the climate-controlled eighth floor or take pictures from the open-air, seventh-floor observation deck. (There is a fee to access the tower.) Four highway overpasses cross the triple-track main line near downtown North Platte, the yard's east throat. The downtown grain elevator is favorite backdrop for railfans, as the city's name is spelled out across the silos.

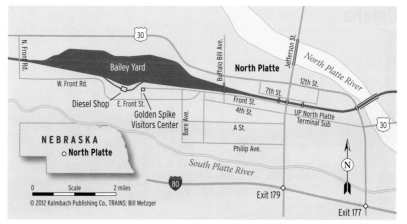

North Platte is in central Nebraska off I-80 fairly close to the Colorado border.

RAILROAD FREQUENCIES: UP: 160.680, 160.935, 160.230, 160.650, 160.545, 161.070, 160.500

TO DO: North Platte sits just off of I-80, so it's an easy stop on your way to the mountain states. The town's Rail Fest in September gives visitors a chance to take a bus tour of Bailey.

NEARBY: If you're not in a hurry, take US 30 from Omaha to North Platte instead of I-80, as it hugs the busy UP main line the whole way. From Gibbon west, the train frequency is so high that as soon as one train passes, the headlight of the next is usually visible. A favorite photo spot on the line is Buttermilk Curve near Brady, 25 miles east of the North Platte terminal.

DIRECTIONS: To reach the Golden Spike Tower, exit I-80 at Highway 83 and go north into town. Turn left onto Philip Avenue. After 3 miles, turn right at Lakeview Boulevard and then left onto A Street. Turn right onto Homestead Road.

Omaha

Dan Munson

The original Union Pacific main line comes into Omaha off the Missouri River Bridge from Council Bluffs, Iowa. The Omaha Sub runs from Missouri Valley, Iowa, through Omaha to Fremont. BNSF has a connection onto the UP here just before the bridge and exercises trackage rights over the bridge to Council Bluffs. UP and BNSF tracks run parallel from the Missouri River Bridge to south Omaha, about 4 miles. The Canadian National has rights over the bridge as well to access their customers in Omaha by both BNSF and UP trackage rights.

ACTIVITY: UP operates approximately 25 trains a day, predominately eastbound trains over this route, and runs westbounds from Missouri Valley to Fremont. BNSF operates 4–6 trains a day, mostly locals and manifests. Watch for small fleets of empty coal trains, detoured off the Creston Sub to the south due to traffic or maintenance-of-way. CN operates a daylight local job that operates over the Missouri River Bridge to BNSF trackage three days a week. Amtrak's *California Zephyr* operates over the BNSF, arriving at night.

TRAIN-WATCHING SPOTS: Great views can be had from the 10th Street Bridge between the former Union Station and former Burlington station. Free parking is available on the bridge. You can fit a camera lens between or under fencing. The view is great from either side of the bridge. Another spot is the Amtrak depot (1003 South Ninth Street) just east of 10th Street on Pacific Street.

RAILROAD FREQUENCIES: UP: 160.740 (road), 160.680 (yard); BNSF: 161.415 (road), 161.100 (yard); CN and Amtrak use BNSF and UP channels.

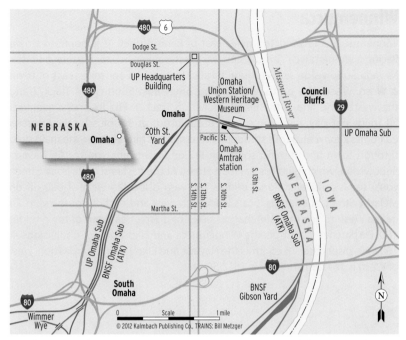

Omaha is located in eastern Nebraska on the Missouri River and the Iowa border.

TO DO: Visit the Durham Museum (801 South 10th Street), the former Union Station, for great railroad displays, historical exhibits, and a restored soda fountain. The Old Market entertainment district is just 2 blocks north of Durham Museum and features plenty of dining and entertainment options.

NEARBY: Just across the river in Council Bluffs, the Union Pacific Railroad Museum (200 Pearl Street) is a must-see, with many exhibits regarding the UP and the American West.

DIRECTIONS: In Omaha, take Exit 454, 13th Street north, off I-80 to Pacific Street. Turn right, go 2 blocks to 10th Street, and turn left. You will see both Union Station and the Burlington station on your right.

NEVADA

Winnemucca

Winnemucca is located 165 miles east of Reno on I-80. It is home to Union Pacific's Winnemucca Subdivision (ex-Western Pacific) to Portola and the Nevada Subdivision (ex-Southern Pacific) to Sparks. Four miles east of town is Weso, where the eastbound line becomes Elko Subdivision Track 2 and the westbound line is the Elko Subdivision Track 1. Freight traffic averages 20 trains per day, with some days topping out at 30, plus locals. Amtrak's *California Zephyr* also rolls through Winnemucca. Third Street is the main drag through town and turning south on Bridge Street gets you to the Nevada Subdivision, which parallels Railroad Street. At the east end of Railroad Street, you'll see a cantilever signal bridge. The yard is located west of I-80 off on Melarky Street. Numerous locals work both west and east out of the yard. To get to Weso to see the interchange, take Third Street east out of town under I-80. Dispatcher 9 controls the Winnemucca and Elko Track 2 Subdivisions at 160.470. Dispatcher 76 controls the Nevada and Elko Track 1 Subdivision, west of Weso is 161.280 and east is 161.550.

Bridgeport

Located near the Delaware River, Bridgeport is home to the 3,000-acre Pureland Industrial Complex, where you can watch and photograph working Baldwins at SMS Rail Lines' operations. Easily accessible from I-295 at Exit 10 or from US 130, Pureland has public grade crossings from which SMS trains can be safely viewed and photographed. SMS has 11 miles of track inside the facility, and you can witness the action on weekdays. The railroad starts most days around dawn, first handling the interchange with Conrail Shared Assets Operations, often with SMS's operating six-motor AS616. If traffic is light, the railroad finishes switching its customers by midday. SMS also serves ethanol and biodiesel business at a transload facility in the park. A short distance from Pureland in Paulsboro is the giant PBF Energy Paulsboro petroleum refinery. Conrail handles all outbound and inbound interchange there, while SMS performs in-plant switching with 24-hour coverage. SMS assigns Baldwins and an EMD to the refinery. However, the SMS job can be seen from public property only for short periods when it switches an in-plant yard, pulling out toward the Conrail tracks, usually midmorning.

Bound Brook

Tom Nanos

Three rail lines run parallel past the Bound Brook train station. NJ Transit operates the former Central Railroad of New Jersey main line as the Raritan Valley Line, which hosts commuter trains from High Bridge and Raritan to Newark and Hoboken. The former Lehigh Valley route is now Conrail's Lehigh Line, the main artery for CSX freights from Philadelphia and Norfolk Southern freights from Harrisburg and Allentown, Pa. The third route is Conrail's Port Reading Secondary, a former Reading branch that begins at Bound Brook and runs east to tidewater at Port Reading.

ACTIVITY: NJ Transit schedules more than 50 trains through Bound Brook on weekdays and 30 on weekends. Most trips start or end at Newark Penn Station, where connections can be made to other NJT, Amtrak, and PATH trains. Freight volume averages around 40 trains a day; action is heaviest from evening through morning, and Monday and Tuesday are much lighter. NS traffic is mainly intermodals, with some unit ethanol, auto rack, garbage, and manifest trains. CSX traffic is split between intermodal, manifest, and unit trash trains. Look for the orange juice train from Florida three times a week. Canadian Pacific runs a triweekly freight between Allentown and Newark.

TRAIN-WATCHING SPOTS: The Bound Brook Station (350 East Main Street) is the area's most popular train-watching spot. The station was built in 1913 by the Jersey Central. At Manville, 3 miles west of Bound Brook, the freight routes to Philadelphia and Allentown split, and track ownership changes from Conrail to the Class I railroads. The junction and a local freight yard can be seen from a shopping center parking lot off Main Street in Manville.

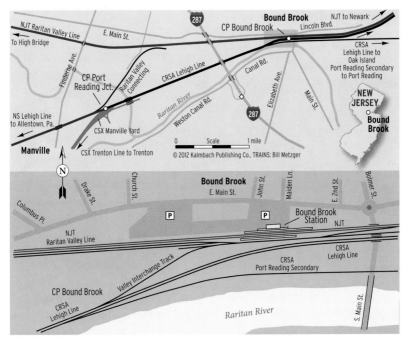

Bound Brook is about 25 miles southwest of downtown Newark.

SAFETY: NJ Transit permits photography from its station platforms. The railroads and local police enforce safety and do not tolerate trespassing on railroad property.

RAILROAD FREQUENCIES: NJT: 161.235 (road); CR: 160.860 (Lehigh Line and Manville Yard), 160.935 (Port Reading Secondary); CSX: 160.980 (Trenton Sub), 160.740 (dispatcher); NS: 161.070 (Lehigh Line)

TO DO: Route 28 (Union Avenue), a half-mile from the station, is the commercial spine of the area.

NEARBY: At Flemington, a tourist destination 20 miles west of Bound Brook, the Black River & Western Railroad runs excursions on a former Pennsylvania Railroad branch to Ringoes. (Other trips depart from Ringoes.) The giant Northlandz model railroad is also located in Flemington.

DIRECTIONS: Take Exit 13 (Route 28) off I-287. Go east about 1.5 miles on Route 28 (Union Avenue). Turn right on Hamilton Avenue and go south a half-mile to the train station. Parking is available at the station.

Three Bridges

Thom Horvath

Located at MP 48 on NS's Lehigh Line is the hamlet of Three Bridges. This is a village with a name that dates back to the 1800s, when it was necessary to cross three bridges spanning the Raritan River's south branch in order to reach this settlement. Its rich railroading heritage can be traced back to the days of the Central Railroad of New Jersey (CNJ) and Lehigh Valley (LV). The CNJ's right-of-way remains in use today mainly by the Black River & Western to interchange freight on a regular basis with NS. Another sign of this location's railroading heritage can be seen at the Three Bridges grade crossing. Off to the right of the grade crossing is the Lehigh Valley station, which is now a private residence.

ACTIVITY: NS runs an estimated 20–30 trains on a regular basis, which are generally intermodal, auto racks, ethanol, or trash. NS 18G and 19G are general merchandise freights and NS H76 is a local freight that interchanges cars along this stretch of the line three times a week. CP's 38Z and 39Z operate between Bethlehem, Pa., and Oak Island thrice weekly. This train arrives in Oak Island in the morning and heads west to Bethlehem the same day.

TRAIN-WATCHING SPOTS: A gravel parking area adjacent to Three Bridge's Main Street grade crossing is a good spot to watch for trains. Regarding photography, the best illumination for eastbound trains is generally late morning. As the day progresses, westbounds receive sufficient sunlight. Winter snows should not be a deterrent in coming here. The plowed snow that piles up provides an elevated mound from which you can photograph trains.

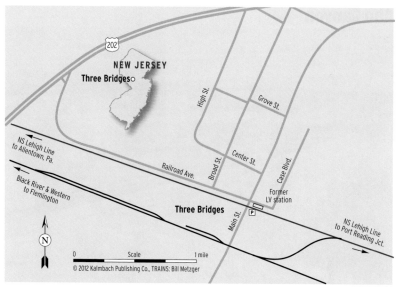

Three Bridges is in the northwest part of the state about 5 miles east of Flemington.

SAFETY: Parking is near the tree line and away from the tracks.

RAILROAD FREQUENCIES: NS: 161.070 (road); Black River & Western: 161.085

TO DO: The Flemington area has numerous hotels, restaurants, and outlet stores to visit while railfanning at Three Bridges.

NEARBY: In Flemington, the Black River & Western offers weekend train excursions to Ringoes. Northlandz is also nearby and bills itself as the World's Largest Model Railroad.

DIRECTIONS: From Route 202, turn onto Railroad Avenue. Then turn right on Main Street and follow it to the grade crossing. The gravel parking area is on the left as you drive over the grade crossing.

Abo Canyon

Ken Fitzgerald

Abo Canyon is between Belen and Mountainair on the BNSF Clovis Subdivision. Here, the BNSF climbs out of the Rio Grande Valley, winding its way around high bluffs, through deep cuts, and over long bridges. Recently, a double track was completed through the canyon to deal with the steady 1.25 percent uphill grade beginning at the west end of the canyon and extending 20 miles east to Mountainair. Five miles of new track were laid and nine bridges built.

ACTIVITY: This is the BNSF Transcon and hosts 60–80 trains every 24 hours. Traffic peaks over the weekend while Tuesday is traditionally the low point. Traffic consists of mainly intermodal and merchandise trains—some as long as 10,000 feet and using distributed power units—with a few loaded and empty coal trains, but there is no passenger service.

TRAIN-WATCHING SPOTS: The BNSF is oriented east to west with eastbound trains having the good light in the morning and westbound trains favored in the afternoon. The Highway 47 grade crossing 4 miles west of Abo Canyon is the closest access point on the west side. Here, at the crossover at Beevers, the land is flat and open. Highway 60 crosses the tracks via an overpass at the east end of the canyon where the terrain is more rugged and scenic. You can park at the south end of the overpass and walk outside the guardrail up to the bridge abutments and safely watch trains. Be careful as the bridge itself is narrow and traffic moves at a rapid pace. Highway 60 follows the tracks on the west side up the grade to Mountainair, and photo locations are numerous from the side of the road. In Mountainair, the Highway 55 overpass at the south end of town provides a great view in the afternoon of westbound trains passing a classic depot.

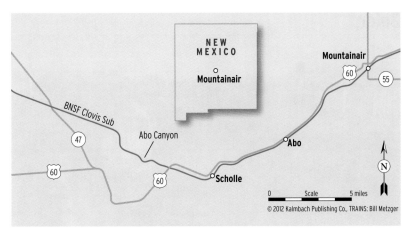

Abo Canyon is located between Belen and Mountainair, roughly 40 miles southeast of Albuquerque.

SAFETY: Do not try to enter Abo Canyon itself from either end. There are no services in the 50 miles between Belen and Mountainair so make sure your vehicle is in good condition and that you have adequate fuel, food, and water.

RAILROAD FREQUENCIES: BNSF: 160.860 (Belen terminal), 160.590 (Belen to Beevers), 161.190 (Beevers to Vaughn)

TO DO: Lodging and dining choices in Mountainair and to the east are minimal. More numerous selections are available in Belen and just north in Los Lunas. Albuquerque is only 25 miles north of Belen and offers a multitude of dining and lodging options as well as entertainment and activities. Salinas Pueblo Missions National Monument and national forests are nearby.

NEARBY: Belen is 25 miles west of Abo Canyon and is a crew change and refueling point for all trains.

DIRECTIONS: Drive southeast out of Belen on Highway 47 for approximately 20 miles to the junction with Highway 60. Take Highway 60 east to Mountainair.

Belen

William P. Diven

The Santa Fe Railway created this town of 7,000 a century ago when it built a low-grade cutoff across New Mexico to get freight traffic off Raton and Glorieta passes to the north. Today, it is more important than ever on BNSF Railway's Chicago-Los Angeles Transcon. All freights recrew in Belen, and most are refueled and inspected, a process that takes 30–60 minutes. At the east edge of town, BNSF's line to El Paso goes south. Just west of the yard office, at Belen Junction, the state-owned tracks to Albuquerque head north. They host New Mexico Rail Runner Express trains to Albuquerque and Santa Fe.

ACTIVITY: BNSF sends about 70 east-west trains a day through Belen—more later in the week, fewer on Mondays and Tuesdays. Two or 3 trains a day in each direction use the El Paso line, and yard crews make several round trips to Albuquerque. There are 7 Rail Runner arrivals and departures weekdays and 4 on weekends, most of which continue to Santa Fe. Amtrak's *Southwest Chief* joins the Transcon at Dalies, 10 miles west of Belen, and gets to and from Albuquerque on a cutoff that melds onto the Belen-Albuquerque tracks at Isleta.

TRAIN-WATCHING SPOTS: You'll see trains enter and leave the west end of the terminal from the Rail Runner station. From the Harvey House Museum parking lot (104 North First Street), you can see the BNSF westbound fueling racks, west-end yard throat, and eastbound arrivals. Northwest of town, where the Transcon crosses Mesa Road, is good on afternoons for catching westbounds leaving Belen. On the east end of the yard, in south Belen, you can watch trains make the big curve out of town at the Highway 109 (Jarales Road) crossing.

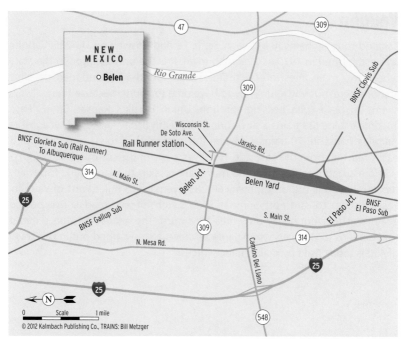

Belen is located on the Rio Grande River in central New Mexico, west of Cibola National Forest and east of Laguna Indian Reservation.

SAFETY: BNSF police frown on trespassing at Dalies because of thefts from trains out of Belen Farther west, reservation police may not look kindly upon photography.

RAILROAD FREQUENCIES: BNSF: 160.860 (Belen terminal), 160.770 and 161.325 (yard operations, east leads), 160.725 and 161.325 (yard operations, west leads), 160.590 (road); New Mexico Rail Runner: 160.410

TO DO: The Harvey House Museum is being restored. You can ride a Rail Runner to Santa Fe, the state capital, and back: a one-way trip takes about 2.5 hours.

NEARBY: Abo Canyon is 25 miles east of Belen. It is accessible from the US 60 overpass at Scholle.

DIRECTIONS: Belen is 31 miles south of the Albuquerque airport via I-25. Locations on the Transcon west of Belen are accessible from Highway 6 and I-40. East of Abo Canyon, follow the Transcon from US 60.

Vaughn

Located roughly halfway between Santa Fe and Roswell on US 285, Vaughn was established in 1919 as a railroad town. It is the only location in the state where two main lines intersect. One visitor found 17 abandoned gasoline stations here, but you're unlikely to have time to count, because there always seems to be a train passing through. Union Pacific's Kansas City-El Paso Tucumcari Line (20 trains a day) tunnels beneath BNSF Railway's Chicago-Los Angeles Transcon (70 trains a day) on the west edge of town, and this spot is easily reached from the east side. However, parts of the surrounding countryside are so photogenic that you may want to skip this landmark. Especially recommended is the US Highway 60/285 overpass 15 miles west of Vaughn. East of town toward Fort Sumner, BNSF's right-of-way road is not posted against visitors, but heavy-duty tires are a must. The handsome stucco depot that harkens to the days when Santa Fe crews also swapped out in this town of 450 is today used by maintenance forces.

Binghamton

Binghamton is located 75 miles south of Syracuse off I-81. The city is at the junction of Norfolk Southern, Canadian Pacific, and New York, Susquehanna & Western routes once part of the former DL&W, Erie, and D&H. There are 10–14 trains daily including several locals. The Chenango Street overpass next to the former DL&W passenger station provides a view of the former DL&W and Erie main lines side by side now used by CP and NS, plus a connection with the former D&H now used by the NYS&W. The NYS&W has a small engine facility east of Chenango Street. Another favorite location is the old Agway Mill off Griswold Street. CP's East Binghamton Yard, located along Route 7, provides viewing opportunities at each end. Other sites to see are these spectacular bridges: Starucca Viaduct at Lanesboro, Pa. (25 miles southeast), and Tunkhannock Viaduct, at Nicholson, Pa. (41 miles south). Parking is available at all sites.

Bear Mountain Bridge

Scott Hartley

Located along the Hudson River 45 miles north of midtown Manhattan, this area offers year-round scenery with a railroad on each bank. CSX's River Subdivision along the west shore is a freight-only route acquired in the 1999 breakup of Conrail. The line is largely single-tracked. Signaled sidings at Fort Montgomery and Haverstraw allow for meets in the area. On the east side of the Hudson, New York's Metropolitan Transportation Authority owns and operates the line as the MTA Metro-North Railroad.

ACTIVITY: The Metro-North Hudson line hosts frequent commuter runs between Poughkeepsie and Manhattan's Grand Central Terminal as well as Amtrak Empire Service trains and the *Lake Shore Limited*, *Adirondack*, and *Maple Leaf*. Freight activity is sparse, with an occasional daytime CSX local, and 2 nighttime road freights in each direction. On the line, you'll see 54 commuter trains, 25 Amtrak trains, and 4 CSX road freights. On the CSX River Sub, you'll see 35 freights daily.

TRAIN-WATCHING SPOTS: The parking lot in the Iona Island Conservation Area Preserve at CSX Milepost 41 is a spot for train watchers that offers good photo opportunities. Other popular locations on CSX include overlooks in Bear Mountain State Park and a pedestrian bridge in Fort Montgomery State Historic Site just to the north. The magnificent Bear Mountain Bridge carries US 6 and US 202 as well as the Maine-to-George Appalachian Trail over the river. Walkways on both sides of the bridge offer stunning views of trains on both shores. Trackside passenger-train photography can be done at the MN stations in Manitou and Peekskill. Both lines curve to permit photographing trains in either direction throughout most of the day. CSX crews call each signal, allowing setup time for pictures.

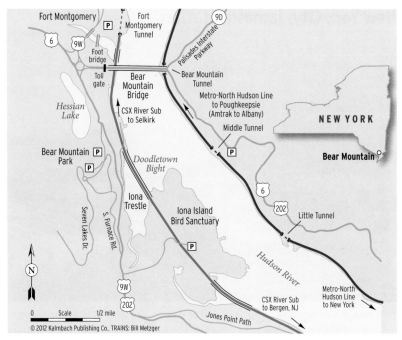

Bear Mountain Bridge crosses the Hudson River in the extreme southeastern portion of the state.

SAFETY: Passenger trains operate at high speeds on MN. The noise of river and air traffic often covers the sound of approaching freights.

RAILROAD FREQUENCIES: CSX: 160.980 (road), 160.620 (dispatcher); Metro-North: 160.950

TO DO: Bear Mountain State Park is a major weekend destination for New Yorkers. Visitors may sightsee, hike, and swim. In fall, foliage viewers can crowd the two-lane roads through the area.

NEARBY: Four miles north of the Bear Mountain Bridge is the United States Military Academy at West Point. CSX trains pass through a tunnel under much of the academy. On MN, old New York Central passenger stations in Peekskill and Cold Spring are now restaurants.

DIRECTIONS: From New York State Thruway (I-87) Exit 16 take US 6 east to the Bear Mountain traffic circle. Iona and Bear Mountain are located off US 9W to the south of the circle; Fort Montgomery and West Point are to the north. Roadside parking for visitors wishing to walk over the bridge is available along Route 9D on the east side.

New York City, Jamaica Station

Joseph M. Calisi

The nearly century-old Long Island Rail Road's Jamaica Station in Queens recently underwent major renovations. The LIRR's hub station also houses the railroad's headquarters. The modernized station features five elevated platforms that serve eight tracks. South of the LIRR platforms, a Port Authority transportation venue, AirTrain JFK, has been added to the mix, carrying 33,000 airport travelers annually.

ACTIVITY: Among all the changes, one constant remains the same—more than 700 LIRR trains daily come and go at a dizzying pace. The new 21st century technology in the rail command center controls 208 switch machines and 144 signals used to route trains through Jamaica. Expect to see a parade of emus (Electric Multiple Units M-3 and M-7) and DE-30AC diesels and DM-30AC dual-mode engines hauling Kawasaki C-3 bilevel coaches. Action is so frequent that merely studying the departure board is sufficient knowledge about train movements, and a scanner isn't really required because the trains are on time. In addition to the commuter action, New York & Atlantic local drill freight makes its late-morning pass-through en route to points east on Long Island using the southern-most tracks away from the platforms.

TRAIN-WATCHING SPOTS: In this post-9/11 world, it is advisable to position your-self only on the ends of the public platforms and take your photos without lingering for too long a time. The station is bordered by now-vintage Jay and Hall Towers, which make for interesting photo props (Jay in the morning, Hall in the afternoon). Note that the photo angles are not all full-sun images but are sometimes on the shady side of the train.

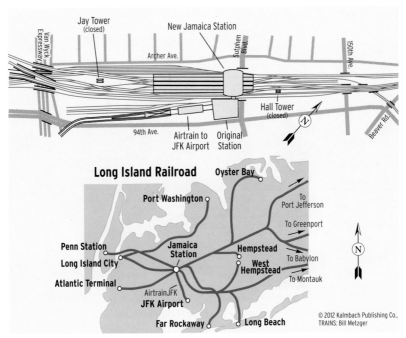

Jamaica Station is located at Sutphin Boulevard and Archer Avenue, 2 blocks south of Jamaica Avenue.

SAFETY: Even though photography is permitted from public areas, be aware that you will be visited by local law enforcement for a cursory background check to make sure you have no outstanding warrants. It is strongly suggested that you notify the LIRR Public Affairs Office (phone: 718-217-5477) of a railfan photo visit to help ease any confrontations involving police or LIRR employees.

TO DO: Situated in the downtown business district of Jamaica, the station is in a major shopping and transportation center that spreads out to Hillside Avenue.

NEARBY: The New York Transit Museum, located at Boerum Place at Schermerhorn Street in Brooklyn, is accessible by MTA.

DIRECTIONS: The station is easily accessible by rail (LIRR, subway, and AirTrain JFK) and MTA-run bus lines. While parking exists, it is difficult to use because it is within a major shopping center area. Penn Station in Manhattan is a 20-minute train ride from Jamaica Station.

Old Fort

Jim Wrinn

Norfolk Southern Railway assaults the Blue Ridge here via a series of loops that allow the railroad to climb out of the North Carolina Piedmont and into the Appalachian Mountains. The railroad spirals for 13 miles, hugging ridges and darting in and out of coves to keep the grade to 2.2 percent, while the direct air route between Old Fort and the top of the mountain at Ridgecrest is only 3 miles. Southern Railway predecessor Western North Carolina Railway built this line in the 1870s, and today it is a secondary route for NS. Eleven bridges and seven tunnels line the route with Jarretts Tunnel, at 123 feet, the shortest, and Swannanoa Tunnel at the crest, at 1,832 feet, the longest. If you're looking for a model railroad come to life, this is the place to visit.

ACTIVITY: Traffic varies, but can be upwards of 12–16 trains per day. Two manifest freights each day travel between Spencer Yard near Lexington and Asheville, but additionally, there are local freights, unit coal trains bound for Duke Energy's Catawba and Belmont power plants, unit wood chip trains bound for Blue Ridge Paper's Mill at Canton, and ballast trains as needed coming off the Murphy Branch at Enka.

TRAIN-WATCHING SPOTS: One of the most unique train-watching locations in the country is the park at Andrews Geyser, a manmade fountain in the heart of the loops where the main line encircles the valley. Additional viewing is available from Mill Creek Road.

SAFETY: Watch for snakes that sun themselves on the ballast. Boots with long jeans are important. During the summer, ticks can be easily picked up while in the dense foliage.

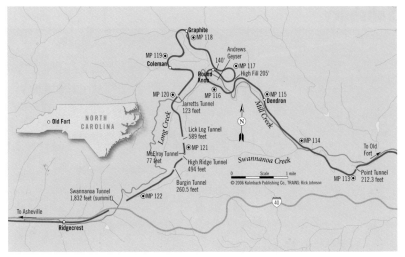

Old Fort is in western North Carolina, about 30 miles east of Asheville and 110 miles west of Salisbury.

RAILROAD FREQUENCIES: NS: 160.950 (road), 160.245 and 160.830 (dispatchers)

TO DO: Old Fort has a few bed and breakfasts. Full service hotels are located nearby in Black Mountain, Marion, Asheville, and Hickory. Mount Mitchell, the highest point in the eastern United States is easily reached off the Blue Ridge Parkway. Asheville is home to the Biltmore House, the largest private residence in the nation, which was built by a descendant of Cornelius Vanderbilt of New York Central fame; building the house was such a huge task that it required a construction railroad!

NEARBY: CSX's own loops on the former Clinchfield run between Marion and Spruce Pine, and it's easy to work both lines over two to three days.

DIRECTIONS: Take I-40 to US 70 into downtown Old Fort. Just west of the depot, take Mill Creek Road. You can follow the old stagecoach road to Ridgecrest, where additional views of the main line are available.

Salisbury

Clint Renegar

Salisbury is well known in the South for constant rail activity. The former Southern Railway Washington, D.C.-Atlanta main line is now a key Norfolk Southern mainline route. The Asheville District, also known as the S Line, stretches west from the Salisbury wye to Asheville. Spencer Yard in Linwood is 6 miles to the north and serves as the termination and origination point for all the manifest freights through Salisbury and as a crew change point for intermodal traffic. Built by Southern Railway in 1979, the yard at Linwood replaced the old Spencer Yard that dated to 1896, which is used for coal and grain train staging, as well as 2 weekday local industry jobs called the Salisbury and Yadkin switchers. The southern tip of the old Spencer Yard can be viewed from the 11th Street grade crossing.

ACTIVITY: About 25–30 trains roll through downtown Salisbury on the NS main line every 24 hours. The majority of Charlotte District mainline trains are manifests, intermodals, and unit coal trains. Salisbury also hosts 8 daily Amtrak trains, the *Crescent*, *Carolinian*, and 2 *Piedmont* trains. The Asheville District sees 4–6 trains per day and also hosts daily locals and runs grain trains as needed.

TRAIN-WATCHING SPOTS: The Salisbury wye off North Lee Street is the most popular train-watching spot in Salisbury. Just south of the wye is the Salisbury depot (215 Depot Street), a restored Frank Milburn-designed Spanish Mission-style jewel from 1908. A gravel parking lot for a local antique shop, the Salisbury Emporium off East Kerr Street, is a great spot to catch southbounds. Another great location nearby is Fulton Street, west of the wye on the S Line. It has a large public parking lot and is a great place to catch trains coming off or awaiting permission onto the Charlotte District.

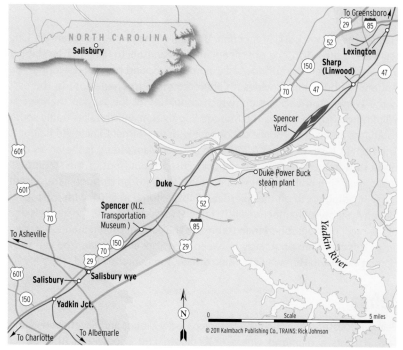

Salisbury is located in the central Piedmont of the Tar Heel state about 45 miles northeast of Charlotte.

SAFETY: Be careful not to trespass on railroad property as you are surrounded by busy mainline tracks on all sides.

FREQUENCIES: NS: 160.950 (road), 160.245 (dispatcher to train), 160.830 (train to dispatcher); North Carolina Transportation Museum: 160.695

TO DO: In historic downtown Salisbury, you'll find shops, ice cream parlors, cafes, and art galleries. Be sure to try some pork barbecue and Cheerwine soft drink.

NEARBY: The North Carolina Transportation Museum is in Spencer, adjacent to Salisbury, and features 14 structures, including a 37-stall roundhouse and 600-foot-long backshop that were part of the steam repair center. It also offers a 25-minute train ride and rolling stock displays.

DIRECTIONS: From Charlotte, take I-85 north and exit at East Innes Street (Exit 76). Turn left on Innes and go into town to Depot Street. Turn right and the depot is on the right. To get to the wye, Lee Street is 1 block west of Depot Street.

Hamlet

Hamlet sits at a critical CSX junction, the hub of the former Seaboard Air Line Railway. To the north, the Aberdeen Subdivision runs to Raleigh. The Hamlet Subdivision extends south toward Columbia, S.C., and beyond to Florida. The Andrews Subdivision provides an alternate route to Charleston. To the east is the Wilmington Subdivision, which continues all the way to the port at Wilmington. To the west is the Monroe Subdivision, which takes traffic south to Atlanta and west to Bostic to connect with the former Clinchfield Railroad. The Hamlet Historic Depot & Museum (2 West Main Street) is the area's best place to watch trains. Six sets of tracks crisscross in front of the station. All trains, including unit coal trains that bypass the yard, go through here, except those heading north on the Aberdeen Sub. Restored in 2004, with its striking Queen Anne style architecture and a famed Witch's Hat dome, the depot is one of the most photographed train stations in the eastern United States. Amtrak's *Silver Star* calls here on its way between New York and Florida. You can view Hamlet Yard from Highway 177 (King Street) and Campbell Road.

Selma

Selma is located about halfway between Rocky Mount and Fayetteville along I-95. It hosts a diamond where CSX's South End Subdivision (the former Atlantic Coast Line main) crosses Norfolk Southern's East Carolina Business Unit at grade. The diamond is on the east side of town, about a quarter-mile from the I-95 exit. Viewing around the diamond is good. Photographing NS eastbounds is great early morning to early afternoon. The bulk of the action is found on the A Line (former Atlantic Coast main) in the form of intermodal, manifest freight, grain, coal, and hopper trains. Weekdays, a local operates from Fayetteville to Selma and back. The NS line sees 1 regularly scheduled through freight every day and a local that runs between Selma and Raleigh; of course, extras can run any time. In addition to the freight action, no fewer than 10 Amtrak trains per day pass through Selma (with 4 calling for passengers): the *Palmettos, Silver Meteors,* and Auto Trains use the A Line straight through town, while the *Silver Stars* and *Carolinians* use a CSX/NS routing via a connecting track along the station itself.

Dickinson

Dickinson is located in western North Dakota along I-94. The former Northern Pacific main line, which is now BNSF's Dickinson Subdivision, cuts through town. This main line usually hosts between 20–25 trains in a 24-hour period. Most are loaded coal trains coming from the Powder River Basin in Wyoming or returning empty from the Midwest. The former Northern Pacific depot still stands at the intersection of Sims and Villard Streets. Other views of the BNSF can be seen along Broadway Street and other grade crossings in town. If you go 35 miles west on I-94, you'll find Medora, a small town located in the Badlands. Medora is home to the Theodore Roosevelt National Park and the Cowboy Hall of Fame. Many beautiful photo locations exist in this area. Check out the view from the Medora Cemetery up on a hill on the west side of town off Chateau Road.

Fargo

Andy Cummings

Fargo is a busy terminal for BNSF along its former Northern Pacific and Great Northern transcontinental main lines. From Fargo, lines radiate east to the Twin Cities and Superior, north to Grand Forks, west to Minot and Bismarck, and south to Breckenridge and Willmar, Minn. BNSF operations are based at the ex-Northern Pacific yard in Dilworth, 3 miles east of Moorhead. Mainline freights and coal trains are fueled and inspected at this point, and crews are changed for all trains.

ACTIVITY: You'll see approximately 40 trains per day plus switching and transfer moves in the terminal. Fargo sees mainline and general freights, intermodals, coal trains, and Amtrak's *Empire Builder*. The busiest line is the former NP Staples Subdivision to the Twin Cities. West of Fargo, the double-track, ex-Northern Pacific line is part of BNSF's main transcontinental route for 28 miles to Casselton, where trains swing onto the ex-Great Northern Surrey Cutoff to Minot. West of Casselton, the ex-NP is mainly a coal train route. Short line Otter Tail Valley operates a weekday freight or coal train from its base at Fergus Falls, Minn.

TRAIN-WATCHING SPOTS: At the east end of Dilworth Yard, the grade crossing at the station of Watts is a safe place to watch trains arriving and departing the yard. In Moorhead, the crossing at 14th Street South offers another place to watch the action. Just east of 14th Street is Moorhead Junction, where the former Great Northern line from Breckenridge and Otter Rail Valley from Fergus Falls cross the ex-Northern Pacific at grade.

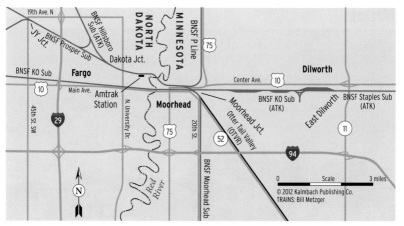

Fargo is in east-central North Dakota on the Minnesota border.

In Fargo, you can park in the lot at the former Northern Pacific passenger station to watch trains. The depot was built in 1898 and is owned by the Fargo Park District; it also houses a senior center. Other city streets in Fargo, Moorhead, and Dilworth offer easy access to the tracks.

RAILROAD FREQUENCIES: BNSF: 160.920, 161.100, 161.160, 161.280, 161.385, 161.415; Otter Tail Valley: 160.425

TO DO: In addition to shops and restaurants in downtown Fargo, for those interested in airplanes, the Fargo Air Museum (1609 19th Avenue North) houses an array of World War II vintage aircraft including a P-51 Mustang, a Douglas DC-3, and an F4U Corsair.

NEARBY: An NP 0-6-0 locomotive, caboose, and depot are on display along US 10 in Dilworth, and an NP 4-4-0 is displayed at Bonanzaville USA in West Fargo. Sixty miles west of Fargo in Valley City, the ex-Northern Pacific main line passes over the Sheyenne River and CP's main line to Portal on a huge, photogenic steel viaduct.

DIRECTIONS: From the east, take I-94 to Exit 6 and drive north on County Highway 11 to the BNSF overpass. This is Watts, where you can begin your exploration. Just north of the tracks is Highway 10 that follows the tracks through Dilworth, Moorhead, and Fargo.

Minot

Steven Welch

BNSF's northern Transcon, its Chicago-Seattle intermodal and freight route, crosses Canadian Pacific's western Canada-Chicago link at grade in downtown Minot at Soo Tower. BNSF's Gavin Yard sits east of the city, although it's mostly inaccessible. At the yard's east end is Surrey, where Devils Lake Subdivision heads east toward Grand Forks, while the KO Subdivision turns southeastward toward Fargo. The Devils Lake Sub handles only Amtrak's *Empire Builder* and local traffic. BNSF crews change at Minot, while CP crews from Harvey run through the city on their way to the Canadian border division point at Portal.

ACTIVITY: BNSF operates around 25 trains daily through Minot. These include intermodal hotshots between the Pacific Northwest and the Midwest, manifest trains, and unit grain trains. Amtrak's *Empire Builder* operates over BNSF. CP operates around 15 daily trains including a host of regular manifest trains plus unit coal, potash, and grain trains from Canada, and a daily intermodal/ automotive train each way.

TRAIN-WATCHING SPOTS: Soo Tower sits behind the Minot Public Library's parking lot at Sixth Street and First Avenue West. A pedestrian bridge jumps BNSF's line between Main Street and First Street East, offering elevated views of the action. The Third Street East Bridge has a public sidewalk from which to watch the action. Don't miss the classic 1912 Soo Line depot, now a transportation museum, where Main Street crosses the CP main line.

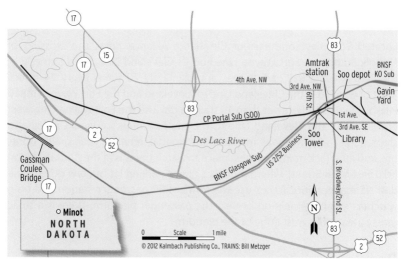

Minot is in the northern part of the state, about 110 miles north of Bismarck.

Six miles west of the city, the majestic Gassman Coulee Bridge rises 117 feet above the valley and stretches on for nearly 1,800 feet. To reach the trestle, take US 52 west from the city to County Highway 17 and turn left. Roughly a quarter-mile up the road, you'll drive underneath the bridge. US 52 follows CP's main line northwest from the city up the Souris River Valley, a scenic stretch of track.

RAILROAD FREQUENCIES: BNSF: 160.920, 161.160, 161.100, 161.250, 160.410, 160.500; CP: 161.370, 161.520

TO DO: Downtown Minot abuts the tracks, and there are plenty of places to eat. Big Time Bistro sits astride the BNSF tracks and sells a wide variety of sandwiches. Minot attractions include the Roosevelt Park Zoo and the Dakota Territory Air Museum.

NEARBY: The Railroad Museum of Minot (19 First Street SE) resides a few blocks south of downtown. The Ward County Historical Society on the North Dakota State Fairground property tells the story of pioneer life.

DIRECTIONS: US 83 runs north-south through downtown and jumps both main lines on an overpass. Business Route 2, the Burdick Expressway, cuts east-west through downtown. Both roads provide easy access to the rail sites.

Alliance

Located 70 miles southeast of Cleveland, Alliance hosts the crossing of Norfolk Southern's Fort Wayne Line and its Cleveland Line, both formerly of the Pennsylvania Railroad. It sees approximately 70 trains every 24 hours, most of which use the Cleveland Line to Cleveland and the Fort Wayne Line to Pittsburgh. Typically, fewer than 10 trains a day use the Fort Wayne Line west of Alliance or the Cleveland Line to the south. Amtrak's *Capitol Limited* also stops here. Traffic includes manifest, intermodal, ethanol, coal, grain, stone, ore, and auto rack trains. The best place to watch trains is at the Amtrak station (820 East Main Street), where there is a gravel parking lot but few other facilities. NS maintenance forces use the former PRR passenger station and train watchers should remain on or near the passenger platform. There is a small grassy area at the west edge of the platform.

Deshler

Deshler, the Crossroads of the Baltimore & Ohio, is located in western Ohio, 15 miles west of I-75 on Route 18. The Willard and Garrett Subdivisions, which meet here, make up the primary CSX freight route between Chicago and the East Coast, hosting approximately 70–80 trains every 24 hours. The CSX Toledo Subdivision sees about 20 trains a day, many of which use one of the three connecting tracks with the Willard and Garrett Subs. Traffic is a mix of manifest, intermodal, auto rack, grain, coal, and ore trains. Crossroads Park, located on West Mulberry Street in the southwest quadrant of the diamond, has a shelter, portable restroom, fire pit, picnic tables, and RV parking. There are no fences, and trains operate on all sides of the park. Train watchers should cross the tracks only at grade crossings and be on the lookout for fast-moving trains.

Fostoria

This Ohio city 40 miles south of Toledo sees more than 100 trains a day and features numerous places for watching them. Two CSX main lines and a Norfolk Southern line cross at Fostoria on three sets of diamonds. A CSX tower operator controls all movements through town. The majority of trains are CSX freights, and unit coal trains abound on the Columbus Sub from Kentucky and West Virginia. Norfolk Southern freight trains include auto rack and RoadRailer trains, along with a handful of unit coal and grain trains. The parking lot of the CSX maintenance-of-way office (the former Amtrak station) just outside the diamonds is a prime viewing area. Locations along Poplar Street and Columbus Avenue, which crosses all three main lines, provide other viewing spots. Fostoria holds an annual railroad festival in September. Groundbreaking took place in 2011 on a railfan park that will be located inside the triangle of diamonds.

Greenwich

Greenwich is located on US Route 224 in north-central Ohio, 60 miles southwest of Cleveland. This junction of former New York Central (Cleveland-St. Louis) and Baltimore & Ohio (Chicago-Pittsburgh) routes sees 75–80 trains every 24 hours. Most trains travel between the two routes on a double-track connection built just before the 1999 Conrail breakup. The bulk of CSX freight traffic between the Midwest and East Coast passes through Greenwich. The Wheeling & Lake Erie has trackage rights on CSX through town to access its route to Cary, Ohio, and to reach CSX's Willard Yard. Traffic is a mixture of manifest, intermodal, auto rack, stone, coal, ethanol, and grain trains. Train watchers may park on a grassy area near the diamond and between the sets of tracks on the east side of North Kniffen Street. Do not park on the railroad property on the west side of Kniffen.

Toledo

Toledo is arguably the busiest rail center east of Chicago, and Vickers Crossing in suburban Northwood is the metropolitan area's hottest spot. Norfolk Southern's ex-Conrail, historically New York Central double-track main between Cleveland and Chicago crosses CSX's double-track Toledo Terminal Subdivision, once part of a belt line circling the city and now CSX's primary route into Michigan as well as the gateway to coal and ore docks on Lake Erie. Daily train counts often exceed 120, with both lines offering steady diets of unit and manifest traffic, and the NS route is also heavy with intermodal trains. Amtrak's *Lake Shore Limited* and *Capitol Limited* ply the NS rails, mostly at night, while CN interchange runs and NS transfers spice up the CSX side. Foreign power visits both railroads frequently. Wales and Drouillard Roads provide easy access to the area, but overpasses scheduled to be built will eliminate the three grade crossings closest to the Vickers diamonds. Two major CSX yards, Stanley and Walbridge, are close by to the south. Traveler services abound at interchanges along nearby I-280 and I-75. NS trains talk on 161.070 and 160.980, while CSX uses 160.230 and 160.635 in the immediate area.

Berea

Craig Sanders

Norfolk Southern and CSX main lines run parallel in this Cleveland suburb. These former Conrail (New York Central) routes are the primary freight arteries of each railroad between the Midwest and Northeast.

ACTIVITY: There are 100–110 trains every 24 hours, split evenly between NS and CSX. Traffic includes intermodal, manifest, coal, auto rack, ethanol, and grain trains. Amtrak's *Lake Shore Limited* and *Capitol Limited* use NS during the overnight hours. The Wheeling & Lake Erie has trackage rights on CSX between Berea and Wellington and on NS between Berea and Cleveland. W&LE operations are conducted as needed.

TRAIN-WATCHING SPOTS: Train-watching activity occurs south of the tracks along Depot Street between Front Street and Rocky River Drive. Most railfans congregate at the west end of a parking lot for the former Big Four station, which still stands. A grassy strip west of this parking lot provides ample room to watch and photograph trains. Although some property owners allow or tolerate train watching, others may ask you to leave their property. The side-walks of the Front Street Bridge over both railroads provide another vantage point. There are high fences over the tracks, but angular unobstructed views are available for photography.

SAFETY: The Depot Street viewing areas are next to CSX, and some trains operate at high speed. Railfans should not cross the CSX tracks or stand on railroad property between the CSX and NS tracks.

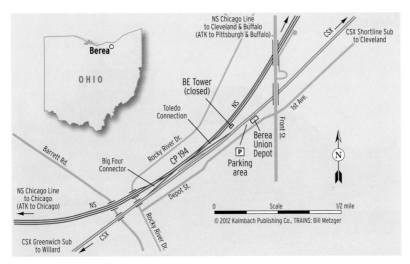

Berea is just southwest of Cleveland near the Cleveland Hopkins International Airport.

RAILROAD FREQUENCIES: NS: 161.070 (road, dispatcher east of Berea), 160.980 (west of Berea); CSX: 160.860 (road), 160.800 (dispatcher)

TO DO: You can find motels at the Bagley Road interchange with I-71 (Exit 235) and restaurants along Bagley Road and Front Street. Berea is 12 miles southwest of downtown Cleveland, where you can visit the Rock and Roll Hall of Fame and Museum, Great Lakes Science Center, *William G. Mather* (a 1925 Great Lakes freighter), and Tower City Center (a shopping center within the former Cleveland Union Terminal). You can also take in the Cleveland Indians, Cleveland Browns, or Cleveland Cavaliers professional sports teams.

NEARBY: Railroad attractions include the Northern Ohio Railway Museum in Chippewa Lake and the Conneaut Railroad Museum. Such Ohio hot spots as Alliance, Bellevue, Fostoria, Greenwich, Marion, and Willard are a few hours away. The Mad River & NKP Railroad Museum is in Bellevue.

DIRECTIONS: Exit I-71 at Bagley Road and take it west to Front Street. Turn right (north), go to Depot Street, and turn left (west). The Big Four station is at Front and Depot Streets. From downtown Cleveland on I-71, or from I-480 in either direction, get off at the exit for Cleveland Hopkins International Airport and take the Berea Freeway (Route 237) past the airport. Turn left (south) onto Front Street.

Marion

Craig Sanders

Three mainline routes converge at Marion's Union Station, built in 1902, which hosted passenger trains of the New York Central (Cleveland-St. Louis), Erie (Chicago-New York), and Chesapeake & Ohio (Toledo-Columbus). The Pennsylvania Railroad (Sandusky-Columbus) also crossed here but had its own station. Norfolk Southern operates the former PRR tracks, whereas CSX owns all other surviving tracks. The NS Sandusky District crosses the CSX Indianapolis Line (former NYC and Erie) on the east side of the station while the CSX Columbus Subdivision (former C&O) crosses on the west side. The eight diamonds can be seen from Marion Union Station Association property.

ACTIVITY: Over a 24-hour period, 75–85 trains pass through Marion. Both railroads have small yards here. NS has the busiest line with a mixture of manifest, coal, grain, and intermodal trains. The Indianapolis Line features a similar traffic mix and is the busier of the CSX routes. The CSX Columbus Sub primarily hosts coal and manifest freights. The Columbus Sub and NS Sandusky District come through Marion on a north-south orientation but are considered east-west routes by their respective railroads.

TRAIN-WATCHING SPOTS: Paved parking is available at the station (532 West Center Street). Although the station is open for limited hours, access to the station grounds is available 24/7.

SAFETY: Fences separate the station from the double-track main lines on three sides, but train watchers should stay off the tracks where the fences end.

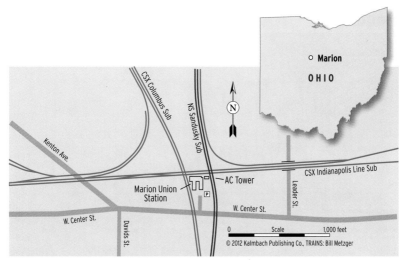

Marion is 50 miles north of Columbus in central Ohio.

RAILROAD FREQUENCIES: NS: 161.190 (road, dispatcher); CSX: 160.860 (Indianapolis Line), 160.485 (dispatcher), 160.230 (Columbus Sub), 160.320 (dispatcher)

TO DO: The Marion Union Station museum is open on Tuesdays and Thursdays, by appointment, or by chance if a volunteer is present. The restored AC Tower, which looks much as it did when it controlled the junction, is open by appointment and on some weekends. The Marion Model Railroad Club is open on Sunday afternoons at the station. Downtown Marion is just east of the station. The Warren G. Harding home and museum (3890 Mount Vernon Avenue) is a restored historical site. The Marion Popcorn Festival takes place the weekend after Labor Day. On hot summer days, you can enjoy the Lincoln Park Family Aquatic Center.

NEARBY: Marion is an hour's drive to hot spots in Bellevue and Fostoria. The Mad River & NKP Railroad Museum is in Bellevue. The Ohio Railway Museum is in the Columbus suburb of Worthington.

DIRECTIONS: From US 23, exit west onto Route 309 (Harding Highway East), which becomes Center Street. Turn right into the station between the sets of tracks.

Wagoner

Mike Condren

In Wagoner, two busy Union Pacific lines that represent the railroad's major links to the Gulf of Mexico cross. One line is the former Missouri-Kansas-Texas route from Kansas City and St. Louis to Houston and Galveston. The other is the ex-Missouri Pacific connection from St. Louis and Kansas City to New Orleans. Both are critical links to the "Chemical Coast" area in Texas and Louisiana on the Gulf of Mexico, which provides fertilizer, plastics, and other petroleum-based traffic. The lines are also important to UP's agricultural business, with grain moving to the Gulf and commodities including soybeans and rice moving north. Between Kansas City and Wagoner, the UP operates the lines as double track, with traffic flowing south on the former MKT route and north on the MP. The town is named after Henry "Bigfoot" Wagoner, a Katy dispatcher.

ACTIVITY: On the UP lines, you'll see approximately 40 trains per 24 hours that include merchandise, unit coal, chemical, agricultural products, and intermodal trains.

TRAIN-WATCHING SPOTS: There are plenty of public access points and photography opportunities as streets parallel both lines (Wagoner Avenue and Smith Avenue are two). The terrain is flat, and you can see and hear trains coming from a long distance. Also, for those with a scanner, there's a talking defect detector on the former MKT north of town that announces southbound traffic.

RAILROAD FREQUENCIES: UP: 160.410 (Coffeyville Sub A), 160.470 (Coffeyville Sub B), 161.220 (Wagoner Sub), 160.875 (Cherokee Sub)

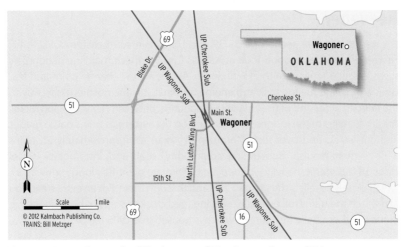

Wagoner is 15 miles north of Muskogee and 50 miles southeast of Tulsa.

TO DO: Camping, fishing, and other recreational opportunities are nearby at Fort Gibson Lake. Wagoner City Historical Museum (231 Church Street) includes a fine collection of historic fashion and artifacts from the city's history. Western Hills Guest Ranch in Sequoyah State Park has various lodging options and activities for everyone. You can float, canoe, or fish on the Illinois River 25 miles east at Tahlequah.

NEARBY: The Three Rivers Museum (220 Elgin Street) is located in the restored former Midland Valley depot in Muskogee and features a 1940s-era diesel switch engine. In Muskogee, you can tour the USS *Batfish*, a WWII submarine on dry land, and restored Fort Gibson, which was a destination point on the Trail of Tears.

DIRECTIONS: Wagoner is at the junction of US 69 and Highway 51. From Tulsa, take the Muskogee Turnpike to Highway 51 and head east into town.

Heavener

Located at the intersection of US 59 and US 271 in southeastern Oklahoma, Heavener provides a good look at Kansas City Southern mainline action. The town, about 50 miles south of Fort Smith, Ark., is a crew change point and features a mainline fueling rack and engine terminal. It is the northern gateway to the railroad's crossing of the Ouachita Mountains. Between Heavener and Mena, Ark., is 45 miles of the toughest railroading on the system as trains battle grades and curves up and over Rich Mountain in Arkansas. Approximately 25 trains a day—merchandise, agricultural commodity, coal, and intermodal—travel through this scenic, heavily wooded area. Views are plentiful along Highway 59, which closely parallels the railroad into and through town. For an extra treat, you can watch the trains roll by while enjoying fried chicken strips or homemade pie in the Southern Belle Restaurant, which is housed in a 1905 railcar.

Tulsa

BNSF's Cherokee Yard in Tulsa is the former Frisco hump yard located at the junction of the St. Louis to Texas former main line of the Frisco and the Avard Sub. This yard also services the line from Kansas City to Texas. Trimmer jobs work the north end of the yard. Transfer runs to the yard at Union Depot downtown depart from the north end. Intermodal trains to Avard Sub connect south of the West 17th Street crossing. Occasional Watco run-through trains are also seen. The best spot for watching is along the service road west of the elevated US 75/I-244 roadway. There is a large parking area just south of the West 17th Street crossing. The BNSF requests that you stay behind the imaginary line from the poles north and south of this lot. The Cincinnati Avenue overpass (closed to vehicular traffic) at Union Depot is another good spot for watching mainline action and switching at the nearby yard. Parking is available on the north side of the tracks.

Waynoka

Waynoka is 140 miles northwest of Oklahoma City on BNSF's double-track transcontinental main line. In 24 hours, you'll see approximately 80–90 trains including hot intermodal Z trains, piggyback trains, and other fast, high-value movements. You can view the trains from the restored Santa Fe Depot (1383 Cleveland Street) and adjacent former Harvey House, which houses a museum. You can follow the trains on a 40-mile trip from Waynoka to Woodward, where the Northwestern Oklahoma Railroad connects with the BNSF. Along the way, one unique vantage point is at Curtis Hill, where you can watch from the bridge over the tracks, which is north off US 412. In Woodward, you can park near the former Santa Fe depot (1000 Kansas Avenue), which is now a BNSF maintenance facility. Much of the land on either side of the tracks is private property; ask permission before crossing fence lines.

Albany

In the heart of Oregon's Willamette Valley, 80 miles south of Portland, is a cluster of railroads still worthy of Albany's historic, rail-inspired name: Hub City. The former Southern Pacific Valley main hosts 10 or more Union Pacific freight trains every day along with 3 daily Amtrak services each way: the *Coast Starlight* and two pairs of *Cascades* corridor trains with Talgo equipment. Albany is the base of regional carrier Portland & Western's southern operations and home to its diesel shop and two yards, both with switchers working two shifts. The P&W dispatches up to 6 trains per day on a variety of routes, with an equal number of trains returning to the yards. Short line Albany & Eastern also comes in from Lebanon on most days with interchange traffic. The Amtrak station (110 10th Avenue) is a great place to catch most of the action, and don't miss P&W's street running on Water Avenue and the impressive bridge over the Willamette River.

Columbia River Valley

Scott Lothes

The crown jewel of the Pacific Northwest's many spectacular railroad routes is the Columbia River Gorge, which extends east from Portland through The Dalles and Wishram, Wash. Union Pacific's Portland Subdivision follows the south bank of the Columbia River while BNSF's Fallbridge Sub hugs the north bank. Both routes include numerous causeways, and the BNSF line features 13 tunnels. BNSF has a modest yard with a local switcher at Wishram, where the Oregon Trunk Subdivision crosses the Columbia River and heads south via the rugged Deschutes River Canyon. Union Pacific maintains a small yard at The Dalles with a switcher to serve its local customers.

ACTIVITY: Both lines are busy, single-track routes with frequent meets at CTC-controlled sidings. The BNSF line is busier with 30–40 trains daily, while Union Pacific runs 20–25 trains on most days. The Portland section of Amtrak's *Empire Builder* runs daily over the BNSF. Both lines host a mix of intermodal, vehicle, merchandise, and grain traffic. From late summer through early winter, loaded westbound grain shuttle trains can be very frequent on the BNSF (empties often return by alternate routes). Additional bulk commodities include coal on the BNSF and potash and soda ash on the UP. Traffic tends to be heavier on both sides of the river in the morning, and a second peak of activity often occurs in the evening on the BNSF. The Oregon Trunk typically sees 4–5 trains per 24 hours.

The Columbia River Gorge is located just east of Portland along the Oregon-Washington border.

TRAIN-WATCHING SPOTS: Both sides of the river offer numerous vistas, but access is easier on Highway 14. The clusters of BNSF tunnels and causeways on either side of White Salmon are also popular. On the UP side, parking is permitted along I-84 if your vehicle is entirely off the paved shoulder. Memaloose State Park offers some trackside campsites and several good views.

SAFETY: Watch your step! Rattlesnakes come out in the warmer months, particularly in the eastern part of the Gorge, and poison oak abounds. Do not leave valuables in your vehicle, as theft is common, especially in popular recreation area parking lots.

RAILROAD FREQUENCIES: BNSF: 161.250 (Vancouver terminal), 161.415 (Washougal to Pasco), 161.100 (Oregon trunk); UP: 160.515 (Dispatcher 1, Portland to Crates), 160.410 (Dispatcher 251, Crates to Hinkle)

TO DO: Vibrant Hood River touts itself as the windsurfing capital of the world and offers plentiful dining and shopping. The Gorge is designated a National Scenic Area between the mouths of the Sandy and Deschutes Rivers, and both sides of the Columbia River have abundant opportunities for outdoor recreation and wine tasting at numerous vineyards. Riverboat cruises are also available.

NEARBY: In Hood River, the Mount Hood Railroad takes you on seasonal excursions and dinner trains to the base of Mount Hood.

DIRECTIONS: From Portland, for BNSF, go north on I-205 to Exit 27 and then east on Highway 14. For UP, go south on I-205 to Exit 22 and then east on I-84. Bridges cross the Columbia at Bridge of the Gods, Hood River, The Dalles, and Biggs.

Allentown

Allentown and adjacent Bethlehem are located 60 miles north of Philadelphia. Norfolk Southern operates a large hump yard and intermodal terminal on tracks once belonging to the Lehigh Valley, Central Railroad of New Jersey, Reading, Philadelphia, Bethlehem & New England, and Lehigh & New England roads. Canadian Pacific has trackage rights over NS to Allentown and New Jersey. Intermodal trains to and from New Jersey as well as Bethlehem-based RoadRailer trains bypass the yard on the south side of the Lehigh River. Expect between 30–40 trains a day, including locals and switching operations on the PB&NE (Bethlehem) and R. J. Corman (Allentown). You can see unit ethanol, garbage, and coal trains anytime. Vantage points in Allentown include South Carlisle Street (NS yard) and Canal Park. In Bethlehem, the Hill to Hill Bridge area is good for NS, CP, and PB&NE action. BNSF and UP power is not uncommon on NS intermodal and ethanol trains.

Erie

Located in extreme northwestern Pennsylvania, Erie and North East are 15 miles apart via I-90 or US Route 20. CSX's Chicago Line (ex-NYC) and Norfolk Southern's Lake Erie District (ex-NKP) operate side by side through downtown Erie and again at North East. Expect 35–40 trains on CSX and 8–10 daily on NS. Erie's Union Station (123 West 14th Street) hosts Amtrak's *Lake Shore Limited*. GE Transportation's locomotive plant is located on Erie's east side at Franklin Avenue. East of the plant between Route 955 and US 20 is the East Erie Commercial Railroad, a test track for new locomotives. The Lake Shore Railway Museum (31 Wall Street) in North East features CSS&SB Little Joe electric No. 802, former NYC GE U25B No. 2500, and ex-Ford Motor Company center cab GE No.1006 among other locomotives and rolling stock. Both CSX and NS trains pass within viewing distance of the museum.

Holmesburg Junction

Holmesburg Junction is located 13 miles northeast of downtown Philadelphia on Amtrak's Boston-Washington Northeast Corridor. This portion of the NEC, once part of the Pennsylvania Railroad, consists of four main tracks, all electrified with overhead catenary. Roughly 110 Amtrak trains (55 each way) fly by here each weekday at speeds of up to 110 mph. Holmesburg Junction is a station on Philadelphia's SEPTA commuter-rail system, and most of SEPTA's 60 daily Trenton Line trains stop here. The freight-only Bustleton Industrial Track diverges northward from the NEC right at the station. Operated by Conrail Shared Assets on its south end and East Penn Railways on its north end, it is generally worked at night. An interesting combination interlocking tower and passenger station sits between the branch and the main line. Homesburg Junction Station (4799 Rhawn Street) is less than a mile from the Cottman Avenue Exit on I-95. Trains approach quietly and quickly so stay alert on station platforms.

Reading

Located 60 miles northwest of Philadelphia, Reading was the hub of all former Reading Railroad operations, which now are part of Norfolk Southern. NS lines from Harrisburg divide to northern New Jersey and Philadelphia here. At Spring Street, there is a classification yard that hosts trains from the Reading & Northern and Penn Eastern Railroads. Weekdays offer 30–40 trains including NS and short line locals. In addition to merchandise and intermodal trains, you'll see extra ethanol, coal, garbage, stone, and steel slab trains. A good variety of photo locations exist as lines go in all directions including a belt line around the city. Penn Avenue in Wyomissing is the place you'll see the most through trains as well as the PRL local. Belt Line Junction along Route 61 (Pottsville Pike) provides a place to see Allentown-bound traffic and the R&N interchange train.

Scranton

Scranton boasts a diverse railroad presence. The Delaware-Lackawanna operates a fleet of Alcos, while CP operates the former Delaware & Hudson as part of its transcontinental system. Steam excursions from Steamtown National Historic Site and a heritage trolley line round out the action. The CP main line marks the end of Depot Street, so go no farther. At the University of Scranton, you can view departing eastbound DL road freights and steam excursions. Scranton's Nay Aug Park has a scenic overlook that provides a stunning vantage point for returning westbound DL trains. At the entrance to Steamtown, DL trains traverse the original D&H main line on a daily basis. Reading & Northern reaches Scranton, serving the Stauffer Industrial Park. The DL switches in Steamtown National Historic Site. CP's Taylor Yard is just south of Scranton. You can view the south end of the yard from Depot Street and from an overlook along Railroad Court.

Harrisburg

Dan Cupper

The capital of Pennsylvania, Harrisburg is the hub of Norfolk Southern freight lines radiating in six directions. It is also the western terminus of Amtrak's electrified 103-mile-long Philadelphia-Harrisburg Keystone Service corridor. Enola Yard, the major freight yard in the area, lies opposite the city on the west bank of the Susquehanna River. Freights run east to Philadelphia and New York via the Harrisburg Line, west to Pittsburgh via the Pittsburgh Line, southwest to Hagerstown, Md., via the Lurgan Branch, south to Baltimore via the Port Road Branch, and north via the Buffalo Line to Canada and western New York. Local freights also run south to York, east to Lancaster, and west to Carlisle.

ACTIVITY: The heaviest action consists of 50 freights a day, plus Amtrak's diesel-powered *Pennsylvanian*, on the NS Pittsburgh Line, and 25–30 freights a day on the NS Harrisburg Line. They include a mixture of intermodal, merchandise, coal, steel, grain, and ethanol loads. Intermodal freight is transloaded at Harrisburg Yard and Rutherford Yard, where double-stack, van, and RoadRailer trains swap blocks. Less frequently, Canadian Pacific (freight) and CSX (coal) trains enter the area. Amtrak operates 13 AEM7-powered, push-pull Keystone trains a day each way on weekdays. Speeds on the corridor reach 110 mph. Amtrak trains serve Harrisburg's restored 1887 Pennsylvania Railroad train station (Fourth and Chestnut Streets).

TRAIN-WATCHING SPOTS: The State Street Bridge and adjacent Harris Tower offer overhead views of the Harrisburg and Pittsburgh Lines. Riverfront Park offers views of the Reading concrete-arch bridge, and the wide berm of Front Street at Rockville Bridge, a historic 3,860-foot-long, 48-stone-arch bridge, provides a safe watching area. The 63rd Street Bridge crosses Rutherford Yard.

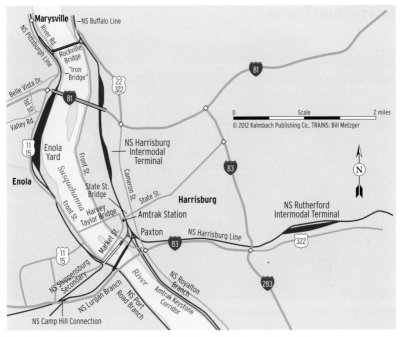

Harrisburg is 100 miles east of Philadelphia on the Susquehanna River.

In Enola, the west side of Rockville Bridge can be seen from the Marysville boat ramp. The Overview Bridge at the west throat of Enola Yard offers a safe, railfan-friendly venue for watching trains.

SAFETY: Traffic can get heavy on US 11/15, so exercise caution if you photograph Enola's hump or engine terminal from that vantage point.

RAILROAD FREQUENCIES: NS 160.980 (Harrisburg terminal), 160.860 (Harrisburg east), 160.800 (Altoona east); Amtrak: 160.635; Middletown & Hummelstown: 161.505

TO DO: The National Civil War Museum is situated in Reservoir Park. Hersheypark, and Indian Echo Caverns are 10 miles east via US 322.

NEARBY: Five miles southeast of Harrisburg lies Steelton, home of the Steelton & Highspire Railroad, and 10 miles southeast is Middletown, home of the Middletown & Hummelstown tourist and freight short line.

DIRECTIONS: From US 11/15 in Enola, turn west on Valley Street, then right on First Street, right on Miller Street, and right on Vista Drive, which takes you to the Enola Overview Bridge. Follow the road (now River Road) another mile to reach the Marysville boat access at Rockville Bridge.

Horseshoe Curve

Alex Mayes

Horseshoe Curve is a 220-degree curve on the former Pennsylvania Railroad's main line through the Alleghenies 6 miles west of Altoona that was completed in 1854. This line is now Norfolk Southern's Pittsburgh Line. The curve was designed to increase elevation 122 feet through Kittanning Gap by constructing a circuitous route to reduce the grade. Today, Norfolk Southern's Pittsburgh Line runs through downtown Altoona, and the nonstop action provides endless enjoyment for the visiting railfan.

ACTIVITY: Both Horseshoe Curve and Altoona see 40–50 trains a day. Traffic includes manifests, intermodals, stack trains, and coal, grain, and other unit trains. Most westbound trains rounding Horseshoe Curve have helper diesels on the rear pushing, and light helper moves (engines only) are seen throughout the day. Amtrak's *Pennsylvanian* runs through this area in both directions during daylight hours.

TRAIN-WATCHING SPOTS: At Horseshoe Curve, the best place to view trains is from the upper viewing area adjacent to the tracks. (A fee is charged.) It is 150 feet above the visitor center and reached by riding a funicular (inclined plane) or by walking up 194 steps. You can also view trains from the ground below. In downtown Altoona, several streets with sidewalks cross over the tracks, offering locations for watching and photographing trains. A pedestrian walkway between the Railroaders Memorial Museum and the Amtrak station is another viewing spot. For an outstanding shot of eastbounds in the morning, try 18th Street from overhead. Norfolk Southern's Juniata Shops are located on East Chestnut Street, and diesels can be viewed from public streets. The North Eighth Street overpass provides a good overhead view of the tracks and servicing area.

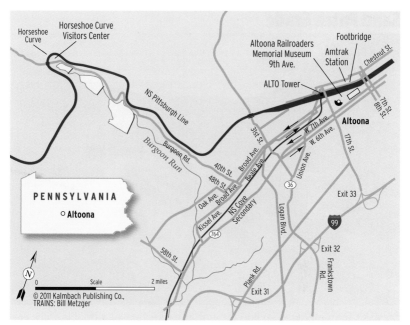

Horseshoe Curve is just west of Altoona, which is about 100 miles east of Pittsburgh.

SAFETY: Most trackage is fenced and posted at Horseshoe Curve and in Altoona. The Pittsburgh Line is a very active, fast main line, so take caution at all times.

RAILROAD FREQUENCIES: NS: 160.800, 161.070, 160.860, 160.980, 160.560

TO DO: The Railroaders Memorial Museum (1300 Ninth Avenue) in downtown Altoona is an interesting place to visit. A combined admission ticket with Horseshoe Curve is available.

NEARBY: Two additional places of interest are 15 miles away in Gallitzin: Gallitzin Tunnels Park and Museum and the Allegheny Portage Railroad Historic Site. Tunnels Park is at the west portal of Gallitzin Tunnel, adjacent to an overhead bridge that provides an outstanding vantage point for west-bound trains in the afternoon.

DIRECTIONS: To get to Horseshoe Curve from I-99, take the US 22 West Exit south of Altoona, and turn right (north) onto Route 764 for 3 miles. Then turn left on 58th Street until it ends. Turn left and follow this road for 2 miles to the visitor center. Downtown Altoona is accessible from the 17th Street Exit off I-99.

Sand Patch Grade

Alex Mayes

On CSX's former B&O main line through the Alleghenies, a double-track line with many scenic photo locations, Sand Patch Grade starts at Hyndman and climbs 1,300 feet to the 2,258 foot summit at Sand Patch, which is just west of the 4,475-foot-long Sand Patch Tunnel.

ACTIVITY: About 25–30 scheduled CSX trains, Amtrak's *Capitol Limited*, and loaded or empty coal, grain, and ethanol trains pass over Sand Patch Grade in a 24-hour period.

TRAIN-WATCHING SPOTS: In Hyndman, the grade crossing provides a good vantage point for eastbounds in the morning and westbounds in the afternoon. To get to the other good locations on Sand Patch, at Hyndman, turn left at the white church on the corner and go west 5 miles to the Fairhope grade crossing. Elevated vantage points on both sides of the grade crossing provide superb locations for early morning eastbound trains. Leaving Fairhope, continue on the road about 4 miles to a sharp hairpin curve to the left, and take this turn. Continue to a T intersection and turn left down a steep and winding road to Glencoe grade crossing for a view of trains in both directions. Leaving Glencoe, go north 200 yards and turn left. This road will turn to gravel in about 2 miles, go 6 miles, and turn left at a sharp turn to the left to reach the Philson grade crossing. Cross the tracks, turn right, and continue on Brush Creek Road until it ends. Turn left, and then right about 400 yards onto Mance Road. The 180 degree curve at the top of the road is a popular photo location for westbounds until noon.

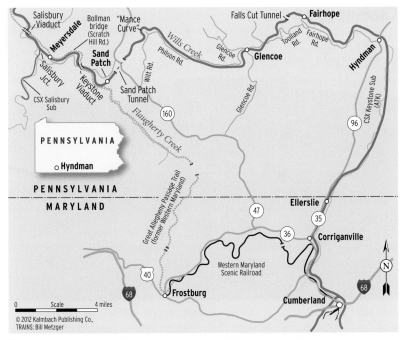

Hyndman is in southern Pennsylvania between Pittsburgh and Harrisburg.

Next, leaving Mance, continue west on Brush Creek Road for 2 miles and turn right onto a steep gravel road to the tracks. Sand Patch is next. Take Brush Creek Road to Route 160, turn right (north), go 500 yards and turn left, then go 2 miles and turn left at the Sand Patch sign, and go over the tracks. West of Sand Patch, good locations include the ex-Western Maryland Railway's Keystone and Salisbury viaducts and the interlocking at Yoder.

SAFETY: This is an isolated, mountainous area, and rattlesnakes and copperheads are seen during the warm months. The roads in the winter months can be treacherous, and winter storms can suddenly develop. Topographical maps and a GPS are helpful in finding your way around.

RAILROAD FREQUENCIES: CSX: 160.230, 160.320, 161.520, 160.410, 160.290

NEARBY: The Western Maryland Scenic Railroad operates steam-powered excursions from the old former Western Maryland Railway passenger station in downtown Cumberland to Frostburg, Md.

DIRECTIONS: From the Pennsylvania Turnpike, exit at Somerset (from the west) or Bedford (from the east) to Hyndman, Pa. From Somerset, take Highway 31 to Highway 96. From Bedford, take Highway 96.

Chattanooga

Steve Freer

Both Norfolk Southern and CSX serve Chattanooga. NS DeButts Yard is 4 miles long and includes a diesel shop, car repair facility, hump and classification yards, and plenty of switching activity. Main lines radiate from Chattanooga toward Cincinnati, Knoxville, Atlanta, and Birmingham. CSX has a small yard in Wauhatchie at the base of Lookout Mountain adjacent to lines to Atlanta and Nashville. Short lines in the region include the Chattooga & Chickamauga Railway and the Sequatchie Valley Railroad.

ACTIVITY: Up to 50 trains per day run through Chattanooga. Norfolk Southern trains can be manifests, intermodals, and unit coal trains, while CSX tends to have mixed, double-stacks, and auto racks. Tennessee Valley Railroad Museum's passenger trains run daily in season.

TRAIN-WATCHING SPOTS: The CSX main line parallels DeButts Yard for its entirety, so spots in this vicinity provide optimum train watching. Seven bridges cross portions of the yard from 20th Street, near the NS/CSX diamonds, to Wilder Street. (Railfan-favorite Coffey's Cliff is adjacent to the Wilder Street Bridge.) The Third Street Bridge allows you to view the NS diesel shop, while Wilcox Boulevard Viaduct provides an overview of the car shop, yard flyover, main tower, and hump lead. Parking is available along road shoulders and in business parking lots near most bridges. For viewing trains on the ex-CNO&TP Rathole line (including Triple Crown service), try the Tennessee Riverwalk parking lot under Tenbridge adjacent to Chickamauga Dam off Amnicola Highway.

SAFETY: Typical safety measures should be followed such as staying clear of tracks and keeping valuables out of sight.

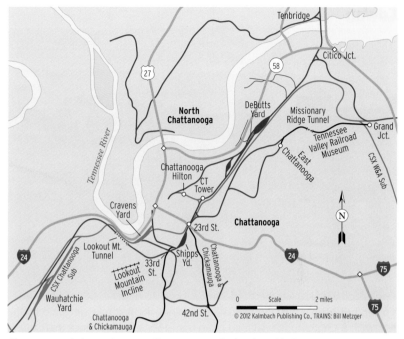

Chattanooga is in southeastern Tennessee on the border with Georgia.

RAILROAD FREQUENCIES: NS: 160.950 (road), 160.245 (dispatcher to train), 160.830 (train to dispatcher), 160.500, 160.905, 161.250 (yard); CSX: 161.370 (Chattanooga Sub), 161.520 (W&A Sub), 160.440 (yard); Chattooga & Chickamauga: 160.455, 160.695; TVRM: 160.425; Sequatchie Valley Railroad: 160.530

TO DO: The Chattanooga area features plenty of attractions, including Lookout Mountain Incline Railway and the Walnut Street Pedestrian Bridge, the world's longest pedestrian bridge. You can visit several Civil War sites including the Chickamauga and Chattanooga National Military Park. Tennessee Valley Railroad Museum excursions range from one-hour Missionary Ridge locals to longer runs into north Georgia.

NEARBY: Other train-watching opportunities include the CSX J Line, which features a steep grade up Raccoon Mountain. The NS line north to Cincinnati is heavily used and provides much action.

DIRECTIONS: From downtown Chattanooga, take Exit 1C from Highway 27 North. Follow Fourth Street west until it zigzags onto Third Street. The Third Street Bridge intersects with Holtzclaw Avenue. A right turn allows access to McCallie Avenue, Bailey Avenue, Central Avenue, and 20th Street bridges. Turn left on Holtzclaw to Wilcox Boulevard Viaduct. Cross near the DeButts Main Tower and turn right onto Riverside Drive to the bridge over the north end of DeButts at Wilder Street.

Cowan

Ralcon Wagner

Cowan has been a bustling railroad town since the first rails were laid by the Nashville & Chattanooga Railroad more than 150 years ago. Since then, heavy trains have required assistance getting over Cumberland Mountain from helper or pusher locomotives due to the steep grades and numerous sharp curves— a tradition that continues today. In addition to being the base for the pusher locomotives, Cowan is the location where the NC&StL's Tracy City Branch once connected with the main line. The former Nashville, Chattanooga & St. Louis Railroad's main line between Nashville and Chattanooga is now a vital part of the CSX network, and the busy CSX line goes down the middle of Cowan.

ACTIVITY: There are approximately 30 trains plus additional pusher movements every 24 hours on this CSX line. Trains vary, but they include unit coal trains, intermodals, and manifests. The helper locomotives add to the action with continuous shuttling and coupling activity.

TRAIN-WATCHING SPOTS: While there are numerous locations for watching and photographing trains in Cowan, because of accessibility, the most popular is the city's spacious and attractive railroad park. The park straddles the track and contains a train-viewing platform, gazebos, historic markers, and the Cowan Railroad Museum that is housed in the restored 1904 NC&StL depot. Adjacent to the depot several pieces of equipment are on display, including a GE 44-ton diesel locomotive, a 1920 Porter steam locomotive, caboose and other pieces of rolling stock. The depot museum, displayed railroad equipment, and abandoned CTC tower across the street are nice elements for train photos. For long or telephoto pictures, the steep grade up the mountain also offers a great background.

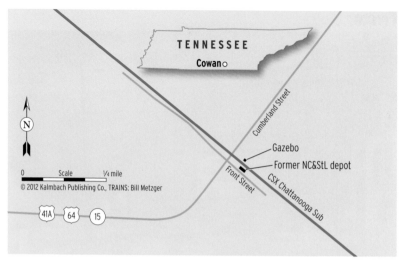

Cowan is located at the foot of Cumberland Mountain in southern Tennessee.

SAFETY: The CSX track through Cowan is always active with a steady volume of trains with pusher engines regularly dispatched.

RAILROAD FREQUENCIES: CSX: 161.370 (road), 161.100 (dispatcher to train), 161.520 (train to dispatcher)

TO DO: Historic downtown offers several restaurants and shops conveniently located near the railroad park. You can view the stone arch bridge over Boiling Fork Creek on Tennessee Avenue South. In Winchester, 6 miles west, you can visit the Old Jail Museum, and a little farther south, experience historic Falls Mill at Belvidere.

NEARBY: The Stevenson Railroad Depot Museum is another great spot for watching and photographing trains, located 35 miles south in Stevenson Ala., just across the state line, where the CSX main from Nashville and Norfolk Southern's line from Memphis merge. Several pieces of rolling stock are on display adjacent to the museum.

DIRECTIONS: Take Exit 127 off I-24 and go south on US 64 toward Winchester for 14 miles. Exit at US 41A ramp toward Cowan. Turn left onto US 41A for approximately 3 miles. Drive to the grade crossing and turn right onto Front Street. The railroad park is on the left. Ample parking can be found on both sides of the track.

Frisco

Ron Flanary

This rural junction of Norfolk Southern (ex-Southern) and CSX (ex-Clinchfield) includes connecting tracks for interchange of trackage-rights trains over both roads in both directions. These movements include south-north CSX trains over NS north of Frisco, and NS trains in both directions via CSX.

ACTIVITY: Frisco sees 30–40 trains per day, with slightly more being CSX trains than NS. Most trains are loaded or empty coal trains, but there are 2 daily scheduled general freight trains on CSX and a nightly general freight turnaround job on NS. CSX also sees some grain and other non-coal traffic. NS local crews working out of nearby Kingsport also add operating interest. Both routes are CTC-controlled, single-track lines, and crews from both roads verbally acknowledge signal indications on the radio—a particularly helpful practice in predicting approaching trains. No scheduled passenger trains run through Frisco.

TRAIN-WATCHING SPOTS: Public secondary roads allow safe access to the north end of the small NS yard, where there's also a photogenic trestle. Carter's Valley Road crosses the CSX/NS junction point just north of Click Tunnel and offers a higher-level viewpoint from a public road. The grade crossing near Waycross allows photography of both CSX and NS movements to and from the north on the CSX main.

SAFETY: There are several safe vantage points in and around Frisco to avoid trespassing on railroad property. A little exploration of the public roads will yield some excellent vantage points.

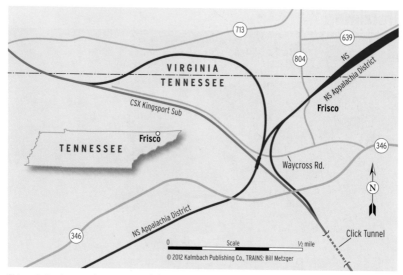

Frisco is in the northeast part of the state on the border with Virginia.

RAILROAD FREQUENCIES: NS: 160.950 (road), 160.245 (dispatcher); CSX: 161.100 (road), 161.520 (dispatcher)

TO DO: Seven miles away, the larger Kingsport offers a wide variety of eating and lodging options, plus other non-rail attractions, including several traditional Appalachian music venues. Camping and RV facilities at Natural Tunnel State Park (25 miles away in Virginia) and other spots are within easy reach.

NEARBY: Speers Ferry, Va. (20 miles north on US 23), has virtually the same traffic levels and features both a developed wayside viewing area along the main highway, plus a secondary road that goes under both Copper Creek trestles (the taller one is 167 feet above the Creek). Just up the road from Copper Creek is the famed Natural Tunnel (a Virginia State Park). This natural cavern turned railroad tunnel (850 feet long and 100 feet high) is a must-see but bring a wide-angle lens to capture the action down in the tunnel itself.

DIRECTIONS: Frisco is reached by Carter's Valley Road (Route 346), which connects with US 23 at the Virginia-Tennessee state line in north Kingsport. US 23 is the northern four-lane continuation of I-26, which in turn is intersected by I-81 in south Kingsport. Kingsport is only 3 miles away.

Harriman

Steve Forrest

Harriman was the eastern end of the old Tennessee Central Railroad. Today, Harriman is primarily served by the Norfolk Southern on its CNO&TP (Rathole) route and its K&O route from Knoxville. CSX also serves Harriman on a very limited level. The former Tennessee Central main is in place as far west as Crab Orchard, but NS only operates it to Rockwood. The western end between Rockwood and Crab Orchard is owned and operated by Franklin Minerals, and there is a good bit of interchange between the NS and Franklin. Emory Gap is west of Harriman, where the Emory River enters the Tennessee Valley.

ACTIVITY: NS operates 40–50 daily trains through Harriman, with about 6–8 of these trains entering or leaving via the K&O. CSX coal trains are sporadic and usually determined by where the TVA buys coal for the Kingston power plant. Two locals are based out of Emory Gap. The first-shift local does most of the work around Harriman and runs several days a week down the main line as far as Dayton. The second-shift local normally works the yard and the industries on the old TC route, including the interchange with Franklin Industrial Minerals. Franklin Industrial Minerals operates ex-NS/SOU B23-7 locomotives in an attractive paint scheme on variable daylight runs.

TRAIN-WATCHING SPOTS: You can view trains from Old Valley Road next to the NS depot at Emory Gap. A few miles north on US 27, West Hills Road crosses over the NS with an excellent overhead view of the double track. For photographers, this is a morning shot as the track is down in a cut with only the east side open. The former Tennessee Central bridge over the Emory River is right next to Highway 27 on a connecting wye. It is used by the locals and Powder River coal trains going to Kingston as they make an unusual pull and shove

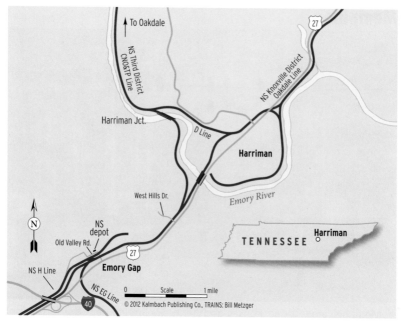

Harriman is about 70 miles north of Chattanooga at the junction of I-40 and US 27. It is about 90 miles south of Burnside, Ky., another hot spot.

move necessary to get to the power plant. Oakdale is to the north, and it is a great spot to watch trains enter and leave the single-track bottleneck through Tunnel 25 and Tunnel 26. From south of Emory Gap to Chattanooga, the NS is a single-track line with numerous sidings and lots of meets.

RAILROAD FREQUENCIES: NS: 160.950 (road), 160.245 (dispatcher to train), 160.830 (train to dispatcher); CSX trains use NS channels while on NS.

TO DO: Harriman contains a number of restaurants, several antique stores, and a few motels. Those motels south of I-40, on request, may provide a room with a view of the railroad.

NEARBY: In Oak Ridge, the Southern Appalachia Railway Museum offers excursion runs behind vintage diesel locomotives and restored passenger coaches.

DIRECTIONS: The Emory Gap depot is located off US 27 on Old Valley Road. US 70 just south of Harriman follows the Franklin Industrial Minerals route out to Crab Orchard.

Memphis

Mike Condren

In Memphis, areas along Kansas and Kentucky Streets near the Mississippi River bridges provide excellent views of BNSF and UP tracks. At the Kansas Street site, you can look directly east down the tracks from the curve in the foreground to the Broadway area, a six-track arrangement (CSX, NS westbound, UP, NS eastbound, BNSF Main 1, and BNSF Main 2). Before Broadway, the CN track crosses at CN Junction, which is controlled by CTC via automatic interlocking. This north-south line is used by Amtrak's *City of New Orleans*, and Central Station is just north of this crossing.

The CN switches the Sugar Services plant just west of Central Station and north of CN Junction. It is the only CN action other than transfer runs through the junction to BNSF Main 2. NS and BNSF also send transfers down the CN using BNSF Main 2 to CN Junction. The UP and BNSF both send switchers down the branch to President's Island, which branches off BNSF Main 2 just west of Kentucky Street.

ACTIVITY: BNSF operates about 24 trains in daylight including unit coal trains to the NS, intermodal trains, and general freight trains. Up to 5 transfer moves are made to the CN from NS and BNSF. The UP runs up to 7 trains to the CN and CSX as well as to its own Memphis Yard. Amtrak's southbound *City of New Orleans* is visible at CN Junction in the summer, especially if it's running late.

TRAIN-WATCHING SPOTS: There are two spots for watching trains near the river. One is at the north end of Kentucky Street where it dead-ends at the tracks. Parking is available at the end of Kentucky Street. Kansas Street is the other location. It is accessible from Riverside Drive by taking Carolina Street east to

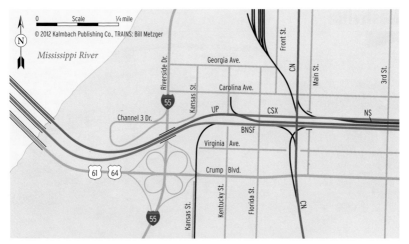

Memphis is in the southwest corner of the state on the Mississippi River.

Channel 3 Drive and then turning south toward the tracks. Parking is available on Channel 3 Drive on the south side of the street.

RAILROAD FREQUENCIES: BNSF: 160.230, 160.695, 161.160, 161.385, 161.415; CN: 161.190, 160.920; CSX: 161.370, 160.440, 161.520; NS: 160.245, 160.830, 160.950, 161.490; UP: 160.320, 160.410, 160.470

TO DO: There are more than 100 barbecue joints in Memphis; try one, try them all. The National Civil Rights Museum (450 Mulberry Street) is located several blocks northeast of Central Station. You can visit Graceland by taking I-55 south, exiting on Elvis Presley Boulevard, and traveling south about a mile.

NEARBY: Amtrak's Central Station (545 South Main Street) is located at the corner of Main and Calhoun. Memphis has several trolley lines that use vintage trolleys. The Main Street Trolley operates downtown and the Riverfront Loop runs along the Mississippi.

DIRECTIONS: Both locations are accessible from I-55. The Kentucky Street dead end is 2 blocks off E H Crump Boulevard (east or west). Kansas Street is several blocks away.

Nashville

Ralcon Wagner

The hub of railroading in middle Tennessee, Nashville sees seven routes converge, five belonging to the CSX. Nashville is also served by the 110-mile Nashville & Eastern Railroad. A commuter service named the Music City Star operates between Nashville and Lebanon over the N&E. All CSX lines connect to Radnor Yard, 7 miles south of the business district, and Kayne Avenue Yard in the heart of downtown. While some trains terminate at Radnor Yard, others continue past Radnor and make a crew change at Kayne Avenue.

ACTIVITY: Approximately 30 or more CSX trains of all varieties run through downtown Nashville each day. Music City Star trains, consisting of former Amtrak F40s and ex-Metra bi-level commuter cars, operate weekdays out of Riverfront Station. The N&E normally operates 1–2 freights Monday through Friday. Cars from the N&E interchange with CSX five times a week at Vine Hill Junction in south Nashville.

TRAIN-WATCHING SPOTS: There are numerous hot spots but the highest volume of trains can be seen in several locations. Kayne Avenue Yard is constantly busy with run-through freights, occasional crew changes, and switching movements. Many intermodal and manifest trains pass through this location daily. The overpasses on Broadway and Demonbreun Streets offer good vantage points. A viewing platform at the rear of the hotel in the former Union Station (1001 Broadway) is open to the public, and the structure makes a nice backdrop for photos. Ground-level viewing is available on 11th Avenue along the west side of the yard.

Riverfront Station is 9 blocks east where Broadway meets the Cumberland River. The area around the station is spacious, making it ideal for viewing

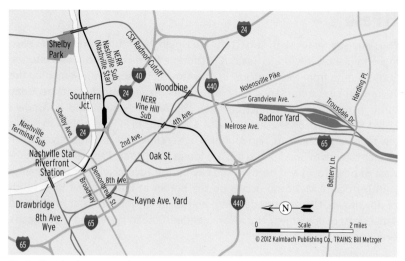

Nashville is in the center of Tennessee at the intersection of I-24, I-40, and I-65.

trains, but parking is limited. For a higher vantage point, both the Shelby Street pedestrian bridge, located almost above the station, and the Korean Veterans Bridge are easy to access.

At Shelby Park, 3 miles east of downtown, you can see frequent CSX freights cross an impressive trestle that spans both the Cumberland River and the east end of the park.

While CSX does not allow access to Radnor Yard, you can photograph trains from the Melrose Avenue overpass, adjacent to I-440 and Nolensville Road. This site affords an excellent view of the north end of Radnor Yard. The Harding Place overpass, situated near Harding Place and I-65, offers a good vantage point of the action at the south end of the yard and activity on the CSX main.

RAILROAD FREQUENCIES: CSX: 161.110, 161.370, 160.410; Nashville & Eastern: 160.365

TO DO: Numerous country music venues, restaurants, and shops line lower Broadway. The Country Music Hall of Fame and historic Ryman Auditorium are also within walking distance. A newer entertainment district called the Gulch at 11th Avenue South and Division Street is 3 blocks south of Broadway.

NEARBY: The Tennessee Central Railway Museum (220 Willow Street) is located minutes away from downtown off Hermitage Avenue.

DIRECTIONS: Broadway and Demonbreun Streets, several blocks apart, run parallel and cross the tracks near 11th Avenue with access from I-40/65.

El Paso

The Lone Star State's sixth-largest city is a Union Pacific hub. Ninety miles east, in Sierra Blanca, the former Texas & Pacific line from Fort Worth links into the Sunset Route from New Orleans. In downtown El Paso, they're joined by the Tucumcari Line from Kansas City. Altogether, expect about 50 trains a day through the Trainway Tunnel between the Amtrak station and downtown Dallas Street Yard. BNSF Railway is also a presence in El Paso, although only a few trains a day show up. And Amtrak's *Sunset Limited* visits three days a week in each direction. Good photo ops are found along West Paisano Drive southwest of downtown and north of the city on the Tucumcari Line. Interchange with Ferrocarril Mexicano occurs on the border at International Yard, south of downtown. UP's intermodal ramp and main freight yard is at Alfalfa Yard 4 miles east of downtown. Not recommended: Cuidad Juarez and the no man's land just west of El Paso.

Flatonia

Flatonia is located between Houston and San Antonio on I-10 and sees 30–40 trains every 24 hours. While still referred to as the Sunset Route, the original Galveston, Harrisburg & San Antonio Line today is UP's Glidden Subdivision between Houston and San Antonio. The old San Antonio & Aransas Pass trackage is known as the Cuero Subdivision running from West Point to the north past Victoria to the south. UP provides the majority of freight traffic and includes all types of trains from intermodal to merchandise, autos, rock, and coal, using just about any locomotive from any railroad or lessor. Amtrak's *Sunset Limited* also passes by at night. In the northwest corner of the diamond, you can view trains from the Rail Park Photo Pavilion, a 40 x 25-foot covered and lighted space that offers a wheelchair ramp along with tables, benches, and electrical outlets. You can also visit Switch Tower 3 and SP bay-window caboose No. 4743 on South Main Street. Communications can be monitored on frequencies 160.665 and 160.410.

Sweetwater

This West Texas town of 10,000, 200 miles west of Fort Worth on I-20, is a crew change point on routes of both BNSF Railway and Union Pacific and the home of one of the surviving pieces of the legendary Kansas City, Mexico & Orient Railway. UP is busier, seeing about 20 trains a day operating over the former Texas & Pacific Line between El Paso and Fort Worth. Its trains swap crews beside a new yard office just south of downtown (but don't look for a yard because there isn't one). BNSF's yard on the northeast edge of town sees about 10 trains a day on its Clovis, N.M.-Temple artery. The railroads run parallel briefly 6 miles east of town to a crossover, Tecific, used three days a week when BNSF routes a westbound freight from Fort Worth over UP. A short line, Texas & Oklahoma Railroad, runs from a BNSF connection south to Maryneal, 15 miles, several times a week to serve a cement plant and crosses under UP west of downtown. When and why to stay away: the town's population doubles during the Rattlesnake Roundup held each March.

Big Sandy

Mike Harbour

The little East Texas town of Big Sandy once had a more railroad-like name. The mighty Texas & Pacific (later Missouri Pacific) and a short narrow gauge road called the Tyler Tap ran alongside each other at a place originally called Big Sandy Switch. The names have changed: MP became Union Pacific, and Tyler Tap successor St. Louis Southwestern (or Cotton Belt to most folks) was absorbed by Southern Pacific and then UP, but Big Sandy is busier than ever.

ACTIVITY: UP's Pine Bluff Sub (ex-SSW) and its Dallas Sub (ex-T&P) provide railfans with more than 40 trains daily, including Amtrak's twice-daily *Texas Eagle*. Intermodal hotshots are frequent visitors as are unit trains and general manifests. Big Sandy is also a popular crew change point, so a fair number of trains will stop on either side of the diamond. You can also enjoy watching eastbound Dallas Sub trains move south on the Pine Bluff Sub. Due to the track arrangement, runaround and backing moves are required before these trains continue their journey toward Tyler.

TRAIN-WATCHING SPOTS: A great place to park and watch from is a gravel lot just north of the diamond (also known as Tower 137, but rarely called such as an actual tower there never existed). An attractive, and now long-gone, union depot once sat here, so it's a great place to look along each main line. Parking is available immediately south along the diamond.

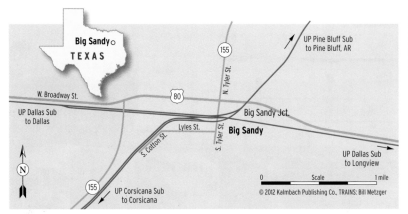

Big Sandy is 100 miles east of Dallas.

RAILROAD FREQUENCIES: UP: 161.145, 160.320, 161.460

TO DO: For outdoor enthusiasts, there are several lakes and a wildlife refuge west of Hawkins, another small town 5 miles west of Big Sandy on the Dallas Sub.

NEARBY: Tyler, a larger city and the starting point of the Tyler Tap, and Longview, a stop on the *Texas Eagle*, are both less than 30 miles away. Both offer motels, hotels, and other amenities. Tyler also has a railroad museum at the Cotton Belt depot (210 East Oakwood Street). The Longview Amtrak Station (905 Pacific Avenue) is another must-see; it's also the fourth busiest *Texas Eagle* stop and was built by T&P in 1940.

DIRECTIONS: From Dallas or Shreveport, take Exit 567 off I-20 and go north on Texas 155 for 10.5 miles. Take a right on US 80 to the first light at South Tyler Street. Take a right and go south for 2 blocks. The gravel parking lot is on the left, just north of the diamond.

Dallas

Ken Fitzgerald

The current Dallas Union Station was built in 1916 and serves as the anchor for services by Dallas Area Rapid Transit buses and light rail, the Trinity Railway Express heavy rail to Fort Worth, and Amtrak's *Texas Eagle*. The UP's ex-T&P Dallas Subdivision runs past the depot connecting the Fort Worth terminal with all points east. The BNSF runs over the TRE from Fort Worth and Irving west to the eastern end of Dallas terminal, where trains head south toward Houston. Short line Dallas, Garland & Northeastern rounds out the mix and performs area switching services.

ACTIVITY: DART light rail trains pass through the station every few minutes during the day. Utilizing push-pull trainsets with the locomotives on the west end, the Trinity Railway Express averages 22 round trips to Fort Worth every weekday and 11 round trips on Saturday. Amtrak's *Texas Eagle* is scheduled to arrive southbound midmorning and northbound afternoons. Union Pacific averages 20–30 freight trains every 24 hours, while the BNSF averages 8–10 trains. Dallas, Garland & Northeastern switchers can pass through the station area at any time on the way to and from various yards and customers.

TRAIN-WATCHING SPOTS: Station platforms provide track-level viewing of passenger and freight trains along with DART light rail trains. Immediately to the east of the station platforms, and easily accessible by foot, is the Houston Street Viaduct, which provides a good location for photographing trains entering and leaving the station on that end with the Reunion Tower and Dallas skyline in the background. The 500-foot level observation deck of Reunion Tower across the street from the station is currently closed for renovation, but otherwise provides a great overall vista.

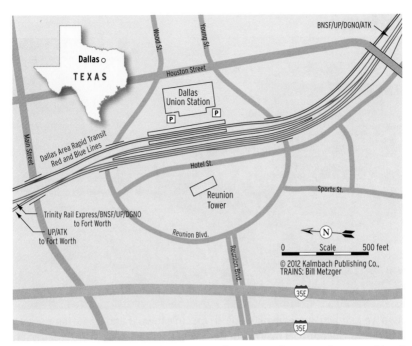

Dallas Union Station is located at 400 South Houston Street on the west side of downtown Dallas.

SAFETY: Security for mass transit in the Dallas Union Station area is divided between Dallas, DART, and Amtrak police along with railroad special agents. While photography is not banned at DUS, if you spend much time here, you can expect to be questioned. Commercial photography is not permitted without advance arrangement. If you plan to spend much time at DUS it is suggested that you email the DART media before your visit. Use of a tripod is not recommended.

RAILROAD FREQUENCIES: UP: 161.145, 160.410, 161.280; BNSF: 161.340; Trinity Railway Express: 161.040; Dallas, Garland & Northeastern: 161.085

TO DO: Dallas is a major city and offers a wealth of choices in lodging, dining, and activities to keep everyone occupied. The JFK Museum and grassy knoll are located a few blocks east of the station.

NEARBY: Riding either the DART light rail system or the TRE to Fort Worth can be fun experiences. One possible destination is the McKinney Avenue Transit Authority, which operates historic trolley cars only 2 miles from DUS and is easily reachable by DART light rail.

DIRECTIONS: Downtown Dallas and the station are easily accessible from I-35, I-30, I-20, and I-45.

Jefferson

Mike Harbour

Two well-known names in railroading cross in a town that became famous as a Texas port. Steamboats may no longer call at Big Cypress Bayou, but Jefferson is still alive with the trains of Union Pacific and Kansas City Southern.

ACTIVITY: A great variety is in store for railfans at Tower 61, the junction so-numbered by the state years ago. Several dozen trains polish the diamond daily, including Amtrak. UP's former Texas & Pacific line is bidirectional through town and hosts everything from the *Texas Eagle* to short manifests powered by a single locomotive. KCS traffic includes unit trains and general freights as well as some intermodals; its right-of-way is ex-Missouri-Kansas-Texas.

TRAIN-WATCHING SPOTS: There's no tower at Tower 61, but it's possible to park along the diamond's south side, which lies almost directly under the US 59 overpass. Better photo opportunities may be found a short distance east from Tower 61 in a parking lot off North Alley Street near the small UP yard between the UP and KCS mains. Trains moving east have several street crossings to whistle for before they hit the diamond, so there's time to move alongside either main to watch them pass. UP will often stage meets east of the yard too, so if a westbound train is waiting, an eastbound movement is likely planned. Downtown Jefferson, the domain of KCS, is a less busy alternative.

SAFETY: Both main lines are active. Also stay alert in this neighborhood.

RAILROAD FREQUENCIES: KCS: 160.260, 160.350; UP: 160.515

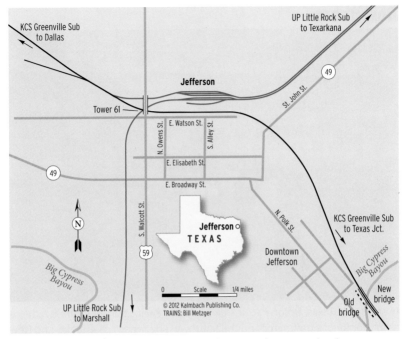

Jefferson is straight east of Dallas near the Arkansas and Louisiana borders.

TO DO: Jefferson's historic downtown offers good food and a number of small retail businesses and antique stores. Look for a hobby shop in a former Iron Mountain business car that once belonged to Jay Gould. (Ask a local about the magnate's curse on Jefferson to get the irony of the display.) A narrow gauge steam train takes riders into the East Texas Piney Woods.

NEARBY: Marshall, the closest stop on the *Texas Eagle*, is about 20 miles south of Jefferson and home to a fascinating passenger station built by T&P still in service.

DIRECTIONS: From Dallas or Shreveport, take I-20 to Marshall and go north on US 59 at Exit 617. Just past the first light at West Broadway in Jefferson, turn right at East Elizabeth Street and then immediately turn left at North Owens Street. The KCS main is directly ahead, so turn left on Watson and follow it to the diamond on your right. To go downtown, take Watson east to North Alley Street and turn right. At East Broadway, turn left and follow it to North Polk Street all the way to the city center. The KCS main is just few blocks east.

Rosenberg

Tom Kline

In southeast Texas, Union Pacific's ex-Southern Pacific Sunset Route is a major artery for freight traffic crossing the Southwest between Los Angeles and New Orleans. Equally important is the BNSF's Galveston Sub that links the country's heartland with Texas ports along the Gulf Coast. These two routes cross at the Tower 17 interlocker near downtown Rosenberg. Adding to the action, the Kansas City Southern hosts a number of freights destined for the Mexican border.

ACTIVITY: In a 24-hour period, the junction at Tower 17 can see up to 45 trains. UP is the major player with a variety of freights, intermodals being the most dominant. BNSF provides numerous manifest, intermodal, and grain trains. It offers the bonus of unit coal trains bound for a generating station in nearby Smithers Lake. KCS punctuates the activity with various export manifest and intermodal offerings, and during very busy periods, up to 6 trains may run each way.

TRAIN-WATCHING SPOTS: There are numerous public places to park and view trains through the Tower 17 area. Of the many local streets around the tracks, the one with the best parking is east of the diamond along Avenue F south of the tracks near the Rosenberg Railroad Museum (1921 Avenue F). First Street crosses over the tracks on a bridge with a protected sidewalk on the east side. For those who like to follow the trains or venture into the countryside, major roadways parallel the main lines west of town: Highway 90 for the UP, Highway 36 for the BNSF, and US 59 for the KCS.

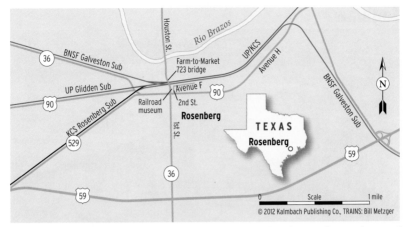

Rosenberg is home to the crossroads of three major railroads 25 miles southwest of Houston.

SAFETY: The Rosenberg Railroad Museum provides a great place to watch trains with its trackside view, and the museum has ample parking and picnic tables under a pavilion near the main lines.

RAILROAD FREQUENCIES: UP: 160.665 (Glidden Sub); BNSF: 161.190 (Galveston Sub); KCS: 161.115 (Rosenberg Sub), 161.565 (train to dispatcher), 160.815 (switching). Listen for KCS trains calling the UP dispatcher for permission to enter and exit the UP.

TO DO: Rosenberg is currently renovating many buildings downtown, and within a few blocks of the railroad are several local merchants and antique shops. The railroad museum hosts a wonderful collection of local railroad heritage displays inside and out with the crown jewel being Tower 17 itself, the original 1903 interlocking tower that controlled the junction until 2004.

NEARBY: You can view KCS's new intermodal yard west of Rosenberg in Kendleton and UP trains passing the restored SP depot in neighboring downtown Richmond and the Brazos River crossing.

DIRECTIONS: To get to Rosenberg from Houston, take US 59 south (Southwest Freeway) and take the Rosenberg Exit. Turn right onto Highway 36, which becomes First Street, and continue north about a mile until reaching Avenue I. Turn right onto Avenue I and go two blocks to Third Street. Turn left onto Third Street and continue north 3 blocks through downtown to Avenue F.

Saginaw

Ken Fitzgerald

Saginaw hosted three railroads: the Santa Fe, Rock Island, and Fort Worth & Denver. Those rail lines are still in use with the ex-ATSF from Fort Worth to Gainesville operating as the BNSF Fort Worth Sub, the ex-Fort Worth & Denver from Fort Worth to Wichita Falls operating as the Wichita Falls Sub, and the ex-Rock Island from Fort Worth to Chickasha operating as the UP Duncan Sub. Massive grain elevators served by their own in-plant switchers make this a busy place during harvest season. All three lines cross at grade next to the Saginaw Chamber of Commerce.

ACTIVITY: From a BNSF standpoint, the diamonds at Saginaw are at the center of a triangle between Saginaw Yard to the south, North Yard to the southeast, and the main Alliance Yard to the north where its intermodal facility is located. The BNSF operates approximately 30 trains a day over the diamonds, consisting of merchandise, coal, and RoadRailers to the Triple Crown facility in Saginaw Yard. BNSF intermodal trains from the Alliance Intermodal facility go north toward Kansas City and west on the Wichita Falls Sub via a connector a mile north of the diamonds. The UP operates approximately a dozen merchandise, rock, and grain trains a day over the Duncan Sub. Amtrak operates the *Heartland Flyer* through Saginaw over the BNSF.

TRAIN-WATCHING SPOTS: The Chamber of Commerce parking lot (301 South Saginaw Boulevard) and grassy area on the west side of the diamonds is a safe and locally accepted place to sit and watch trains. On sunny days, photography is only good in the afternoon once the sun has come around to the west side of the tracks.

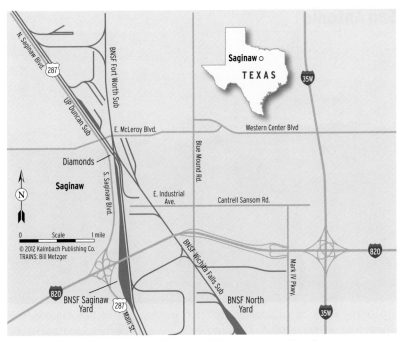

Saginaw is located less than 10 miles north of downtown Fort Worth.

RAILROAD FREQUENCIES: BNSF 160.650 (Fort Worth Sub), 160.920 (Wichita Falls Sub), 161.370 (Saginaw Yard), 161.235 (North Yard), 161.355 (Alliance Yard); UP: 160.740 (Duncan Sub)

TO DO: Fort Worth is a major city, so there are numerous options for lodging, food, and entertainment. Fort Worth has a museum district west of downtown, and the Fort Worth Stockyards district is between Fort Worth and Saginaw. It offers shopping, dining, and activities and features daily passenger trains operated by the Grapevine Vintage Railroad.

NEARBY: Another pleasant and scenic area is the Trinity River Bottoms linear park just north of downtown Fort Worth. The grassy park runs along the south bank of the Trinity River and passes under three rail lines where you can photograph BNSF, UP, Amtrak, and Fort Worth & Western trains. You can park on the levee on the west side of Samuels Avenue on the south side of the river and walk to the river bottom and the paved bike trail.

DIRECTIONS: From the I-820 Loop around Fort Worth, go to the north side of Fort Worth west of I-35 and take the Business 287 Exit. Head north on Saginaw Boulevard about a mile to the Chamber of Commerce parking lot on the right.

San Antonio

Carl Lehman

The Grassy Field, as local railfans call it, is the hot spot in San Antonio. It is situated on the south edge of downtown on the east-west ex-Southern Pacific Sunset Route main line. Here, the ex-Missouri-Kansas-Texas line leaves the main line, 2 blocks west the Beckmann Branch leaves the main line going northwest, and the Rockport Branch goes south. The Beckmann Branch connects with the ex-Missouri Pacific main line northwest of the Grassy Field at Tower 109. There are double crossovers just west of the Grassy Field and a busy interchange track at Tower 105. All tracks in San Antonio are now Union Pacific. (The towers in San Antonio have been torn down, but railroaders still often refer to their locations.)

ACTIVITY: Approximately 35 trains pass the Grassy Field in a 24-hour period, half or more in daylight. These include mixed freight, double-stacks, auto racks, coal, gravel, grain, and 2 Amtrak trains. DPUs are used on many trains. Trains using the Beckmann Branch include gravel trains and Amtrak's southbound *Texas Eagle*. Trains using the Rockport Branch are coal trains to a power plant and a local that switches industries. The ex-Katy line is used for northbound trains, and the ex-MP line is used by southbound trains (the only trains not seen from the Grassy Field). Often seen are pool trains and run-through power from BNSF, CSX, NS, KCS, and FerroMex.

TRAIN-WATCHING SPOTS: Besides the Grassy Field, other hot spots include the Amtrak station (350 Hoefgen Street); historic Sunset Station (1174 East Commerce Street); Towers 105 and 121; Kirby, SoSan, and East Yards; and the junctions just south of SoSan Yard.

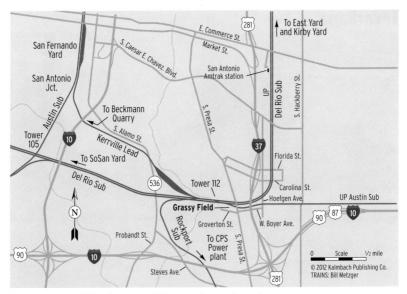

San Antonio is 200 miles west of Houston in southern Texas.

The ex-SP locomotive shop is an emissions-testing facility, and locomotives from all over the country show up. The newly constructed intermodal facility south of town has two ex-Montana Rail Link SD9s for switching.

SAFETY: The Grassy Field abuts the busy double-track main line, and most trains move through the area at speed. You can hear train horns a few blocks from the Grassy Field, which gives ample warning of their approach.

RAILROAD FREQUENCIES: UP: 160.515 (east road); 161.550 (west road); 160.500, 161.430, 161.115 (yards); Amtrak: 160.440

TO DO: A mile north of the Grassy Field is downtown San Antonio with the River Walk, Alamo, and many excellent restaurants. Stretching south from downtown along the San Antonio River are four other Spanish Missions dating from the early 1700s, all open to the public.

NEARBY: The Texas Transportation Museum on Wetmore Road just north of the airport offers rides behind an ex-Air Force diesel, and 25 miles north of San Antonio is the New Braunfels Railroad Museum.

DIRECTIONS: From north or south I-37, exit at the Florida and Carolina Exit. One block east is Hoefgen Avenue, turn right on it to West Boyer. Turn right on Boyer and go to South Presa. Turn left and then immediately right on Groveton Street. The Grassy Field is on the right, and parking is available there.

Texarkana

Mike Harbour

At one time, Texarkana featured four railroads: St. Louis Southwestern (Cotton Belt), Texas & Pacific, Missouri Pacific, and Kansas City Southern. Today, only the latter exists; the other three have long been assimilated into Union Pacific. Fortunately for railfans, this city still offers plenty of action thanks to a busy pair of UP lines (between St. Louis and Texas) bisected by the equally active KCS main from Kansas City to the Gulf of Mexico.

ACTIVITY: Between the two railroads, fans can catch more than 50 trains daily, including Amtrak. The *Texas Eagles* are hosted by UP, which runs dozens of manifest, intermodal, and coal trains between them. KCS offers a similar, but smaller, menu that lacks only passenger runs.

TRAIN-WATCHING SPOTS: Tower 42 is the grade-level crossing of the single-track KCS and the former MP and former Cotton Belt lines. While the tower disappeared in the 1990s, a large electrical cabinet sits at the site still labeled for the 1904-era interlocker. While there's no public property at the KCS-SSW crossing, a gravel parking lot is close by, as is a shady spot south of the Cotton Belt. The SSW-MP crossing is visible to the east. Sadly, there's a modern-day hobo jungle near the diamonds, too, so visitors should stay alert.

A safer, less-active alternative is just east at the city's historic Union Station (100 East Front Street). Amtrak takes up only the east corner of this sprawling edifice (the Bowie County Correctional Center is on the west end), but it's a nice place to sit, relax, and watch trains up close and personal, as well as catch switchers working the MP and SSW yards south of the facility. The state line runs right through the station and platform.

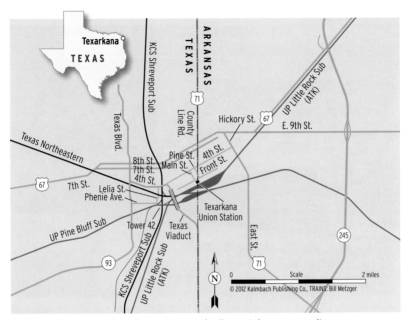

As its name suggests, Texarkana sits atop the Texas-Arkansas state line.

SAFETY: Except for the abandoned ex-T&P line west of the KCS crossing, most tracks are active.

RAILROAD FREQUENCIES: KCS: 160.260,160.350; UP: 160.515, 161.550

TO DO: Texarkana's downtown has only a few places to eat, but there are several sites worth visiting: the Museum of Regional History, Discovery Place Children's Museum, and Ace of Clubs House. The majority of restaurants are located along State Line Avenue. Those on the west side of this north-south thoroughfare are in Texas, and those on the east side are in Arkansas. Some accommodations are located here, but more choices lie along I-30 to the north and west.

NEARBY: Northeast Texas has plenty of outdoor activities and there are parks and lakes in both states.

DIRECTIONS: To get to Union Station from Dallas or other points west of Texarkana, take Exit 223 and go south on North State Line Avenue, and once downtown, turn left on Pine Street and then right on Front Street. The station is on the left. For Tower 42, take Front Street to Main Street and head west on West Fourth Street to Lelia Street. Go south on Lelia to Phenie Avenue and turn left.

Echo Canyon

Alex Mayes

Union Pacific's scenic double-track main travels through the Wasatch Range east of Ogden, which is UP's Evanston Subdivision, going through both Echo Canyon and Weber Canyon. The tracks run parallel to I-84 from Ogden east to Echo, and then closely follow I-80 northeast most of the way to the Wyoming border.

ACTIVITY: About 28–35 trains pass through the two canyons in 24 hours. They include intermodal, stack, auto rack, coal, and grain trains. Trains tend to run fleeted, with a half-dozen in rapid succession, followed by long periods of inactivity. There is no passenger service on this line.

TRAIN-WATCHING SPOTS: Weber Canyon begins near Peterson and ends near Croydon. There are several places to pull over on the shoulder of I-84, park, and set up for a shot. The Utah Highway Patrol is generally tolerant of this practice. Heading east from Ogden on I-84, you'll see a pair of tunnels on the left about a mile after entering the canyon where you'll be able to pull over on the shoulder. At Devil's Slide, a huge natural chute formed by two parallel limestone outcroppings running up the side of the mountain near Croydon, the visitor parking lot is a convenient viewing spot. At Morgan, there are a few good afternoon locations near Route 66 along the tracks.

Between Weber Canyon and Echo Canyon, a flat, open area stretches for about 12 miles. Although there are limited photo opportunities in this area, at Henefer, 3 miles east of Croydon, the Route 65 overpass spans the tracks and provides an excellent vantage point. Route 65 ends just north of the tracks and connects with Echo Canyon Road, which provides access to many good photo locations through Echo Canyon. Turn right on Echo Canyon Road, go through

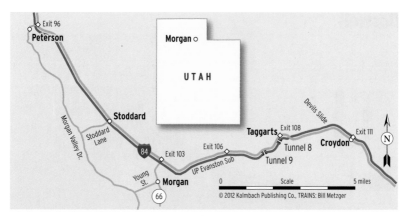

Weber and Echo Canyons are southeast of Ogden in northern Utah.

the town of Echo, and drive a few miles. In the distance, you'll see stunning red rock formations on the north side of the tracks that provide a picturesque background, especially for westbounds in the afternoon. Park on the shoulder and set up on the rocks, which are a few feet above the tracks.

RAILROAD FREQUENCIES: UP: 160.350, 160.410, 160.515

TO DO: In addition to train watching, wildlife watching is especially good in the hills on the north side of the tracks near the red rocks in Echo Canyon, where you can see elk, mule deer, fox, and an occasional moose.

NEARBY: The Utah State Railroad Museum, located in the former Ogden Union Station (2501 Wall Avenue) has an interesting selection of preserved steam and diesel locomotives and other artifacts. The museum also houses a firearms museum, a classic car museum, and a restaurant.

DIRECTIONS: From Ogden, take I-84 and head east about 18 miles. The west end of Weber Canyon begins at Peterson, and ends at Croydon. Echo Canyon begins a few miles east of the town of Echo, and I-80 runs through the canyon.

Doswell

Alex Mayes

At Doswell, CSX's RF&P Subdivision crosses with the Buckingham Branch Railroad. CSX's line is a busy double-track, north-south main line, which was the former Richmond, Fredericksburg & Potomac Railroad. The Buckingham Branch Railroad is a former east-west Chesapeake & Ohio single-track line that crosses CSX on a diamond. The Buckingham Branch Railroad runs between Richmond and Clifton Forge, its Richmond and Allegheny Division. Adjacent to the diamond is the former joint RF&P/C&O passenger station, now used by the Buckingham Branch Railroad, and the long abandoned HN Tower.

ACTIVITY: On CSX, expect to see 20–25 regularly scheduled freights and about 18 Amtrak trains in a day. Additionally, there may be loaded and empty coal trains, grain trains, and the Tropicana Juice Train that carries citrus products from Florida to New Jersey. There is a small yard in Doswell used by the Buckingham Branch to assemble trains and set off cars to be picked up by CSX. CSX also sets off cars on a siding next to the yard to be interchanged with the Buckingham Branch. Traffic on the Buckingham Branch is mostly westbound CSX empty coal trains en route from the export piers at Newport News to Clifton Forge that show up sporadically. The Buckingham Branch operates Mondays through Fridays in Doswell and usually switches cars in the morning with older model EMD diesels. A Doswell-Richmond turn and a Doswell-Gordonsville turn run each weekday.

TRAIN-WATCHING SPOTS: There are several train-watching spots off Doswell Road, which crosses both CSX and the Buckingham Branch, that provide vantage points for photography. (For optimum photography, use a 200-250mm lens.) Since trains on both lines usually appear with little warning, listening to

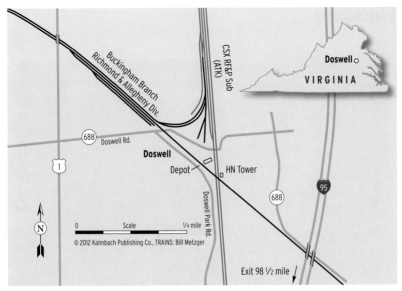

Doswell is in central Virginia between Richmond and Fredericksburg on I-95.

a scanner is very helpful. Southbound CSX trains will call the signal at North Doswell a mile to the north, and westbound Buckingham Branch trains will call the signal east of the diamond.

SAFETY: Visitors should not trespass on either CSX or Buckingham Branch property; property lines are posted and employees are instructed to report trespassers.

RAILROAD FREQUENCIES: CSX: 161.490, 161.550, 161.520, 160.410; Buckingham Branch: 160.470, 160.455, 160.710

TO DO: Kings Dominion, a very large theme park, is located 3 miles east of Doswell on Route 30. The park is open seasonally.

NEARBY: Nine miles to the south is the town of Ashland, where CSX runs in the old downtown section in an island in the middle of Railroad Avenue. Several restaurants and stores are located on Railroad Avenue. A few Amtrak trains stop at the old RF&P depot in Ashland.

DIRECTIONS: Heading north on I-95 from Richmond, take Exit 98 (Route 30) and go west to US 1. Turn right (north) on Route 1, go 1 mile, and turn right on Doswell Road to the tracks.

Lynchburg

Gerry Callison

Lynchburg marks the crossing for Norfolk Southern's ex-Southern Railway main line from Washington to Atlanta with the former Norfolk & Western main from Roanoke to Norfolk and CSX's former Chesapeake & Ohio James River Line from Clifton Forge to Richmond and Newport News.

ACTIVITY: The former Southern main sees 15–20 trains per day, including passenger, mixed freight, and intermodal. The former N&W and CSX lines each see 10–15 trains per day, with volumes varying by level of coal and grain shipments, which dominate traffic on both lines. Both of these lines tend to be directional in nature, as eastbound coal traffic on the former N&W line takes the former Virginian line along the Staunton River, and westbound coal empties on CSX take the former C&O Mountain Division. NS also operates a secondary line to the south that serves local industries and two power plants.

TRAIN-WATCHING SPOTS: CSX's James River Line highlights trains with magnificent mountain scenery along a canal towpath. One such location is the James River Outpost, a park where the Blue Ridge Parkway crosses the railroad and river. Ruesens Dam, located in western Lynchburg, is another noteworthy location. One of the best photo locations on NS is the former Southern main line, which crosses the James River on a dramatic trestle. This bridge can be photographed from the north, where Route 685 crosses the tracks (to the north, Harris Creek trestle is also visible) or from the south at Riverside Park. Photo locations along the former N&W include Possum Creek trestle, Eastbrook Curve, and Beaver Creek trestle, all a few miles east of town. NS operates Kinney Yard on the former N&W and Montview Yard on the former Southern.

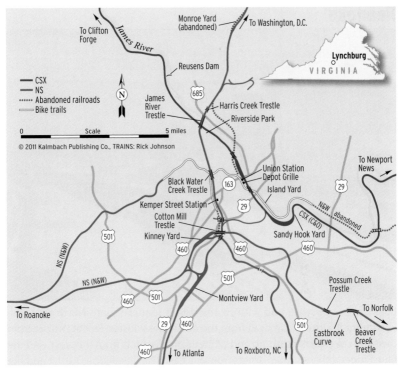

Lynchburg is northeast of Roanoke in central Virginia.

RAILROAD FREQUENCIES: NS: 161.190 (ex-N&W), 160.950 (ex-Southern), 160.275 and 160.530 (yards); CSX: 160.230 (road), 160.320 (dispatcher), 160.530 (yard)

TO DO: Lynchburg offers first-class amenities and entertainment. One restaurant of note is the Depot Grille, located in the former N&W freight house downtown. This restaurant offers excellent contemporary, Virginia-inspired cuisine, features railroad memorabilia, and has a dining area on a porch with great views of CSX's James River Line. You can take a scenic drive along the Blue Ridge Parkway, and the area features historic estates, such as Point of Honor and Thomas Jefferson's summer home of Poplar Forest.

NEARBY: Lynchburg has unique remnants of rail history. In addition to hosting Amtrak, Kemper Street Station has been restored and contains a bus terminal and nature museum. The original N&W main line through downtown has been converted into a paved bike trail. Going west, riders can take the trail through a tunnel and under the active Black Water Creek trestle.

DIRECTIONS: From Roanoke, take Highway 220/221/460 east to Lynchburg.

Roanoke

Samuel Phillips

Roanoke is a busy NS hub with six main lines funneling into North Yard. The Shenandoah District comes in from the north, the Winston Salem District from the south, the Christiansburg and Whitethorne Districts from the west, and the Blue Ridge and Altavista Districts from the east. The Blue Ridge District and the Altavista District connect at Tinker Creek at the east end of Roanoke.

ACTIVITY: You can easily see 20–30 trains in a 12-hour period while visiting Roanoke. Traffic ranges from coal and grain trains to manifests and hot inter-modal trains. The North Yard at Roanoke is the crew change point for five different districts and a main destination point. The South Yard, situated roughly 2 miles south of Roanoke's North Yard, sees only loaded coal and grain trains via the Whitethorne District. This is also where the bulk of the loaded traffic is located. The South Yard is a crew change point, and it features a diamond with the Winston Salem District.

TRAIN-WATCHING SPOTS: Downtown Roanoke contains several excellent train-watching spots. The David R. and Susan S. Goode Railwalk parallels the tracks from Market Street to Warehouse Row. Along the way, you can also view historic railroad memorabilia and listen to a radio scanner. (David Goode was a NS president.) A pedestrian walkway crosses over the tracks and is a great place for photographing trains. It offers some great angles with interesting buildings in the background. You can access the walkway where Centre Avenue NW intersects with Henry Street NW or off First Street and Norfolk Avenue from the other side of the tracks.

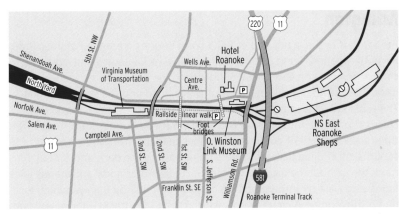

Roanoke is situated in the heart of the beautiful Blue Ridge Mountains in southern Virginia.

The Market Square Walkway is an enclosed glass bridge from Hotel Roanoke over the tracks to Market Street. For a preview of rail activity, go to roanokerailcam.com. The web cam is mounted on top of Hotel Roanoke.

RAILROAD FREQUENCIES: NS: 161.0250 (Blue Ridge and Altavista Districts), 160.4400 (Roanoke and Winston Salem Districts), 161.1900 (Christiansburg and Altavista Districts), 161.2500 (yard)

TO DO: In downtown Roanoke, you will find gift shops, nice places to eat, and a seasonal farmers market. The Taubman Museum of Art is just off Market Street, and 15 art galleries are within several blocks.

NEARBY: The O. Winston Link Museum of rail photography and Virginia's Museum of Transportation are within walking distance of the bridges, both are must-see attractions, and they offer a combined admission.

DIRECTIONS: Take I-581 off I-81 to Exit 5. Take Williamson Road and turn right on Shenandoah Avenue to downtown.

Arlington

Arlington is at the south end of CSX's Long Bridge across the Potomac River. Recently opened, Long Bridge Park provides a vantage point adjacent to control point RO on CSX's RF&P Subdivision. The park features a raised esplanade that provides excellent views of the railroad and the surrounding area. The esplanade is about 30 feet from Track 3, the closest track. Tracks 2 and 3 cross Long Bridge into Virginia, and at RO, Track 1 diverges from Track 2. The three-track alignment continues for more than 10 miles south through the suburbs. All Virginia Railway Express trains pass by the park, and Amtrak runs trains throughout the day. CSX freights, including intermodal and orange juice trains, also pass by throughout the day. Another nearby train-watching location is the Monroe Avenue Bridge, which crosses the tracks 4 rail miles south of RO. From this bridge, you'll enjoy excellent views of southbound trains with the U.S. Capitol building in the background. You can reach the park from I-395 at Exit 10A while heading northbound and from Exit 9 while southbound.

Clifton Forge

Clifton Forge is situated in west-central Virginia on I-64 near West Virginia. CSX's former C&O main travels through the Alleghenies between Clifton Forge and Russell, Ky. Traffic is mostly eastbound loaded coal trains en route to the export piers at Newport News and empties heading west back to the coalfields. Grain trains headed east, and grain empties headed west, are also seen. CSX traffic levels can be sporadic, with a dozen trains seen during daylight hours some days, and only a few on other days, and 2 scheduled CSX manifest trains currently on this line. Amtrak's *Cardinal* runs over the Huntington Division East in both directions. At Clifton Forge, there is a major freight yard and engine servicing facility, as well as an Amtrak station downtown (307 East Ridgeway Street), and you can view trains from the station parking lot. As you follow the line west of Clifton Forge, you'll find many scenic locations for photographing trains, including those with structures, tunnels, and rock cuts. In isolated, forested areas, rattlesnakes and copperheads are seen, so a first aid kit, snake bite kit, and a cell phone are recommended.

Tacoma

Tacoma and surrounding areas offer numerous viewing opportunities for BNSF and UP freights, the Tacoma Rail short line, and a variety of passenger trains. BNSF's Seattle Subdivision with its double-track main line (three tracks through Tacoma) provides the most action. Union Pacific's Seattle Sub connects to the BNSF mains. Tacoma Rail handles container service for the city's port as well as other freight traffic. Passenger rail includes Amtrak's *Coast Starlight* and *Cascades* regional service and Sounder commuter trains. Yards include BNSF's Tacoma Yard, complete with turntable, UP's Fife Yard, and Tacoma Rail's Muni Yard. Viewing spots include the Freighthouse Square area (25th Street) and the nearby Amtrak station (1001 Puyallup Avenue) and Dome Station (610 Puyallup Avenue). Backdrops for scenic rail photos abound: the waters of the Puget Sound, a unique lift bridge (Bridge 14 at Chambers Creek), the twin Tacoma Narrows bridges, the Olympic mountains, and Mount Rainier. Tacoma's historic Union Station (1713 Pacifc Avenue), a marvelous example of Beaux Arts architecture, now is home to a federal courthouse, but still worth a visit. Frequencies are BNSF: 161.415 (road), 161.100 (switching), 161.010 (switching); UP: 160.515 (road), 160.410 (switching); and Tacoma Rail: 161.145, 161.070, 161.445, 161.295, 161.190, 161.475.

Edmonds

Robert Scott

Referred to as the Scenic Subdivision, this heavily used BNSF, former Great Northern, CTC main line is the primary traffic route to Canada and to points east from the Seattle area. At Everett, 18 miles north of Edmonds, the northern Transcon turns east to cross Stevens Pass toward Minneapolis and Chicago. North of Everett, the Bellingham Sub follows Puget Sound north to Vancouver. One section of single track is located in Edmonds and another is 10 miles to the north. Depending on the time of day and traffic levels, trains can be held on double track for opposing traffic for some time.

ACTIVITY: About 25 daily mainline trains run along this corridor. A large percentage of priority intermodal traffic in the area uses this route as does container and auto train traffic from the Seattle and Tacoma ports. Bulk traffic includes empty grain trains and coal trains. Manifest traffic between Seattle and Vancouver and garbage trains round out the freight traffic. During the week, 14 Amtrak trains operate along this line including the daily *Empire Builder* and *Cascades* to Vancouver. Eight commuter trains known as Sounders operate between Everett and Seattle.

TRAIN-WATCHING SPOTS: One of the best and most popular train-watching locations is along Sunset Drive just north of the Washington State Ferry Dock (adjacent to MP 18). A few free parking spots can be found along this roadway. The Sounder depot south of Main Street (210 Railroad Avenue) is also a popular location. With the BNSF main line hugging the Sound, Richmond Beach, Picnic Point, and Carkeek Park are popular locations for photography—and beachcombing.

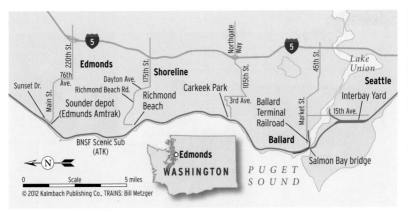

Edmonds is 17 miles north of Seattle along Puget Sound.

A few miles south in Ballard, you'll find the Salmon Bay Bridge, which is another great train-watching location. Adjacent to the Hiram Chittenden Locks in Commodore Park, the bridge is a single-leaf bascule. Ballard Terminal Railroad is next to the Locks, and BNSF's Interbay Yard is just south of the bridge. Adjacent Balmer Yard receives and generates manifest traffic for this line.

SAFETY: Trespassing is strictly enforced as this corridor is popular with beachgoers who regularly use the tracks as access.

RAILROAD FREQUENCIES: BNSF: 161.160 (Seattle terminal dispatcher), 161.250 (North Branch dispatcher), 161.100 (Seattle east dispatcher)

TO DO: Many local restaurants, pubs, bakeries, and cafes are within walking distance in downtown Edmonds. Ferries can take you to many locations including Seattle, Vancouver Island, and other interesting destinations.

NEARBY: The Northwest Railway Museum is 45 miles east in Snoqualmie, Mount Rainier Scenic Railroad is 90 miles southeast in Elbe, and Cascade Tunnel is 70 miles east.

DIRECTIONS: Edmonds is located just off I-5. You can exit at Highway 104 and take it all the way to the ferry dock.

Spokane

Bruce Kelly

BNSF routes from Seattle and Portland converge here into a busy corridor used by northern-tier trains to and from the Midwest and Texas. A BNSF branch also heads north to Chewelah. Union Pacific trains serving Spokane or running to Canada use BNSF track between Napa Street (2 miles east of downtown) and Fish Lake (12 miles to the southwest). Yards located east of downtown include Erie Street (used for BNSF storage and BNSF/UP interchange), UP Yard (used by UP's Spokane-Hinkle trains and locals), and BNSF's large Yardley/Parkwater terminal. Most BNSF crew change and train refueling operations happen at Hauser Yard in northern Idaho, 20 miles to the east.

ACTIVITY: BNSF moves 50 or more trains daily through Spokane including intermodals, manifests, unit grain, unit coal, and vehicle trains. UP handles 8–14 trains daily that are manifests, unit grain, and unit potash. Additionally, UP takes coal trains south from Spokane three or more times per week. Amtrak's *Empire Builder*, scheduled to stop late at night, splits into two separate sections here for Seattle and Portland.

TRAIN-WATCHING SPOTS: Latah Creek Bridge, on the city's west side, is where trains come and go via three separate routes. Parking and viewing spots can be found along Sunset Boulevard, Inland Empire Way, and other side streets. A new parking lot for the Fish Lake rail trail puts you beneath the Y where Latah Creek Bridge splits. Napa Street interlocking, the single busiest spot in Spokane, can be viewed from the south side off Crestline Street or from the north off Trent Avenue. Overpasses at Freya Street and Fancher Road provide views of BNSF yard action.

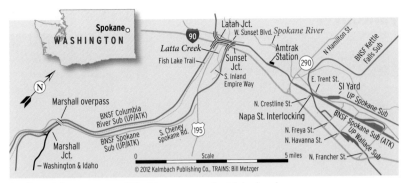

Spokane is in east-central Washington near the Idaho border.

RAILROAD FREQUENCIES: BNSF: 161.250, 161.100, 161.160; UP: 160.740

TO DO: Sunset Junction Model Trains, on Sprague Avenue just east of Division Street, has a view of BNSF from its parking lot. Frank's Diner (1516 West Second Avenue) serves good food in a vintage railcar right next to BNSF tracks. Riverfront Park, site of the 1974 World's Fair and home to the former Great Northern station clock tower, has a tour train, carousel, sky ride, and playgrounds.

NEARBY: Marshall Canyon has roadside views of trains working the moderate grades on two separate tracks. Fish Lake Trail provides additional public access to train-watching locations. Gatto's Pizza in Cheney has window seating with a view of BNSF and UP trains.

DIRECTIONS: To reach Marshall Canyon and Fish Lake Trail, take US 195 south from I-90. Turn right onto Cheney-Spokane Road and continue south. Bear right where Spokane-Cheney Road and Cedar Road split. Park safely off the roadway at either end of the Marshall overpass or along the next big curve at Scribner. Fish Lake Trail access is at Scribner Road (just south of Marshall) and also at South Myers Park Road.

Vancouver

Scott Lothes

Pacific Northwest railroading converges on Vancouver to make it the busiest location in the region. From a wye that surrounds the unique, two-sided Amtrak station, BNSF double-track main lines fan out in three directions. The Seattle Subdivision heads north through Vancouver Yard to Seattle, while the Fallbridge Subdivision goes south (timetable west) across the Columbia River to Portland and east into the Columbia Gorge.

ACTIVITY: Traffic is heaviest on the Seattle Sub, where BNSF's 20–30 daily trains share the route with 12–18 Union Pacific trackage-rights trains, as well as 4 Amtrak *Cascades* each way plus the *Coast Starlight*. Nearly all of those BNSF trains operate in the Columbia Gorge, joined by a few that originate and terminate in Portland and Vancouver, as well as the Portland section of Amtrak's *Empire Builder*. All Union Pacific trains cross the Columbia River to get on and off their home rails in Portland. BNSF operates several daily switchers and local freights out of Vancouver, and regional carrier Portland & Western comes into the Vancouver Yard from Tigard, Ore., to interchange cars in the afternoons Tuesday through Saturday.

TRAIN-WATCHING SPOTS: The Amtrak station (1301 West 11th Street) is in the middle of the wye, and there is ample free parking immediately to the north. Farther north, the West Mill Plain Boulevard overpass has a wide sidewalk with overhead views of the yard and Seattle Sub. BNSF trains going between the Seattle and Fallbridge Subs frequently stop to change crews at one of the grade crossings on the northeast leg of the wye.

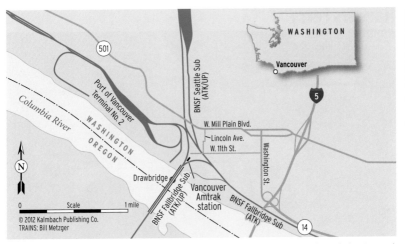

Vancouver is located just across the Columbia River from Portland, and the Amtrak station is at the western end of West 11th Street.

SAFETY: Stay alert, as multiple trains are frequently moving simultaneously on multiple tracks in different directions. Heed all No Trespassing signs and stay out of the way of Amtrak station staff and passengers.

RAILROAD FREQUENCIES: BNSF: 161.250 (Vancouver terminal), 161.100 (Seattle Sub), 160.650, 161.010, 161.415, 161.220 (yard)

TO DO: Downtown Vancouver, just a few blocks to the east, has several shops, restaurants, cafes, and a seasonal farmers market on the weekends. Across the river, Portland can fill several vacations' worth of itineraries. Don't miss the downtown Powell's City of Books but head to their Beaverton branch for many railroad titles.

NEARBY: The Steel Bridge in downtown Portland is a one-of-a-kind, double-deck, telescoping lift bridge with a pedestrian path next to the lower-level railroad tracks. The Oregon Railway Heritage Foundation in Portland runs occasional trips behind steam locomotives.

DIRECTIONS: Going south on I-5, take Exit 1C, turn right on East 15th Street, left on Franklin, and right on West 11th Street. Going north on I-5, take Exit 1B, turn left on West Sixth Street, right on Columbia, and left on West 11th Street.

Harpers Ferry

Alex Mayes

Harpers Ferry sees the junction of the former B&O double-track main line between Washington D.C., and Pittsburgh, now CSX's Cumberland Sub, and CSX's Shenandoah Sub south to Strasburg, Va. The switch connecting the two lines is actually inside the tunnel across the Potomac River in Maryland. Both the double-track main and the single-track secondary line exit the tunnel and cross the river into West Virginia on separate trestles.

ACTIVITY: About 25–30 scheduled CSX trains, 2 morning eastbound and 3 afternoon westbound MARC trains, and Amtrak's *Capitol Limited* ply the main line in a 24-hour period. Loaded and empty coal, grain, and ethanol trains also run on the main. MARC trains run only on weekdays. The Shenandoah Sub usually sees 3–4 loaded and empty stone trains running to and from a quarry in Millville, 4 miles south of Harpers Ferry, as well as 1-2 trains running to or from Winchester, Va.

TRAIN-WATCHING SPOTS: Westbound trains emerging from the tunnel, and trains on both trestles are best photographed in the afternoon. Trains emerging from the tunnel are best seen from the south passenger platform of the Amtrak/MARC station (Potomac and Shenandoah Streets). This location is located within Harpers Ferry National Historic Park, and a nominal fee is charged for entrance. This is a very popular tourist destination, especially during the summer and on weekends, and parking may be difficult. The best way to see and photograph trains on the trestles is to walk to the south bank of the Potomac River and stand between the trestles. Midafternoon lighting is ideal for both trestles.

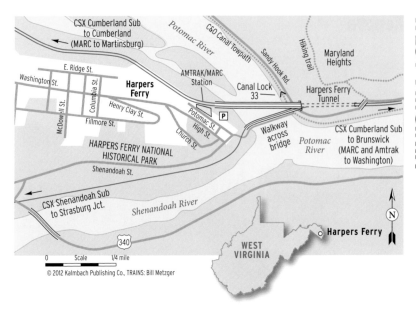

Harpers Ferry is located at the confluence of the Potomac and Shenandoah Rivers near the Virginia and Maryland borders.

You can get a spectacular morning view of eastbounds crossing the river from the mountain above the tunnel in Maryland (Maryland Heights). However, parking on the Maryland side of the river is very limited, and the climb to Maryland Heights is via a steep and very rough trail. There is no access to the Maryland side from the park.

RAILROAD FREQUENCIES: CSX: 160.230, 160.320, 161.520, 160.410, 160.290

TO DO: Harpers Ferry is an intensely interesting place to visit. There are 100 19th century structures in the park, many of which are open to the public. Additionally, there are hiking and biking trails along the towpath of the C&O Canal. Canoeing, tubing, kayaking, and whitewater rafting trips are available on the two adjacent rivers during the summer.

NEARBY: Point of Rocks, Md., is 12 miles to the east, and Shenandoah Junction is 7 miles to the west. CSX's yard and MARC servicing facilities are in Brunswick, Md., 5 miles to the east.

DIRECTIONS: From US 340, take the entrance into the national park (just west of the Potomac River) and follow this road until it ends. Turn left and look for places to park on the street or in the station parking lot.

Kenova

Chase Gunnoe

As one of the busiest railroad communities in West Virginia, both CSX (Ex-Chesapeake & Ohio) and Norfolk Southern (Ex-Norfolk & Western) operate double-track main lines through the city. A rail to river short line operated by Kanawha River Terminal hosts an active interchange with the two large roads. CSX also operates a small interchange yard with NS just east of the distinctive over/under crossing, while NS hosts a small yard used to classify traffic for local industries.

ACTIVITY: Kenova sees 40–60 trains a day, with Norfolk Southern producing slightly more traffic. NS operates numerous intermodal, merchandise, grain, and coal trains, while CSX contributes primarily coal trains (loads and empties go in both directions here) and 3 manifest freights operating in each direction daily. Amtrak's *Cardinal* operates over CSX on a triweekly schedule, making station stops in Huntington (6 miles east) and Ashland, Ky. (7 miles west). The NS route is also part of the Heartland Corridor, a new and growing double-stack intermodal lane created after a number of restrictive tunnels, mostly in West Virginia, were enlarged, daylighted, or bypassed. This new high-capacity route expects to see much traffic growth in the years ahead.

TRAIN-WATCHING SPOTS: Several public vantage points throughout downtown Kenova provide a variety of perspectives. The former N&W double-track bridge carrying the NS Kenova District crosses the Ohio River near 13th Street. The bridge can be seen from miles, allowing you to work numerous photo angles from public access points.

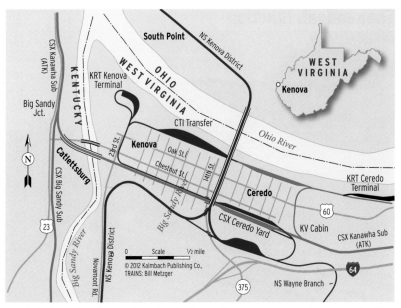

Nestled along the Ohio and Big Sandy Rivers, Kenova is a strategic rail spot in West Virginia, neighboring both Ohio and Kentucky.

RAILROAD FREQUENCIES: NS: 161.250 (road, dispatcher), 160.440 (Kenova Yard); CSX: 160.230 (road), 160.410 (dispatcher)

TO DO: The area has a number of lodging options (including RV and camping sites) near Kenova, particularly in Huntington (east) and Ashland (west). Commercial districts in Huntington, Catlettsburg, and Ashland offer a diverse sampling of eating establishments. Around Halloween, stop in and see the Pumpkin House with its thousands of carved pumpkins.

NEARBY: Located in the heart of railroading operations for the former Chesapeake & Ohio, there are numerous locations of interest nearby. CSX's Russell Terminal is the originating point or crew change location for most trains in the region.

DIRECTIONS: From I-64, exit on Highway 75 (Sixth Street) and head downtown to the tracks.

Shenandoah Junction

Alex Mayes

At Shenandoah Junction, CSX's former B&O main between Washington D.C., and Pittsburgh, now the Cumberland Sub, crosses with Norfolk Southern's former N&W Hagerstown, Md., to Roanoke main, now the H Line. Norfolk Southern's single-track line crosses over the CSX main. Although there is a connection between the two lines here, traffic is no longer interchanged between the two railroads.

ACTIVITY: About 25–30 scheduled CSX trains plus 2 morning eastbound and 3 afternoon westbound MARC trains, and Amtrak's *Capitol Limited* travel on CSX during a day. The line also sees loaded and empty coal, grain, and ethanol trains. MARC trains run only on weekdays. Norfolk Southern runs about a dozen manifest, intermodal, stack, and grain trains a day during daylight hours.

TRAIN-WATCHING SPOTS: Morning views of eastbound trains on CSX are visible from the Ridge Road grade crossing just west of the NS overhead trestle and from the embankment on the south side of the CSX tracks. Photographing NS trains on the overhead trestle is also good here in the morning. Afternoon shots of westbound CSX trains snaking through an S curve can be taken near the foundation of where the old passenger station stood. Photographing afternoon trains on the NS trestle is also good from this location. Southbound NS trains can be seen at the Shenandoah Junction Road crossing throughout most of the day.

SAFETY: Both lines are active throughout the day with trains running at 40 mph or higher.

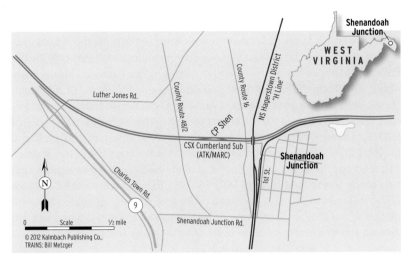

Shenandoah Junction is located in the eastern panhandle of West Virginia 7 miles west of Harpers Ferry.

RAILROAD FREQUENCIES: CSX: 160.230, 160.320, 161.520, 160.410, 160.290; NS: 161.190, 161.250, 160.440, 161.205

TO DO: This is a remote location with no major stores, restaurants, gas stations, or other services nearby. There is a small convenience store in the town.

NEARBY: Other nearby hot spots are Point of Rocks, Md., 19 miles to the east, and Harpers Ferry, 7 miles to the east. CSX's yard and MARC servicing facilities are in Brunswick, Md., 12 miles to the east. Lodging, major stores, and restaurants are located in Martinsburg or along I-70 in Frederick and Hagerstown, Md.

DIRECTIONS: Shenandoah Junction is located just east of Route 9 between Martinsburg and Charles Town. From Route 9, take the Wiltshire Road Exit and go east 200 feet, turn right onto Charles Town Road, and then left on Shenandoah Junction Road. After crossing the tracks (the Norfolk Southern line), turn left on Ridge Road and take this road to the end. You can park here, and the CSX main is 100 feet ahead.

Magnolia Cutoff

CSX's very scenic former B&O main line runs through the northern section of the eastern panhandle of West Virginia. The Magnolia Cutoff was built by the B&O in 1914 above the original main line between Paw Paw and Orleans Road. About 25–30 scheduled CSX trains and Amtrak's *Capitol Limited* pass through Magnolia Cutoff in a 24-hour period. Additionally, there are loaded and empty coal, grain, and ethanol trains. The gravel service road, which was the original B&O right-of-way, parallels the tracks for most of the length of the Cutoff, and provides access to the four tunnels and two trestles over the Potomac River. This road has deep ruts and potholes in many places and is especially rough east of the abandoned town of Magnolia. The four tunnels on the Cutoff are being enlarged to increase overhead clearances and are scheduled for completion in late 2012, so access may be restricted. This is a very isolated location with no services nearby; also be aware of rattlesnakes and copperheads.

Thurmond

Thurmond rests deep in West Virginia's New River Gorge at the end of a 7-mile-long, one-lane (paved) road that winds down Dunloup Creek from US 19, 12 miles north of Beckley. The former Chesapeake & Ohio main line was the only "Main Street" the town ever had, and the remaining storefronts still abut the high iron. Traffic varies widely on CSX's New River Subdivision, which depends primarily on coal. The route can host up to 6–8 unit coal trains and 1–2 unit grain trains daily, all eastbound, with equal numbers of westbound empty trains. There is also a pair of daily manifests and Amtrak's triweekly *Cardinal*, which makes flag stops at the beautifully restored depot (at the intersection of Highways 2 and 25), which is now an interpretive center for the National Park Service and a great place to watch the action. A local from Quinnimont swaps cars a few times per week with R. J. Corman, which provides freight service up Dunloop Creek and also loads 2–4 CSX coal trains each week. Nearby hiking and biking trails follow abandoned coal branches.

Milwaukee

Five railroads operate in the area. Canadian Pacific owns the former Milwaukee Road south to Chicago and west to the Twin Cities. Canadian National's main line passes west of Milwaukee toward Chicago. CP and CN each host 15–20 freights daily. Union Pacific operates up to 6 through freights each day and a swarm of locals. Wisconsin & Southern's area operations include its terminal in Milwaukee and local lines. Amtrak operates 7 daily *Hiawatha* round trips to Chicago and the *Empire Builder*. Duplainville, about 15 miles west of Milwaukee, is a prime viewing spot. The CP and CN main lines cross at a diamond. Railfans often park on Marjean Lane along the south side of the CP tracks. Several grade crossings off Duplainville Road on the CN afford nice photo locations. Located in the Menomonee Valley, Muskego Yard is CP's major facility, and you can see it from several large bridges with sidewalks. UP's Butler Yard is in Milwaukee County's northwest corner. You can view the yard from the Hampton Avenue Bridge. North Milwaukee Yard is home to the Wisconsin & Southern; CN's Saukville and West Bend local interchanges cars here.

La Crosse

Steve Glischinski

The crossing of two main lines, combined with Mississippi River Valley scenery, make La Crosse a great place to visit for rail action. BNSF's ex-Burlington Chicago-Twin Cities main line crosses Canadian Pacific's former Milwaukee Road Chicago-St. Paul Line, just south of the BNSF Yard, where BNSF trains change crews. Across the Mississippi River in La Crescent, Minn., at River Junction, CP's Dakota, Minnesota & Eastern (ex-Iowa, Chicago & Eastern and Milwaukee Road) main line from Iowa joins the CP main line to St. Paul. Union Pacific has trackage rights over Canadian Pacific from Tunnel City through La Crosse to Winona, Minn.

ACTIVITY: Approximately 40 mainline, general freight, grain, and intermodal trains pass through La Crosse on BNSF each day. CP hosts approximately 15–20 trains daily, including coal trains, manifests, and intermodals. UP runs a freight as needed, while DM&E has 2 trains scheduled each day. Amtrak's *Empire Builder* stops twice daily at the former Milwaukee Road depot on CP.

TRAIN-WATCHING SPOTS: The La Crosse Amtrak depot (601 St. Andrew Street) is a good location for watching trains. The CP/BNSF diamond at Grand Crossing, about a mile east of the depot, is best viewed from the Gillette Street overpass, which offers good views of eastbound BNSF and CP trains. For dramatic views of the valley, make the drive up to Grandad Bluff Park. Grandad Bluff is the largest bluff in the area and is well known for its scenic overlook of La Crosse, with the added benefit of overlooking the BNSF main line. In addition to enjoying the view, you can explore several hiking trails. Just up I-90 at Dakota, Minn., you'll find an overlook that provides great views of the CP main line and the Mississippi River.

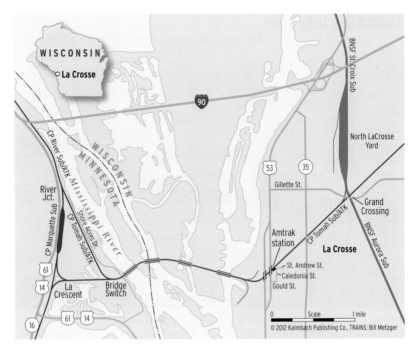

La Crosse is situated on the Mississippi River in west-central Wisconsin.

SAFETY: Use caution at the Gillette Street overpass since the shoulders are narrow.

RAILROAD FREQUENCIES: BNSF: 160.695 (La Crosse-St. Paul), 161.100 (La Crosse-Savanna, Ill.); CP: 161.520 (Milwaukee-La Crosse), 160.770 (La Crosse-St. Paul); DM&E (IC&E): 161.370

TO DO: Downtown La Crosse is a busy retail area with a variety of interesting shops. In Riverside Park, you can view International Friendship Gardens, stroll along the Mississippi River, or take a paddle wheeler cruise on the river. The Swarthout Museum (112 Ninth Street South) highlights the history of La Crosse.

NEARBY: At Copeland Park along Highway 53, a railroad display features the Grand Crossing interlocking tower, Burlington 4-6-4 No. 4000, and Milwaukee Road caboose 0359. At Sparta, 29 miles east of La Crosse, is the Elroy-Sparta State Trail, one of the first rail trails in the country. The 32-mile former Chicago & North Western line includes three tunnels.

DIRECTIONS: To reach the La Crosse Amtrak depot, take Exit 3 off I-90 to Highway 53 South. Follow 53 until it crosses above the railroad tracks. After crossing, turn left on Gould Street and take another left on Caledonia Street until reaching St. Andrew Street.

Saunders Junction

Steve Glischinski

Saunders is the junction of BNSF's Lakes Subdivision line from Superior and its Allouez Subdivision from the railroad's taconite facility in Superior. Passing under and connecting to the junction is CN's ex-Duluth, Missabe & Iron Range Superior Subdivision line that links CN's former Duluth, Winnipeg & Pacific, Missabe, and Wisconsin Central lines. Canadian Pacific and Union Pacific have trackage rights on BNSF through the junction to reach BNSF's Hinckley Subdivision main line to the Twin Cities, which breaks off at Boylston, about 5 miles west of Saunders. At Saunders, UP freights swing off BNSF and use the CN to reach to South Itasca Yard. Just north of Saunders Junction is the former Duluth, Winnipeg & Pacific Pokegama Yard.

ACTIVITY: On CN, you'll see approximately 20 trains per day, including transfers, through freights, and UP trains. BNSF's line sees about 25 trains daily, including CP and UP trackage-rights trains.

TRAIN-WATCHING SPOTS: Highway 35, just north of the junction, crosses over both the CN and BNSF's Allouez Line and offers excellent photo opportunities. Just north of Highway 35, the CN and the Allouez Line cross the Nemadji River on large bridges that are a short walk from Highway 35. To get closer views of BNSF trains, head south on Highway 35 about a mile where the road and railroad run parallel.

RAILROAD FREQUENCIES: BNSF: 161.100 (road), 161.250 (Superior Yard), 160.605 (Duluth trackage); CN: 161.295 (road south), 160.860 (road north), 160.350 (ex-DM&IR Duluth to Iron Range), 161.415 (Pokegama Yard), 160.230 (Proctor Yard), 161.280 (Duluth Ore Dock); CP: 161.520 (Superior Yard), 160.770 (Duluth Yard); UP: 161.175 (Itasca Yard)

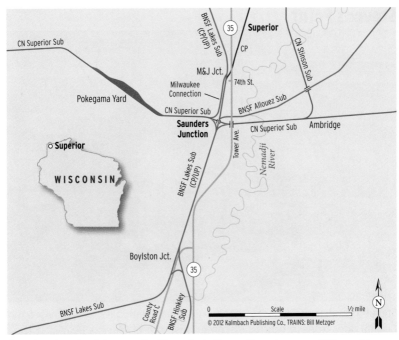

Saunders Junction is just south of Superior in the northwest corner of Wisconsin.

TO DO: In Superior, the Richard I. Bong World War II Heritage Center (305 Harbor View Parkway) includes a restored P-38 Lightning. Stop by the aerial lift bridge in Duluth's Canal Park and watch shipping activity at the Twin Ports for the journey across the Great Lakes. Adjacent to the bridge is the Lake Superior Marine Museum and Army Corps of Engineers Maritime Visitor Center. Admission is free.

NEARBY: The Lake Superior Railroad Museum in Duluth (506 West Michigan Street) has one of the finest collections of railroad equipment in the country. Most of the museum's exhibit space is enclosed at Duluth's restored Union Depot complex. The museum focuses on railroading in the Lake Superior region and features a giant DM&IR Yellowstone Mallet. During the summer, the North Shore Scenic Railroad operates excursion trains out of the museum along Lake Superior's North Shore to Two Harbors. Another tourist line, the Lake Superior & Mississippi Railroad, offers 6-mile rides out of Duluth on weekends from June to October.

DIRECTIONS: From I-35 in Duluth, follow the US 2 Exit. Cross the Richard I. Bong Bridge over the St. Louis River into Wisconsin and follow the signs for Highway 35. Saunders Junction is 5 miles south of downtown Superior on Highway 35.

Stevens Point

Steve Glischinski

Stevens Point is the nerve center for Canadian National's former Wisconsin Central operations in central Wisconsin. Just east of Stevens Point at a location called Hoover, the 233-mile Superior Subdivision connects to the Neenah Subdivision. The Superior Sub passes through Stevens Point and heads northwest, terminating at Carson, west of Proctor, Minn. Another line, the 19-mile Plover Subdivision, heads south from Stevens Point to Plover and west to Wisconsin Rapids. Appropriately named Junction City, where CN's former Milwaukee Road Valley Subdivision crosses the Superior Sub, is 12 miles west of Stevens Point. The two lines are joined by connections in all four quadrants of the crossing, so trains can move in any direction out of Junction City.

ACTIVITY: Roughly 25 trains pass through the area each day. They vary from manifests and intermodals on the Superior Sub to coal trains, long-distance locals, and local trains feeding the huge paper mills in nearby Wisconsin Rapids on the Valley Subdivision.

TRAIN-WATCHING SPOTS: In Stevens Point, the Water Street crossing immediately west of the large former Soo Line passenger depot offers excellent afternoon views of westbound trains. Patch Street parallels the Stevens Point Yard on the south side, and some trains run through Stevens Point from North Fond du Lac using a mainline bypass parallel to the street. A few miles east, the old Highway 18 crossing, at a point called Orchard, is the end of two tracks from Point Yard and is a quiet place to watch trains.

At Junction City, the Center Avenue crossing on the east side of the Valley Sub crossing and the Court Avenue crossing on the west side are both good safe spots to see trains snaking through the various connecting tracks.

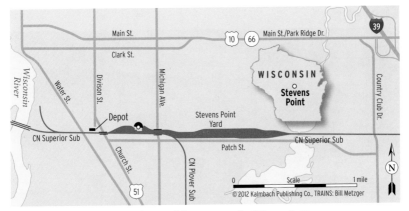

Stevens Point is in the central part of the state on the Wisconsin River.

RAILROAD FREQUENCIES: CN: 160.785, 161.295, 161.385, 160.260, 160.335, 161.385, 161.250

TO DO: Wisconsin is known for its beer, and you'd be hard pressed to find a better combination of trains, beer, and food than Mike & Betsy's Hiawatha Bar (817 Main Street) in Junction City. It sits in the middle of the two north legs of the wye along the Valley Subdivision.

NEARBY: Dairy State Cheese in Rudolph, at Highway 34 and County Road C is a family-owned and operated store and cheese production facility. Visitors can view master cheesemakers at work from two observation windows and sample more than 100 types of Wisconsin cheese.

DIRECTIONS: To reach the depot in Stevens Point, take I-39 north to Exit 158, and head west on US 10. Turn left (south) on Division Street 11 blocks to Depot Street; you will see the station straight ahead. To reach Junction City, return to Division Street heading north and turn left on Clark Street. Cross the Wisconsin River and follow County Road HH that follows the CN tracks west. About 4 miles east of Junction City, HH intersects with Highway 10. Go straight on Highway 10 into town.

Cheyenne

Mike Danneman

Once hallowed ground where some of the largest steam locomotives in the world tested their mettle storming the grades of Sherman Hill and the main line through Cheyenne, the busy route still stirs the soul of a train watcher. Located on Union Pacific's Overland Route main line, Cheyenne is a crew change point and has a frequently busy yard. Leaving Cheyenne westbound is an impressive four-track main line. The main line splits at Borie, located 10 miles west. Two tracks head west for Sherman and the Laramie Mountains. The other tracks head south to Speer, with one track headed west out of Speer through Harriman, connecting with the old main line at Dale Junction. The fourth track continues south as the main to Denver.

ACTIVITY: Traffic can vary depending on the day of week, but usually 50–70 trains a day run on UP's main line through Cheyenne and over Sherman Hill.

TRAIN-WATCHING SPOTS: At the west end of Cheyenne Yard, the BNSF's former Colorado and Southern main from Denver to Wendover crosses over the UP main. The Southwest Drive grade crossing yields a good place to view the action, with parking nearby. One of the best and easiest locations to watch trains headed up the grade west of Cheyenne is along old US 30, which is now Highway 225 or Otto Road. Several grade crossings can be reached on public roads on Sherman Hill. County Road 234 crosses two mains just east of Dale Junction. At Tie Siding off US 287, Hermosa Road crosses all three mains. Another good location for action is just east of Cheyenne where the main line climbs east out of town over Archer Hill.

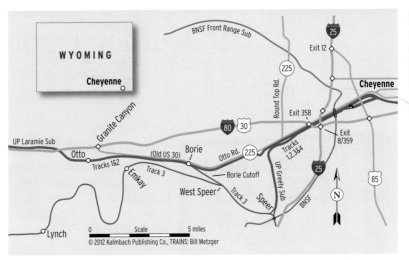

Cheyenne is located in the southeast corner of Wyoming 100 miles north of Denver.

SAFETY: Many areas around Sherman Hill are still fairly inaccessible. Too many gates left open and other problems with trespassers over the years have made local ranchers less tolerant of visitors. Stay on main roads and avoid private roads and private property.

RAILROAD FREQUENCIES: UP: 160.470 (Laramie Sub), 161.145 (Greeley Sub); BNSF: 161.160 (Front Range Sub)

TO DO: The renovated former UP depot now houses the Cheyenne Depot Museum (121 West 15th Street), which tells the story of Cheyenne during the construction of the Transcontinental Railroad and features other historical displays. Several times a year, UP's historic steam and diesel engines operate out of Cheyenne for special events. For some western rodeo fun, check out Cheyenne Frontier Days in July.

NEARBY: Nearby (in Wyoming terms), Powder River Basin and the flood of coal trains that haul the black diamonds to faraway places is 150 miles to the north. To serve this operation, more than 100 trains a day traverse BNSF's multiple-track, 127-mile Orin Subdivision. Situated at the coal line's north end, Gillette connects with Douglas at the south end via Highway 59. East-west roads along the Orin Sub take you to the tracks, and many of them have bridges that provide excellent vantage points for viewing the action. The line's operational highlight is a 21-mile stretch of four-track main line over Logan Hill between Bill and Nacco Junction. The Steckley Road overpass, at the summit of the hill (a 1 percent climb each way), is a great place to watch from.

DIRECTIONS: Cheyenne is located at the crossroads of I-80 and I-25.

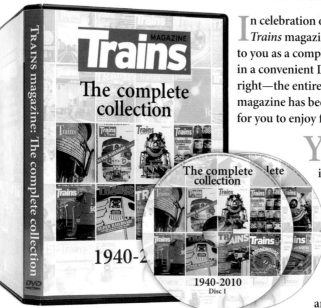